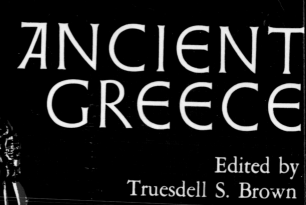

ANCIENT GREECE

Edited by
Truesdell S. Brown
University of California,
Los Angeles

Sources in
Western Civilization

Herbert H. Rowen,
GENERAL EDITOR

SOURCES IN WESTERN CIVILIZATION

Ancient Greece

ANCIENT

Sources in Western Civilization

GENERAL EDITOR, *Herbert H. Rowen*

RUTGERS UNIVERSITY

GREECE

EDITED BY

Truesdell S. Brown

UNIVERSITY OF CALIFORNIA, LOS ANGELES

THE FREE PRESS, NEW YORK

Collier-Macmillan Limited, London

To my daughter, Priscilla Jane Collins

CONTENTS

viii

SOURCES IN WESTERN CIVILIZATION

Ancient Greece

INTRODUCTION

It is hard to decide when Greek history began and when it ended, since a high degree of civilization was attained by Greek-speaking people before the time of Homer, and continued for half a millennium after the loss of political independence. In this book the end of Greek history is assumed to coincide with the loss of freedom for mainland Greece in 146 B.C., though writers of a later date are included where they represent an earlier tradition. This problem of beginnings was one which the Greeks themselves attempted to solve, for they were the first people to conceive of the past in terms that we still recognize as historical. That is, the Greeks became interested in the past because they were curious to know what happened and why, rather than because they needed to find support for the cult of a god or the rule of a dynasty or even, as sometimes happens today, because they wished to reinforce an ideology. However, this curiosity did not develop early, and when it did manifest itself in the fifth century B.C. much of the Greek past had become even more obscure to them than it now is to us. They found it impossible to go back confidently beyond the old poets.

1. The Epic Tradition

Poetry preceded prose as a form of literature among the Greeks, as among other peoples generally, for reasons that are fairly obvious. Prose literature presupposes a knowledge of reading and writing while poems were composed to be memorized and sung or recited, at a time when the Greek alphabet was not yet in use. Although Greek had been written much earlier (1200 B.C.?) in the script known as Linear B, which has been found in Crete as well as on the mainland, this was a syllabary, not an alphabetic, script, the use of which was forgotten during the migrations that terminated the

Mycenaean Age. The epics are the earliest Greek poems known to us. Their content was preserved by the rhapsodes, or wandering bards, who entertained aristocratic audiences far and wide in the Greek world with their recitals. Theirs was a hereditary craft, and its practitioners undoubtedly combined, altered and sometimes, if they were sufficiently talented, added verses of their own, until the existence of established written texts controlled their innovations.

Ancient taste can hardly have erred in selecting the *Iliad* and the *Odyssey* out of the great body of epic literature recounting the deeds of legendary heroes and, as it were, canonizing them. Fragments are all that remain of the rest. Homer, to whom the *Iliad* and the *Odyssey* were attributed, was traditionally a blind poet of Chios, known to us as to the Greeks themselves only through fictional biographies. The Homeric controversy, though it is not resolved, burns less brightly now than it did fifty years ago; yet like other scholarly debates it has had important, sometimes unexpected, results. Who Homer was, whether the same poet wrote either or both poems, or whether they had multiple authorship, will probably never be known. It might even be urged that the questions are meaningless when stated so simply. Excavations during the past century have provided us with an archaeological background for the Age of Heroes: Troy, Mycenae, Tiryns, Pylos and Orchomenus are known to us as real places; yet they live and breathe only in the poems themselves [1].*

The ancients believed that the Trojan War and other episodes of the Age of Heroes had to do with real events and real people but that the poets had supplied sensational details and improbable motivation in order to make their poems attractive. Xenophanes, a sixth century Ionian philosopher who liked to shock his contemporaries, went so far as to call Homer a liar, not because of the tale of Troy, but because he depicted the gods in human shape; Plato, in his *Republic*, attempted to bowdlerize Homer for the sake of the future citizens of his ideal state. But everyone read Homer, most gentlemen knew long passages from both poems by heart, and the dramatists drew freely from epic materials for their plays. Thucydides, a most skeptical historian, quite seriously compared the Trojan with the Peloponnesian War. Even as late as Augustus, the celebrated geographer Strabo defended Homer as a knowledgeable geographer in the teeth of modernists like Eratosthenes. But even Eratosthenes could

* Bracketed numbers refer to the numbers of selections given in the text.

not break away from tradition entirely, for it was he who established the standard date for the Fall of Troy (corresponding to 1183 B.C.).

It may be added that the *Homeric Hymns,* as they are called, though written in the language of the epics, are undoubtedly of later authorship, probably the work of the rhapsodes.

Like the authors of the *Homeric Hymns,* Hesiod [2] also wrote in dactyllic hexameter and used the epic language; but there the resemblance ends. In Hesiod we have left the court for the farm, and strife on the battlefield for the grim struggle to wrest a living from the soil of Boeotia. The author, unlike Homer, is a three-dimensional figure. Our information about him, so far as it is trustworthy, depends on what he tells us in his poems. His father lived in Cymē on the coast of Asia Minor, which he left at some indeterminate period to try to better himself by moving to Greece. He settled down in the village of Ascra, the exact location of which is still uncertain though it seems to have been in the neighborhood of Thespiae. There Hesiod and his younger brother Perses grew up, and there the father died, leaving a modest estate to be divided between them. The fame of Hesiod's poems later led Cymē to claim him as her own but we have no way of knowing whether he was born before or after his father settled in Ascra. The most widely read historian of the fourth century B.C. was Ephorus, who was born in Cymē, and it may well be that it was he who trumpeted Cymē's claims to Hesiod. We are told that Perses obtained more than his just share in the division of the estate by influencing the judges, but of course our only informant is the disgruntled Hesiod. After squandering his own patrimony Perses appealed for help to his thrifty brother, threatening him with a lawsuit if he refused. This is the background for the *Works and Days,* which is written as a long epistolary admonition to Perses. No greater contrast can be imagined to the aristocratic society portrayed in the *Iliad* than the farming community of the *Works and Days,* where the rewards of honest toil, the dangers of idleness and the deviousness of "gift-devouring kings" are depicted for Perses' edification, along with illustrative stories like that of Pandora and the Ages of Man. The author, for all his cynicism, is deeply troubled by the problem of evil in the world, but he professes his faith in the ultimate triumph of Right.

Quite different is the other important poem by Hesiod, the *Theogony,* not included in the selections for reasons of space. In it we can trace the beginnings of what would later be a Greek sense of history. As the title indicates, this poem is concerned with the origin of the gods; despite its rambling style, with digressions that divert us from the main theme, it shows an effort to systematize the accounts of the present world order. The author must have sifted quantities of religious material in his search for a coherent story, a process utilized long before in the ancient east but the author is no longer a priest serving the interest of a cult in Heliopolis, Memphis or Babylon. He is a poet who wants to know.

It is a tribute to Hesiod's influence that later on the unlikely story was told that he had met Homer in a poetic contest in Chalcis and won the prize. Strange but less suspect, since we can see no motive for a falsification, is the assertion that Hesiod was murdered. He had followers, however, who continued the task of harmonizing the stories about gods and heroes, working out a consistent chronology for them in terms of generations. The various heroes were related to one another and to the gods and their careers were grouped around famous legendary enterprises such as the Voyage of the Argo, the Calydonian Boar Hunt and the Return of the Heraclidae. When the historian arrived on the scene he found that the methods used by the mythographers could lead to solid results when applied to real men and real events.

2. *The Ionian Greeks*

In 494 B.C., fifty years before Herodotus went out to Thurii, and probably more than two hundred years after Hesiod's father migrated from Cymē to Ascra, the city of Miletus was brutally sacked and then demolished by the Persians of Darius. Exercising our privilege of hindsight and blinded by the brilliance of the period that lay just ahead for European Greece, we are perhaps too ready to think it was all for the best, as we do with Hastings, or the Armada, or Yorktown. But was it really? In 494 Miletus held the position that Athens occupied ninety years later as the intellectual center of the Greek world, the "School of Hellas." In 404 there were those who proposed to level Athens to the ground and sell her people into slavery. Had this happened, would it too have been regarded by twentieth century pundits as a good thing? It would not be surprising, for what could they know of the Academy, the Lyceum, the Stoa and the Garden, if the philosophers who made them famous had found no congenial environment in which their ideas could germinate?

Equally unknown would be the major Attic orators and the whole New Comedy of Menander and later imitators all the way down to Molière. Yet Miletus, too, suggests a brilliant might-have-been, and surely Greek developments after 494, much as we admire them, were drastically affected by its destruction. There was loss as well as gain which the thoughtful student will not overlook.

Just as the Mycenaean civilization was intimately associated with older Asiatic cultures of the ancient east, so the Ionian Greeks of the seventh and sixth centuries reflect a give-and-take between East and West. It is no accident that the epic arose among the Greeks of Asia at a time when European Greece was still parochial nor that western philosophical speculation began in Ionia. It has long been customary to see a great gulf separating Greek thought from that of earlier peoples. We like to say that the Babylonians and Egyptians worked things out by rule of thumb while the Greeks classified their observations and sought for theoretical explanation. Though they may contain an element of truth, such generalizations are unfruitful because they imply that in some mysterious way the Greeks were not as other men, that they revolutionized human thought by sheer genius, almost without effort. This is merely to restore the element of mumbojumbo that we credit the Greeks with eliminating. It obscures the fact that western philosophy is an achievement of the human spirit, not the casual discovery of a few bright men in Miletus. The time for it was ripe. It is a fortuitous circumstance that its formulation, when it came, was in the Greek tongue.

Thales, Anaximander, Anaximenes — those are the three famous names associated with the foundation of western thought in the city of Miletus. We know them only through later writers, for their own works were soon superseded and disappeared. The interpretation of what they were about depends at best on Aristotle, who discusses them in his *Metaphysics* (mid-fourth century B.C.), and at worst on writers like Diogenes Laertius, whose chief virtue is the lack of any original ideas of his own but who lived centuries later in the third century A.D. This is not the place to discuss the theories of Thales, Anaximander and Anaximenes, but it should be noted that all three were mathematicians. The bond between mathematics and philosophy is perhaps the single most important influence of the Greeks on later western thought. The Milesian School, as it came to be called later, was primarily concerned with finding a rational explanation for the world and man's place in it rather than with establishing rules of behavior. The freedom to speculate without regard for politics, morals or established opinions generated a tough-minded curiosity about people, places and things: the thinkers were exuberant, highly personal and sharply critical. The tradition among scholars of confidence in one's own opinions and contempt for those of others got off to a good start.

The new spirit of inquiry was not long confined to speculation about the universe. Prose writers appeared — the logographers as they are called — who interested themselves in less recondite matters, such as the description of foreign countries and the strange peoples who inhabited them, based on reports by Greek merchants and travelers. The most famous of these is Hecataeus of Miletus. Like Anaximander, but unlike Herodotus, he illustrated his writings with a map. We still have a fragment of his preface, in which he says: "Hecataeus the Milesian is speaking. In what follows I write what I believe to be the truth, for the Greek accounts strike me as being just as ridiculous as they are numerous" (*F.Gr.H.*, No. 1, fr. 1a). This candid observation may be supplemented by that of Heraclitus of Ephesus: "Much learning does not improve the intelligence or it would have had that effect on Hesiod and Pythagoras, and also on Xenophanes and Hecataeus" (*Ibid.* T 21).

The fall of Miletus, which ended the Ionian revolt, also put an end to the intellectual leadership of the Asiatic Greeks, but we can still hear echoes of it in Herodotus' account of Egypt [3], particularly his somewhat belligerent remarks on the geographical boundaries of Libya and Asia and his discussion of the Nile flood. But when Herodotus wrote these were only memories. Athens was in her prime. How the Athenians felt earlier, however, is shown by the story that when Phrynichus presented his play on the *Capture of Miletus* the audience was moved to tears and the dramatist fined two hundred dollars for reminding them of their troubles.

3. The Background of the Persian War

We must now consider the political developments that led up to the Persian War.

The bronze age civilization of Mycenae and Tiryns had already given way to what has been called the Dark Ages of Greece long before Homer and Hesiod were born. That change is thought to have been both technological and social in character; it occurred when the last waves of invading Greek-speaking peoples overwhelmed the Aegean area towards the end of the second millennium B.C. Economically and socially the growing dependence on iron was of utmost significance. Copper deposits were relatively rare, but iron could be found in usable quantities in many parts of Greece and the surrounding islands. This availability of iron broke the monopoly of the merchant princes and opened the way for the local independence of smaller geographic areas; it also made possible the Greek city-state or polis with which we are familiar. Warfare became less a matter of the prowess of individual heroes and more the concern of a disciplined middle class armed primarily with shield and spear; the fighting man could learn his trade reasonably well without becoming a professional warrior. Agricultural tools were also improved and the stony soil of Greece reluctantly yielded a better return to support an increasing population. Technological advances were slow, however, lagging painfully behind the needs of all but the most fertile areas, like Thessaly and Boeotia. Elsewhere starvation was the alternative to migration or development of specialized export goods to be exchanged for grain and other necessities. The result of these pressures, as well as other factors, was the Great Age of Greek Colonization. This was a new movement of the Greek peoples that established the highwater marks of Greek expansion before the time of Alexander the Great.

The Greek colonists followed the path of least resistance along the coastlands of the Mediterranean and the Black seas, where a few resolute men could make a landing and defend themselves against the earlier inhabitants. There was no central planning or national direction of these efforts except in so far as the shrewd pronouncements of Apollo in Delphi may have exerted some slight control. Our knowledge of this colonial period is poor, depending on Greek writers of a later date; however, they did have information at their disposal which is no longer available to us. Thucydides, who is frequently our best authority, knew the dates which the various cities recorded for their foundation. The results of excavation in modern times tend generally to increase our respect for the great Athenian historian, particularly for his relative chronology. Nowhere were the colonies more concentrated than in South Italy, which is commonly referred to as Magna Graecia, and in Sicily. The colonies proved no more amicable in their mutual relations than the city-states of Greece and Asia Minor that had sent them out. Nor was harmony achieved even when the stiffening resistance of Carthaginians and Etruscans threatened their existence and called a halt to further settlements. Cooperation was rare, incomplete and short-lived. Nevertheless, one giant did emerge from the confusion; this was the city of Syracuse, which was easily the most populous of all Hellenic cities by the time of the Persian War, retaining her importance even when Athens reached her highest point in the Age of Pericles. To satisfy the aspirations of the colonial Greeks, particularly in the West, foundation legends were created or adapted which insensibly merged the historic tradition of real colonists and real founders with the Trojan War and the activities of heroes after that war. One such example will be found in the Diodorus-Timaeus passage [4].

The effect of the colonial movement was also great on the Greeks at home; it created new tastes, new markets and new problems. As the migration slowed to a trickle, more gradually here and more rapidly there, the older Greek states had to find new methods of meeting their economic difficulties. They did this in a variety of ways, in response to pressures which varied greatly from region to region. One partial solution, found in only the more advanced states of Greece and Asia, was the governmental innovation known as *tyranny*. This experiment was usually short-lived, as Aristotle points out in his discussion of tyranny [5], but after the tyrant had been overthrown a more sophisticated government than the old landed aristocracy usually took its place. However the unending variety in the Greek city-states prevented any pattern from appearing. Asia Minor is a good instance. The Ionian cities, the most economically advanced in the Greek world, soon found themselves unable to resist the pressure of their Asiatic neighbors and fell before the diplomacy and arms of the Lydian kings. About 550 B.C. Lydia herself gave way to Cyrus and the Empire of Persia, and the Greek cities came to be ruled by citizen-tyrants who themselves owed obedience to Persia. Later it was one of these tyrants, Aristagoras of Miletus, who raised the standard of a revolt that ended with the destruction of Miletus in 494. Darius of Persia then reversed his field by abolishing the tyrannies and ruling the Greeks in Asia through constitutional governments! In Sicily, where Carthage was an ever-present danger, tyranny of a different sort grew up in Syracuse and other cities. The continual threat from without made the tyranny indispensable. At the time of the Persian War Gelon was in control of Syracuse [6]. But in Greece proper tyranny had largely disappeared by that date. Sparta, as she developed her own remarkable institutions [13] became the declared foe of tyranny. Corinth, Sicyon and Megara had long ago emerged from tyranny with constitutional governments; Corinth had the most stable oligarchy of the three. Athens was unique. The whole of Attica enjoyed Athenian citizenship. Athens' economic development had been charted for her by the reforms of Solon (594 B.C.), who encouraged the cultivation of the vine and the olive rather than cereals. This progress was accelerated under the tyranny of Pisistratus. His successor Hippias was overthrown in 510 to be replaced by a popular government established by Clisthenes. Thereafter Athens' rise was rapid. Her assistance to the Ionian cities aroused the wrath of Persia, whose attempt to restore Hippias in 490 was prevented by Miltiades and an Athenian army at Marathon. Almost ten years of grace were granted to the Greeks before Xerxes' well-publicized attack by land and sea brought about the greatest degree of cooperation ever achieved voluntarily by the Greeks — under the leadership of Sparta. Even this effort was far from unanimous.

4. Athens Between the Wars

The resounding defeat of Persia and the deliverance of Greece was largely the work of Athens [6], and it was Athens that capitalized on the results. The most reliable account of the period between the wars is Thucydides' cryptic narrative [7], but we also have a critique of the imperial democracy written by an unknown oligarch who knew Athens well [8]. The hegemony of Athens was brought to a close by Sparta and her allies in 404 B.C.; it had lasted longer than that of Sparta or Thebes was destined to do. After the Battle of Chaeronea in 338 B.C. Philip of Macedon imposed a measure of unity on mainland Greece. The time between the retreat of Xerxes' army and the outbreak of the Peloponnesian War (479–431 B.C.) was the high period not only for Athens but for all democratic society in the ancient world. We need to understand something of the inner workings of that democracy to appreciate its achievements, for there are vast differences between democracy as we know it and as the Greeks knew it in the fifth century B.C.

The most obvious difference is size. There were no more and probably less than 40,000 qualified voters, that is male citizens over twenty years of age, at the peak, before the Great Plague of 430 B.C. The rest of the population of approximately 300,000 was made up of women, children, metics (resident aliens) and slaves. However uncertain these figures are, the proportion of voters in the total population (about 13 per cent) is not far off. Yet to the Greeks 40,000 citizens seemed a recklessly large number. Aristotle twits Socrates (i.e., Plato) for postulating a city with 5000 full citizens, for it would "require a territory as large as Babylonia" (*Politics* 1265a 14). Under these circumstances, how can we speak of Athens as a democracy at all? There is another side, however. If the Athenian proportion held in the United States and we assume a population of 180,000,000, there would be 24,000,000 persons with a right to go to Washington and cast a vote for every bill presented in Congress, to debate it on the floor or question its constitutionality. More than 3,000,000 of this number would be selected annually by lot to act as federal jurors for the year, with no appeal against their decisions to a higher court and no presiding judge to direct their verdict. The Athenians expected and demanded that every citizen devote a large amount of his time to the service of the state, so that while the proportion of the citizens to the total population may seem small the proportion of the total population actively determining public policy was enormous. Most of us merely choose between alternative candidates presented to us by political parties; once they have been chosen we have no further say until election time comes around again. In Athens the citizens ruled directly and they were never averse to showing their displeasure by fines, dismissal or banishment of their most distinguished citizens. The best proof of the conscientiousness of the ordinary Athenian is given by the Old Oligarch [8, especially III]; this testimony is all the more convincing because it comes from an ill-wisher.

Nevertheless, effective government also requires professionals. It is no accident that the leaders were all men of means, usually from the old families, elected year after year to the responsible post of strategus (general), which gradually became more and more a political office. While military incompetence could lead to dismissal of a strategus, his election depended on his ability to influence the majority by speaking in the Assembly. This was not easy. Public speaking was an art in the fifth century, and even those who only listened demanded a first-rate performance. But the well-to-do alone could afford the time and money needed for such training. Teachers of rhetoric were in great demand and exorbitant fees were sometimes paid for their services. Such teachers, and learned men generally, were called "sophists" — wise men — by the Athenians. In the fourth century, after the Athenian empire had fallen, moralists like Plato blamed the failure on irresponsible democratic orators and the men who taught them. Others found fault with intellectuals like Socrates for undermining the old respect for law and religion. Plato's genius still makes us think of a sophist as one "who makes the worse appear the better reason," a venal and superficial manipulator of words; yet Socrates himself was often caricatured as a sophist on the comic stage (we have a brilliant example in Aristophanes' *Clouds*). Even men without political aspirations were forced to learn public speaking, because in Athens the defendant was expected to plead his own case in court; he might hire a ghost writer but he had to give the speech.

Another reason why statesmen came from the well-to-do class was that most citizens made their own living. They could take time off to attend the Assembly when important issues were at stake but they were not free to make a career out of politics. Annual offices, like membership in the panel of 6000 jurors or service on the Council of Five Hundred came to be salaried, and pay was also provided for the thousands who rowed the naval vessels — a fact that helps explain the esprit de corps that distinguished them. But their compensation was not high enough to embarrass the government while the Delian Confederacy held together.

To round out this sketch of the democratic society it should be noted that many Athenians were engaged in small business enterprises, as retailers, shippers and manufacturers, but not a few of them worked as hired laborers. Farming was still a leading occupation, with a substantial number of citizens owning small farms. Only citizens could own real property in Attica. There were also entrepreneurs on a larger scale, not all of whom were Athenians. This flourishing economy was first seriously threatened when the presence of Spartan troops forced a general evacuation of the countryside during the Peloponnesian War.

It is against this background that the literature of fifth century Athens should be read. Also worth keeping in mind is the fact that Aeschylus fought in the ranks at Marathon and that Sophocles served as one of the imperial treasurers (443 B.C.) and was even elected strategus (440 B.C.). Poet, philosopher and man of action were often combined in the same person during these remarkable years.

5. *Slavery as a Greek Institution*

Forty thousand citizens, even when supplemented by twenty thousand metics, would have been insufficient to maintain the Athenian Empire without the institution of slavery. Athens was a slave state, but it was a slavery very different from that of modern times. In antiquity slavery varied greatly from place to place and at different periods in the same place. Aristotle, who lived in the fourth century, a time of criticism and analysis, discussed and justified "natural slavery" [9], little realizing how his arguments would later be used in a very different context by Calhoun and others to justify Negro slavery in the American South.

In Homeric society we read about slaves like Odysseus' swineherd Eumaeus and the female servants in the palace who made themselves agreeable to Penelope's suitors, or Briseis, whose charms brought about a rupture between Agamemnon and Achilles. Some slaves were well-born ladies captured when their cities fell; they employed their time with weaving and other household tasks when too old to share their master's bed. But well-born slaves, male or female, were never numerous. Later, while war continued to be an important source of slaves, they were also recruited in other ways, particularly as a result of indebtedness. A man in difficulties borrowed on his land; when he had no more land to offer he pledged his person. This practice still continued at least down to the fourth century [see 12, Lysias XII, 98], but not in Athens, where a law of Solon's (594 B.C.) forbade the enslavement of Athenian citizens for debt.

Probably the leading method of acquiring slaves in the fifth century was by purchase. There were professional slave dealers, whose trade flourished especially in backward areas such as Thrace, where men, women and young children could be obtained at a low price. Records indicate there was also a considerable market for slave girls in Syria. But while there were many barbarian slaves in Greece there were also Greek slaves. The institution of slavery therefore had no racial basis. From time to time an entire Greek city was "andrapodized" — that is the whole population was put on the block (sometimes after the men of military age had been executed).

Matters did not go ordinarily quite that far (Mytilene had a very narrow escape from being "andrapodized" [10]), and it was the usual practice to ransom captives for a fixed sum. Slavery was also inflicted as punishment for offenses against the state.

Probably the most galling form of bondage in the fifth century was that which afflicted the agricultural serfs of Sparta, the helots. Many of them were descended from the Greeks of Messenia, which was finally conquered by Sparta in the Second Messenian War (mid-seventh century B.C.). Their servile status was hereditary. They were treated by Sparta with an impersonal brutality which left them little hope for improving their lot. In general agricultural slavery seems to have been a survival from more primitive times and was not prevalent in more advanced areas like Attica. They were still a factor in faraway Corcyra, however [see 11, Thucydides, III. 73].

Aside from these serfs the condition of bondage was usually temporary. In Athens the slaves constituted a skilled labor force. Thucydides tells us that some twenty thousand of them got away during the Spartan occupation of Attica in 412 (VII. 27), which was a body blow to the Athenian economy. We also have a number of inscriptions listing Athenian slaves who had been granted freedom. Their occupations are noted and many craftsmen are included. Such slaves were not distinguished from citizens or metics in what they did, in how they dressed [see 8, I, 10-11] or in the amount paid for their services by employers. One explanation is that the demand for skilled workers forced slave owners to offer special inducements to the slave, since he could not afford to keep him unless he performed skilled and therefore highly paid tasks. The best inducement was a promise of freedom, allowing the slave to set aside purchase money from his earnings.

The slave had one great advantage over the free worker: he was not subject to military conscription. Contrary to a popular notion, slaves were not used to row the Athenian triremes and only in a moment of desperation did any city-state call on them for military duties. When this did happen, they were also promised their freedom as a reward.

Slavery, then, was not usually permanent. We have no sure way of estimating the number of slaves in Attica nor the number owned by the average Athenian. Statements by orators mentioning estates left by well-to-do persons suggest that fifty slaves is an unusually high figure, though less reliable sources go as high as 1000, which

is fantastic. The slave was a person in Athens, not a "thing" as in Roman law. He could give testimony in court but was subject to torture, unlike the citizen. It is a commonplace of the Attic orators to criticize an opponent for not allowing his slave to be put to the torture. However, when a slave was freed in Athens he became a metic, not a citizen, as in Rome. There were instances where a former slave — the banker Pasion for example — not only acquired freedom but citizenship as well — but bankers are very special people. It may be added that mining was the worst form of servitude. While some needy Athenians did mine silver at Laurium the ore was usually excavated by slaves; the cost in human misery was appalling. The modern reader finds it hard to reconcile the genial picture we have of Xenophon from the *Anabasis* and the *Memorabilia* with his proposal in the *Revenues of Athens* that the Athenians solve their economic problems by living entirely on the work of a multitude of slaves in the silver mines of Laurium.

6. *The Peloponnesian War*

The military strength and economic resources of Athens were never greater than in 431 B.C. when the long threatening war finally broke out between the Peloponnesian League, with Sparta at its head, and the Delian Confederacy guided by Athens, under the leadership of Pericles. A generation later, in 404 B.C., the final decision had been reached; the triumph was Sparta's for the moment but ultimately it was Macedonia's and then Rome's. The war ended the only attempt to unite the Greek states under the hegemony of one of their number which had any prospect of success. Thucydides saw the war coming, anticipated that it would be of great significance, and decided in advance to be its historian. His biography, like that of Herodotus, is known to us only through the History he wrote, since the "Life" by Marcellinus and other accounts of him are late and untrustworthy. Clearly a man of influence — otherwise he would not have been elected a strategus — he must have had information on the inner workings of Athenian policy of a type not available earlier to Herodotus; as a prominent exile after the loss of Amphipolis, he evidently came to know much about the Spartan leadership. His influence on later historians was — and still is — immense; Xenophon, Theopompus and probably the competent unknown, a part of whose *Hellenica* turned up in Egypt, all began their histories where Thucydides breaks off in 411 B.C. His imitators were legion, including the Roman Livy, who paraphrases him in introducing the Second Punic War (Book XXI). It is not easy to select a part of Thucydides, since all of his History should be read, but two of the passages chosen have independent value. The first [10] touches on a subject of perennial interest, the question of punishment as a deterrent to crime; and the second [11] anticipates Burke and others who have considered the effects of revolution on human society. The most moving narrative, the account of the Syracusan expedition, is too long to be included.

We gain some insight into the feelings of the man in the street by reading Aristophanes' comedies. Here we find all the scandal about Pericles and other bigwigs so rigorously excluded by Thucydides, as well as biting remarks about Euripides' plays, new-fangled ideas in education and Socrates and other sophists. The joys of peace are described in the midst of war, and scenes of bawdy humor alternate with lyrical passages of great beauty. Nothing is too high or too low to escape the notice of this brilliant scoffer. Fraud in high places, informers, the price of food, homosexuals, Persian agents, utopian states, the law courts, deserters, bragging soldiers, Boeotian peasants, leading statesmen — all these and more are served up to be laughed at by appreciative audiences. But as the war went on the comedies became more reticent about current politics: it was no longer a subject for laughter. While all the Athenians who had not gone to Syracuse were waiting anxiously to hear the outcome of that fateful expedition, Aristophanes treated them to a play of sheer fantasy, in which the birds decide to build a city of their own, Cloudcuckooland, between the world of men and the gods — far from tax collectors, recruiting officers and the other stern realities of life. Yet Aristophanes was awarded only the second prize. He was more successful with the *Frogs,* in which Aeschylus and Euripides dispute for the chair of tragedy in the underworld. By this time (405 B.C.) the war was nearly over. It is strange that Athens could appreciate such a play at such a time and that an Athenian could write it.

Further light is thrown on the period by that engaging rascal Andocides. An Athenian blueblood, we know of him only because of his involvement in the still mysterious incident of the mutilation of the Hermae. On the eve of the sailing of the Syracusan expedition (415 B.C.) a group of young revelers went out one night and hacked up the sacred images that many pious Athenians had before their houses. Charges and counter-charges soon led to the recall of Alcibiades from Sicily and his desertion to Sparta, which contributed importantly to the failure of the expedition and the loss of the war. Andocides turned state's evidence and was forced into exile. His three orations all represent unsuccessful attempts to have his rights as a citizen restored. Andocides was no professional orator but his speeches are composed with spirit. They give us a lively picture of the upper-class Athenian, of which he was, to be sure, a somewhat tarnished specimen. His speech *On the Mysteries* lends new meaning to the narrative of Thucydides.

It was also during the Peloponnesian War that Socrates carried on his special mission, whenever he was not serving as a footsoldier. Socrates left no writings so that we depend chiefly on three men who did know him and wrote about him, Aristophanes, Plato and Xenophon. Of these Plato alone gives a sense of his greatness. Aristophanes merely uses him as a convenient representative of the educational ideas he abhorred. That the playwright was not personally hostile to him is shown by Aristophanes' role in Plato's *Symposium.* Xenophon simply could not understand what Socrates was trying to do but he does give us a delightful picture of him in his *Memorabilia* as a kindly man with a sense of humor and all the conventional virtues. Plato understood Socrates but he also outgrew him, and attributed to him ideas that were really his own. Efforts to separate the Socrates of history from the Platonic Socrates have not been entirely successful, but independent evidence of Socrates' influence as a thinker is furnished by the so-called Socratic Schools founded after his death by men who admired him as much as Plato did but were influenced by him in other directions. The Socratic dialogue also appears as a new literary form, with spiritual descendants all the way down to the *Imaginary Conversations* of Walter Savage Landor.

We are unfortunate in viewing this critical period almost exclusively through Athenian eyes. It is not that we do not find them sharply critical — for example, the *Trojan Women* of Euripides was a scathing indictment of Athens' treatment of Melos — but we would like to know how the struggle was regarded by neutrals and enemy cities. So uncertain is our evidence that even today there are those who maintain in the face of Thucydides that Athens was popular with her allies. All we can be reasonably sure of is that once Sparta took over the direction of Greek affairs there were many Greeks who looked back on Athens' rule with great longing.

7. The Fourth Century

The years between the fall of Athens and the victory of Philip of Macedon at Chaeronea (404–338 B.C.) are just as important historically as the much-heralded fifth century both in literary and scientific achievements and in political significance. But no historian of the calibre of Herodotus or Thucydides recorded them. Xenophon's *Hellenica* stops with the Battle of Mantinea in 362 B.C. and at no time does he rise to the level of his incomparable predecessor. Xenophon's narrative of the great adventure in which he served first as a volunteer in the army of the Younger Cyrus (401 B.C.), then as a leader who brought the Greeks safely back from Persia (the *Anabasis*) is much better reading, but it deals only with this episode. For the main narrative after 362 we depend on the fragments of historians like Ephorus and Theopompus, the "Lives" of Plutarch and the uninspired narrative of Diodorus Siculus. On the other hand the Attic orators furnish an abundance of detail about life in Athens. For the early period Lysias is the best witness [12]; then we move on to Isaeus (who specialized in breaking wills), the long-lived Isocrates, who kept asking outside princes to rescue the Greeks until Philip took him at his word, and finally Aeschines and Demosthenes. Among the most exciting political developments during the fourth century was the Syracusan Empire of the Elder Dionysius, which foreshadowed the super-state of Alexander and the Successors. Dionysius had as his historian a wealthy Syracusan named Philistus, who wrote as the convinced advocate of dictatorship. The loss of Philistus' history is regrettable. Alexander thought it worth sending for in the midst of his campaigns. Another western Greek was Pytheas of Massilia, a scientific navigator who sailed past Gibraltar into the outer sea as far as Britain or beyond and wrote an account of what he saw. While Pytheas is known only through scattered references, we do have an interesting compilation entitled *Periplus* ("voyage around") *of the Mediterranean,* written in the fourth century and mendaciously attributed to Scylax, an explorer at the time of Darius I. There is also a contemporary writer from

Stymphalus in Arcadia, Aeneas Tacticus, who wrote about siege warfare, and his work is not without interest for the social historian.

Politically the future seemed at first to lie with Sparta, whose institutions were criticized by Aristotle and compared with those of Crete in the light of later events [13]. Meanwhile Athens went through a "time of troubles" under the provisional government of the Thirty Tyrants, described for us with vigor and hatred by one of its victims, the orator Lysias [12]. When the old democracy was restored the Athenians behaved with moderation, though the condemnation of Socrates (399 B.C.) cast a deep shadow. He was condemned for both good and bad reasons: partly because his searching questioning did threaten Athens' democratic institutions, partly because the Athenians hoped to be rid of their own bad conscience by putting to death the "gadfly" who would not let them alone (see Plato's *Apology*).

As the years passed the Greeks became disenchanted with Sparta and the new free world they had looked forward to after the defeat of Athens. Disenchantment became complete when the Peace of Antalcidas (386 B.C.) — the King's Peace as they called it — was forced upon them by a Spartan-Persian entente which included the renewed surrender of Asiatic Greece to Persia. Economically European Greece was less prosperous than before; it was not a disastrous falling off but was very perceptible. Money was hard to come by. Defense costs rose as warfare became more specialized and therefore more expensive. Citizen armies began to give way to mercenary troops; this change threatened the very foundations of the autonomous city-state. Even able and patriotic leaders like King Agesilaus of Sparta and Iphicrates of Athens found it necessary on occasion to enter the service of a foreign power.

Dissatisfaction with things as they were led to literature depicting things as they ought to be. Plato's *Republic* and his unfinished *Critias* still stir us, though the *Seventh Letter,* whether written by Plato or by someone close to Plato, shows the dangers of trying to convert dreams into political realities. Xenophon's *Cyropaedia,* a historical novel centering around the founder of the Persian Empire but betraying the Spartan leanings of its author, has a charm of its own. More widely read than either Plato or Xenophon was the wily Ctesias, whose works were probably in Alexander's knapsack. Nearchus of Crete, a close friend of Alexander with a reputation for probity, tells us that one of the reasons for the grim march back from India through the Gedrosian waste was Alexander's determination to outdo Semiramis, and Semiramis was known to the Greeks through Ctesias [14].

Two years before he died Philip of Macedon accomplished the objectives he had set for himself of making Macedon strong internally while externally she controlled the policies of the Greek states. The final step was taken when, after stubborn resistance, Athens and Thebes were defeated at Chaeronea in 338 B.C. Demosthenes had seemingly done the impossible in bringing Athens and Thebes together, but partial cooperation among the Greeks no longer sufficed as it had in the time of Xerxes. Conspicuously absent was Sparta, whose help might have postponed the day of reckoning. Later Sparta tried resistance on her own only to be crushed by Alexander's viceroy, Antipater. Immediately after Alexander's death Demosthenes and Athens made a last attempt in the Lamian War. Chaeronea marked, however, the real end of the old order.

8. The Hellenistic State System

Two years after Chaeronea, as he was about to take personal command in the war against Persia, Philip was assassinated by a young Macedonian nobleman named Pausanias. We will never know just what happened immediately afterwards but when the dust had settled Philip's son Alexander, twenty years of age, was seen firmly seated on the Macedonian throne. Neither then nor later did Alexander falter in his relentless pursuit of aims known only to himself. Thirteen years later (323 B.C.) in Babylon he died, exhausted by his own victories and bequeathing the whirlwind to be reaped by the generation that succeeded him. It is not certain that anyone, even his bosom friend Hephaestion, ever really knew Alexander. It is certain that we do not; how else could such widely different views be held about him by so many otherwise reliable historians? His career made a vivid impression on the youthful Plutarch, who wrote more than four hundred years later [15]. More important for us than the fascinating question of what Alexander would have done or tried to do had he lived out his time is consideration of the new political combinations that emerged under the Successors and the effect of this new situation on Greece and the Greek people.

Alexander's failure to leave a grown son to succeed him left the fate of the Macedonian royal house chiefly dependent on his infant son, his half-witted brother and his terrifying mother, the indomitable Olympias. The generals with whom he had conquered Persia and invaded India found themselves torn between their loyalties and their ambitions; Alexander's veterans exercised a malign influence as the one unchallenged force in the eastern Mediterranean. Forty-two years later, in the summer of 281 B.C., the last of Alexander's generals, Seleucus Nicator, was murdered by the bastard son of another of Alexander's commanders, Ptolemy the Thunderbolt. All chance for a reunited empire died with Seleucus. A precarious balance of power was in the making instead. Outside of Greece two great kingdoms survived from the wreckage: the Seleucid Empire, with holdings in Asia Minor linked by a thin line of communications with the central area of Syria and Mesopotamia, and stretching out eastward to the borders of India; and Ptolemaic Egypt, with special interests in Cyrenaica, Cyprus, Coele-Syria and in the islands and coast of the Aegean Sea. In Greece the old city-states remained with greatly diminished powers; they were threatened by the Macedonian kingdom to the north, where the throne had just been seized by the adventurer Ptolemy the Thunderbolt. Two years later, in 278 B.C., a last ingredient was added to the brew with the arrival of Celtic invaders from the Danube region, the Galatae; they swept down through Macedonia, killing Ptolemy on the way, and penetrated south all the way to Delphi. When they were driven out of Greece, some of them were ferried over to Asia where they eventually settled down; in the meanwhile their depredations enabled Pergamum to become an independent kingdom at the expense of Seleucid rule in Asia Minor. The establishment of Antigonus Gonatas, named for his grandfather the general of Alexander, as ruler of Macedonia, completed the main lines of the Hellenistic state system.

In the second half of the third century, this system proved inadequate to check the spread of Roman power. The same disease that almost allowed Persia to conquer the Greek mainland early in the fifth century now proved fatal to Greeks and Macedonians alike. The Romans were able to play one state off against another with ludicrous ease until, as Polybius tells us [18], they found themselves after some fifty-three years (220–167 B.C.) without a rival in the Mediterranean. Rome did not drop the pretense of "freeing the Greeks," however, until it suited her convenience. Macedonia became a Roman province in 148 B.C., while Greece was subjected two years afterwards when Corinth was destroyed.

Despite the failures of the Hellenistic state system its results were not all negative. Alexander is credited with establishing seventy cities [see 15, 5]; this is an evident exaggeration but he and the Successors did build many new cities while modernizing old ones all the way from Egypt to India. Military reasons may have been paramount with them, but these cities brought about permanent economic changes in western Asia. Coined money replaced barter and the new system continued even when the Parthians took over the Seleucid territories. It can be said that the cosmopolitan city, the metropolis, was a Hellenistic development. Seleuceia, Antioch and Alexandria were the most famous examples of cities that transcended political boundaries, miniature replicas of the life of the whole eastern Mediterranean, centers of trade, art, manufacturing and amusement. Still more important was the prevalence of the Greek tongue and Greek institutions — watered down but still Greek — in the eastern part of what was soon to be the Roman Empire. Here Hellenism was so deeply rooted that the Romans, after opposing it in favor of local native cultures, finally adopted it as their own. Had the practical good sense of the Romans failed them, not only would the Empire have been of short duration but the diffusion of Christianity, with all that followed from it, would have been drastically affected. The Roman learned not only from the failures of the Successor states but from their successes.

A summary of the political history of this turbulent period would be confusing rather than instructive. Something of the flavor of the times can be gained from the story of the remote city of Heraclea on the Black Sea, preserved for us by the happy accident that Photius had in his library a copy of the work of Memnon [17]. Of special interest are the experiments made by the Greeks with federal government in the twilight of their political independence. Two federations in particular, the Aetolian and the Achaean leagues, have been much admired, and were perhaps more cited than understood by the Founding Fathers in their debates over a constitution for the United States.

9. Social and Economic Developments

Alexander's conquests had a profound effect on the economy of Greece, which fell away slowly but steadily from the booming days of the Athenian Empire. The reasons for this decline are not obvious, and it is well to avoid easy generalizations, yet the fact itself is undeniable. Unstable conditions may have been both cause and effect. The ferocity with which the Greek cities continued to wage war on one another before Philip temporarily checked their belligerence still shocks anyone who turns from the nobility of Plato's writings to the reality of contemporary events. This constant state of warfare also tended to impoverish all but the wealthiest states. It was often better in many ways for a Greek businessmen or artisan to carry on his work under the loose rein of the Great King than in the contaminated atmosphere of the autonomous cities of Greece. It was not even possible in those troubled times to keep the city-states from seizing the treasures of the gods, the accumulation of centuries of pious giving. The Phocians, hard pressed by their Theban neighbors, looted Delphi and melted down sacred objects of gold and silver to find pay for their soldiers. A scandal resulted but there was no lack of volunteers to fight against Apollo provided their scruples were relieved by somewhat higher wages. None of this would have happened had the economy been in a healthy condition. Export trade was declining, however, in favor of more favored regions, such as the Asiatic coastland and the nearby islands, as well as Sicily and the West. When Alexander captured Susa and Persepolis he found enormous quantities of silver and gold ingots which he turned into coin. Lavishly bestowed by the conqueror on his soldiers, this money soon found its way to the market places. Much of it was used to satisfy the new demand for goods from Greece. The result was a rise in prices and an economic revival for many Greek cities. Improvement was not permanent, however. By the third century Greece had lost its advantage and the economic center of gravity shifted eastward; Rhodes replaced Athens as a leading port for the exchange of goods and cities like Miletus prospered as terminal points for the eastern caravan trade. At the same time new cities such as Alexandria developed specialties of their own, perfumes, cosmetics, cameos, costume jewelry, fine fabrics, which were generally preferred to the products of Athens and Corinth. Heracleides in the second century tells us of the poverty of Athens in his time, though he gives a very different impression of agricultural areas like Boeotia [19].

The Successor kingdoms, notably Egypt and the Seleucid Empire, present a different picture economically. The chief concern of their rulers was how to attract Greeks to live in their lands. They needed technically trained experts of all sorts; professional soldiers were of primary importance. But in order to support their expensive military establishments and the Greek bureaucracy which they superimposed on the older governmental structure they needed to increase the productivity of their countries. There would have to be changes in agricultural methods, as well as the introduction of new industries and the feverish exploitation of mines. The Ptolemaic economy, which is known best, was regulated by the government down to the smallest detail. The tax system was ingenious and efficient, with one group of officials guaranteeing the honesty of another. At the very bottom was the native Egyptian field hand, who was carefully allowed just enough sustenance to keep him reasonably healthy and hopelessly poor. All that can be said in favor of the system is that it worked so well that the Romans later adopted it.

The first part of the Hellenistic period was marked by a wave of emigration from Greece. Skilled artisans, businessmen, professional soldiers and engineers were attracted by the prospects of great wealth to be acquired in the new monarchies. Many settled down and raised families. Often they married natives but they tried to bring their sons up as Greeks and they clung to their privileged positions. The new cities in Asia were all provided with theaters, town halls, gymnasiums and temples to the Greek gods. Officers formed clubs and their families kept up the old traditions. Nevertheless a reverse trend set in by the third century and more Greeks were returning to Europe than were going out to settle in the East. There was still a great deal of fluidity, however. Traveling companies of entertainers toured the new cities, giving plays or improvising skits of their own. On the other hand the priests of Isis and the "Great Mother," along with their ceremonial processions, became a common sight in Greece, as the older cultures of the ancient east made their influence felt.

10. Intellectual Developments

In one realm, that of philosophy, Athens maintained her supremacy. But there were no more giants after the death of Aristotle in 322 B.C. Aristotle had worked out a system of logic which he applied to all forms of knowledge in the effort to establish the general principles of each. Less brilliant than Plato he was infinitely more patient and his curiosity was unlimited. He had a flexible mind, although we are apt to think of him as dogmatic and intolerant because his conclusions were accepted as gospel for so many centuries. Metaphysics, biology, political science, ethics, art, poetry. rhetoric and the history of philosophy all came within his range of interests. After Aristotle, however, the natural and exact sciences tended to be neglected by the philosophic schools and were forced to strike out for themselves. In Athens the overriding interest was in ethics, the study of how men ought to behave. The old gods failed to meet the needs of the new era. Men, both dazzled and frightened by the enlargement of their world, felt uncertain of the future. Thoughtful people sought something in the series of bewildering changes which could give meaning to their lives. The answers furnished by philosophers were widely different but all aimed at making the individual independent of external circumstances. Most successful was the Stoic School, founded by Zeno of Citium, whose ancestry was probably Phoenician. The Stoics pictured a world order operating in accordance with immutable laws. Everything that would happen had already been determined and could not be prevented. The wise man was the one who accepted this, whose will was in tune with natural law. Such a man knew that all was for the best and that by identifying himself with natural law he became the master of his own destiny. He could rise above agonizing physical pain or the loss of worldly goods or even the death of a son, because of his conviction that such things had to be and were good.

Epicurus, an Athenian who founded his own school, the Garden as it was called, thought differently on these matters. Instead of fate, destiny, world order, there was only chance. Borrowing the mechanistic hypothesis of the Atomists, he viewed the world as made up of tiny particles of many shapes whose continual movement led to an endless variety of combinations and permutations which had accidentally brought about the particular arrangements of atoms that constituted the universe of his own day. There was no plan and nothing was permanent but neither was there anything to be afraid of. Pleasure was desirable but pleasure meant merely the absence of pain. Knowing this the wise man refused to become involved in the senseless activities of those around him. He avoided pain by engaging in intellectual pursuits, which were agreeable but not emotionally disturbing and had no unpleasant aftermath. If even these proved fatiguing he might at any time remove himself from the scene. Meanwhile he lived unworried by thoughts of divine vengeance. The gods either did not exist or, if they did, had no interest in humanity. Epicureanism continued to win converts but never in large numbers. Most men live by their illusions and Epicureanism had nothing to offer them. Epicurus' doctrines are presented most persuasively in the beautiful lines of Lucretius (*De Rerum Natura*). There were other schools also, notably the Skeptics and the Cynics; the Academy and the Lyceum continued to honor the teachings of Plato and Aristotle.

Alexandria took the lead in mathematics and the sciences, partly as a result of the generous support given by the Ptolemies. The Library of Alexandria was the largest in the Greek world. Scholars were encouraged to come to Egypt to pursue their researches. Medicine developed rapidly with royal support; Herophilus and Erasistratus were two famous physicians in Alexandria during the third century. In geometry Euclid is still remembered and his textbook was used in European schools until very recently. Astronomy made advances and not only at Alexandria. The high point was probably the discovery of the precession of the equinoxes by Hipparchus of Nicaea, much of whose work was done in Rhodes. Aristarchus of Samos came to Alexandria and promulgated the heliocentric theory but the data available was insufficient to substantiate his daring hypothesis. The great mathematical genius of antiquity, Archimedes, was a Syracusan who studied in Alexandria and then returned to Syracuse; he was killed by a Roman soldier when Marcellus captured Syracuse in 212 B.C. Among Archimedes' achievements were the foundation of statics, the discovery of the law of specific gravity and a remarkable number of practical inventions, including war machines and a new way of pumping water. As a geometer he solved problems later reserved for calculus.

Even more versatile was Eratosthenes, nicknamed "Beta" by scoffers who said that he was second-best in everything. Certainly he was a poor second to Archimedes in mathematics but as a geographer he had no equal in antiquity. He had the good sense to recognize the importance of Pytheas' voyage to Britain and made use of it in his treatise (Polybius denounced Pytheas as a liar). He set high standards in the theoretical aspects of geography but was handicapped in descriptive geography by the inaccuracy of the reports available to him, reports like those of Megasthenes on India [16] and Patrocles on the Caspian Sea. He did arrive at a creditable figure for the circumference of the earth, however, and maintained that it was possible to sail around the world.

There was a wider reading public in the Hellenistic period than in any previous time. Books were easier to obtain thanks to the cheapness of the papyrus of Egypt and the parchment which made Pergamum a household word. The older writers were copied and recopied, with Homer easily the popular favorite. There was also a new fashion in poets and poetry, where novelty of subject matter and learned allusions were admired, as well as experiments in new verse forms. The short epic of Lycophron, the *Alexandra,* still survives to puzzle commentators and challenge the translator. More understandable is the *Argonautica* of Apollonius Rhodius, an epic on Jason and the Golden Fleece which shows an interest in love as a psychological experience.

The only historian of whom we have more than a collection of fragments is Polybius. His remarks on what history is about, particularly his insistence on the unity of all history, are truly remarkable. If Herodotus did not settle on his real subject until he had already written the earlier part of his History, Polybius began with his main theme in mind — the conquest of the Mediterranean world (the *oecumene* as he called it) by Rome in a period of fifty-three years (220–167 B.C.). Unfortunately Polybius disregarded the excellent advice he gave to other historians — to tell the truth without prejudice — whenever he came to write about his native city of Megalopolis or its enemies [18].

When everything else had changed the Greek athletic games continued. Pausanias gives us a vivid account of the history of the Olympic Games from mythical times down to the second century A.D., when he lived [19]. The Roman gladiatorial games and spectacles in which animals were slaughtered in the arena were not able to dim the Greek fondness for racing, throwing the discus and wrestling. When the Olympic Games were abolished in 392 A.D. by the Emperor Theodosius I, the spirit of ancient Greece was truly dead.

1

The World of Homer

THIS PASSAGE from the Iliad is our earliest picture of a Greek city both
at peace and in war. The selection from the Odyssey which follows
shows Homer's ideas of the outer world of the uncivilized savage and how
he lived. This theme recurs in later writers, though as the Greeks learned
more about geography the "natural savage" is pushed farther and farther
back either in space or time, sometimes as the noble child of nature and
sometimes as the brute depicted here, the spiritual ancestor of Caliban.

a Iliad, xviii, 462-617

THEN THE lame god answered her: "Take courage, and may
the things you dread never happen! If only I had the power to
keep ill-sounding death away from him, when his fated day arrives!
But splendid arms he shall have, a wonder to any who sees them of
the cities of men."

Having spoken he left her there and went off to his bellows, turning them on the fire and urging them to the task. Now all the
bellows blew into twenty crucibles, and they blew on the fires with
every kind of blast, now increasing now lessening their intensity as
Hephaestus desired and as the work required. Unyielding bronze he
threw into the flames, tin and precious gold and silver. Then he set
his great anvil on the anvil block. With one hand he wielded his
mighty hammer, grasping the fire tongs with the other.

First of all he made the shield great and strong, then he ornamented it all around, enclosing it with a triple gleaming rim, and
fastening to it a silver-studded shield strap. He emblazoned the five-
folded shield with many devices of his own imagining.

Upon the shield he portrayed the earth, the heavens and the sea,
the tireless sun, the full moon and all the constellations that crown
the heavens: the Pleiades, the Hyades, mighty Orion and the Bear,
also called the Wain, which turns itself around watching Orion, and
never dips into the baths of Ocean.

Thereon he made two cities of mortal men. In the first weddings were being celebrated. Brides were escorted from their chambers and up through the town with flaming torches as the marriage song rose high. Noble youths whirled in dance to the continued music of flute and lyre. Women watched admiringly from before their doors. Also people were crowding into the market, where a contest was taking place. Two men disputed over the price of a man slain. The first swears he will make full payment, calling on the people to witness, while the other refuses to accept any recompense as sufficient. Both profess a willingness to abide by the award of an arbiter. They are loudly applauded, for supporters are present on each side. The Elders are seated on polished stones in a sacred circle, while loud-voiced heralds, scepters in their hands, go from one to the other in turn, as they pronounce judgment. In the middle lie two talents of gold as a reward for the one deemed to have given the fairest judgment.

Two armies lay besieging the other city, but they were of divided counsel, some urging total destruction, others favoring a sharing of all the fine things in the city. But the men of the town had not given up, and were arming themselves for an ambush. On the walls stood their dear wives and small children along with the men smitten by old age. The rest went forth, led by Ares and Pallas Athena. Both these were of gold with golden garments, conspicuous as gods should be, with mighty and splendid arms. The people were represented on a somewhat smaller scale. The townsmen, in sufficient numbers to form an ambuscade, waited by a river where all the livestock were accustomed to drink, and there they stood encased in ruddy bronze. Two scouts were stationed at a distance from the soldiers to be on the outlook for sheep and cattle with crumpled horns. The animals came along at a brisk pace, followed by two shepherds playing merrily on their flutes; for they expected no harm. Perceiving them, the townsmen swiftly drove off the herds of cattle and the flocks of fine white sheep, slaying the shepherds. When the besiegers in their place of assembly heard the loud noise of the cattle, they quickly jumped on their high-stepping horses and gave chase. Arriving posthaste they halted and joined battle on the banks of the river. They struck one another with lances of bronze. Then came Strife, Confusion and dire Death, who seized on one who was wounded but still alive, then on another as yet unscathed, and dragged a third through the press by his feet, already a corpse. The shoulders of Death's garments were wine red with human blood. Thrusting themselves in and fighting like living beings, they even snatched dead bodies from one another.

And then he fashioned a field of soft earth, rich farm land, broad and three times ploughed. In that field were many ploughmen driving their yokes back and forth and then around. Whenever a ploughman reached the turning place at the end of the furrow, then a man would come up to him and place a cup of honey-sweet wine in his hands. And then he would turn the plough, pressing on to reach the boundary marking the end of the ploughed land. Though wrought in gold the soil grew dark behind as though it were really being furrowed, for this was an amazing feature of the work.

And then he carved an estate with waving grain, where reapers were harvesting with sharp sickles in their hands. Grain fell thick and fast by handfuls into the swathes. Three men stood binding it into sheaves, while behind them boys busily gathered the grain, bringing it up in their arms. And the lord with his scepter, glad of heart, stood silently by in the cutting. At a distance under an oak tree heralds were making preparations for a feast, dressing a great ox they had sacrificed, while women strewed quantities of white barley meal for the harvesters' dinner.

Next he wrought in gold a large and beautiful vineyard weighed down with fruit. The bunches of grapes were dark on vines propped up with silver poles. Around and about it he drew a blue enamel ditch and a hedge of tin. There was a single path which the vintagers used in harvesting the grapes. Light-hearted youths and maidens carried off the honey-sweet fruit in plaited baskets. In their midst a boy played delightfully on a clear-toned lute, singing the beautiful Linus song in his sweet child's voice. The others followed him, joyously beating time with tripping feet.

Then he made a herd of straight-horned cattle in tin and gold, lowing as they hurried from the corral to pasture beside a noisy stream and a thicket of reeds. Four golden herdsmen ranged the cattle in ranks, followed by nine white-footed dogs. Two frightful lions seized a roaring bull from the front ranks of the cattle, and dragged him off bellowing loudly. The stout dogs went in pursuit. But the lions meanwhile tore asunder the great bull's hide, gulping down his innards and the black blood. The herdsmen urged on the swift dogs, but in vain, for they refused to close with the lions, merely moving up and barking then backing off.

Next the lame one made a pasture in a pleasant valley, a large pasture with gleaming white sheep, shepherds' huts, stalls and covered sheep folds.

Then the lame god made a skillfully designed dancing hall like the one Daedalus formerly built in broad Cnossus for beautiful-haired Ariadne. And there young men, and young women well worth the cattle price were dancing, holding one another by the wrist. The girls wore garments of fine linen, the men well-woven tunics, slightly glistening with oil. The ladies wore fair headbands while their partners carried golden daggers with silver baldrics. They danced lightly with responsive feet, just as when a potter, sitting with the wheel fitted into his hands, makes trial of it to see how it will run. Sometimes they danced with one another in lines, and a goodly crowd stood around enjoying the delightful spectacle. Also two tumblers whirled round and round among them leading the dance.

Next he depicted the Ocean stream at the outermost edge of the skillfully made shield.

But when the great shield was finished and made strong, then he fashioned a breastplate brighter than flame, and a massive helmet carefully fitted to the temples and beautifully ornamented. To the helmet he fastened a crest of gold, and he also made greaves of fine beaten tin.

And when the illustrious lame god had completed all the weapons he took them, and offered them to the mother of Achilles. She flew down from snow-clad Olympus like a hawk, bearing the gleaming armor of Hephaestus.

b Odyssey, *ix, 105-542*

WE SAILED on from there[1] with sad hearts until we reached the country of the lawless and insolent Cyclopes, who neither plough nor plant anything by hand, apparently trusting to the immortal gods. Everything grows without sowing or cultivation, including wheat and barley and grapes yielding fine wine, for the rain of Zeus nourishes them. They have neither laws nor meeting places, but live on mountain tops or in hollow caves governing their wives and children, but with no care for one another.

Stretching along outside the harbor lies a heavily wooded by no means despicable island, not too near and yet not very far away from the Cyclopean mainland, and on it wild goats have multiplied in great numbers. Man has not set foot there nor have hunters landed on that island, toiling through the brush and pushing on to the tops of the hills. Nor has it ever been inhabited by shepherds or farmers, but it remains unsown and unploughed, producing bleating goats but not sharing in the destiny of man. For the Cyclopes have no red-prowed ships nor are there shipwrights among them to build well-timbered ships able to reach the cities of men—crossing the sea from port to port as men are wont to do. Otherwise they would have culti-vated the island for themselves, for it is not a bad spot and would yield all things in season. There are pleasant well-watered meadows on the coast of the gray sea. The grapevines never waste away, the land is easy to cultivate, and grain would always stand tall at the season of mowing, for the soil underneath is rich. Then too an inlet offers good anchorage where no rope is needed, or mooring stones fastened to the stern. Rather, the ship may be left on the beach until such time as the sailors need it and the winds are blowing. But at the far end of the bay, water flows sparkling from a spring in a sub-terranean cave, and poplars grow around it. That is the place we sailed to, guided by some god. The night was dark without enough light to see by. For there was a heavy pall around our ships and the moon could not be seen in the heavens, overpowered by clouds. No one set eyes on the island nor did we notice the long waves rolling off shore until we beached our well-timbered ships. When they were grounded we took down all the sails, then we stepped out on shore, sleeping soundly while we waited for divine day.

When morning began and rosy-fingered dawn appeared, then we roamed over the island, marvelling. And now the nymphs, daughters of aegis-bearing Zeus, aroused the goats from their mountain lairs so my comrades might eat. We hurriedly retrieved our curved bows and long-socketed javelins from the ships, dividing our company into three parties, and let fly with our missiles. Straightway god granted us success in our hunting. Twelve ships there were that followed me, and nine goats fell to the lot of each, while ten were set aside for me alone. All that day we spent feasting on this ample supply of meat and drinking sweet wine until the sun went down. The red wine in the ships was not yet expended, some remained, for we had each provided ourselves with many amphoras when we sacked the sacred city of the Cicones. And we perceived the land of the Cyclopes, which was not far away, and smoke rising and the noise of sheep and goats. When the sun set and disappeared in the darkness, then we went to rest on the shore of the sea. When morning began and rosy-fingered dawn appeared I called everyone together, and addressed them as follows: "Trusty comrades, the rest of you wait here, while I go in my ship with my own crew to find out about these men, who they are, and whether they are dangerous savages inaccessible to reason, or hospitable men of a god-fearing disposition." Speaking thus, I went on board ship, ordering my comrades to embark and cast off the stern cables. They climbed in at once, took their places at the oarlocks, and sitting well in order smote the gray sea with their oars. When we approached land, which was not far, we saw at the very edge near the sea a spacious cavern roofed over with laurel trees, where many flocks of sheep and goats were resting. All around it was an enormous court, closed in by rocks set firmly in the ground, by tall pine trees and oaks with lofty foliage. And there a monster of a man was wont to sleep, who tended his flocks far away. He sought no companionship but lived apart, a lawless spirit. And this monster was a sight to behold, he resembled no bread-eating mortal but was rather like some forested peak in the high mountains, where one stands apart from all the rest.

Bidding the rest of my trusty comrades wait there to watch the ship I went ashore with twelve men whom I picked as the bravest. Moreover, I carried a goatskin of sweet dark wine which Maron, the son of Euanthes the priest of Apollo, the custodian of Ismarus, had given me. We had spared him with his wife and child, dreading the divine wrath, for he dwelt in the grove of Phoebus Apollo. On me he bestowed splendid gifts: seven talents of fine gold he gave me, also a silver mixing bowl, and for me he drew twelve whole amphoras of unmixed sweet wine, a divine gift. Not a female slave or handmaid in his household knew about it, but only he, his dear wife and the housekeeper. And whenever he drank the sweet red wine he would fill one cup and pour it into twenty measures of water, whereupon a divine aroma rose from the mixing bowl, and it was not easy to refrain. Filling a great skin with this I carried it, and also brought provisions in a knapsack. Straightway my bold spirit looked forward to meeting an enormous man, all muscle, a savage without concern for law or right doing.

In no time at all we reached the cave, but we did not find him inside, as he was grazing his sleek flocks in the pasture. Entering the cave we looked around, admiring everything: quantities of cheese drying in baskets; pens crammed with lambs and kids — those born in the spring, those born in the summer and the newly born all separately confined; and bowls all overflowing with whey, also buckets and small pails ready for milking. Then my companions pleaded with me to take the cheese and depart; to drive the kids and goats out of their pens onto our swift ship and to sail away over the salt sea. But I was not to be persuaded, though it would have been greatly to my advantage, for I was determined to see him and find out whether he would offer us his hospitality. But certainly he was not apt to be a pleasing sight to my companions.

Then we kindled a fire, and after offering sacrifice we took cheese and ate. We remained inside waiting for him to return from the pasture. He arrived carrying a heavy load of dry wood to prepare his supper, throwing it down inside the cave with a resounding crash. We fled in terror to the innermost recesses of the cave, while he drove all the milk animals from the fat flock into the spacious cavern, leaving the rams and he goats outside in the high-fenced courtyard. Then he lifted up an enormous rock and set it in the doorway. Twenty-four stout four-wheeled wagons could not have moved it from the ground, so heavy was the towering stone that he placed in the doorway. Seating himself he milked all his ewes and she goats in turn, and under each he placed a new-born lamb. Then, immediately scooping out half of the white milk he placed it in woven baskets, while half he poured into bowls where he might find it to drink for his supper. After he had finished his hurried chores he kindled a fire.

Then, spying us, he spoke as follows: "Strangers, who are you? From what place have you sailed a watery path? Pray, on what business have you roamed recklessly over the sea like pirates? For surely those who wander about bringing ill to alien peoples take their lives in their hands."

When he spoke our hearts gave way at the harsh sound of the monster's voice. Nevertheless I answered him in these words: "Truly, we are Achaeans driven off our course from Troy by every kind of wind over the abyss of ocean. Striving to reach home we have come by other paths on a different course, doubtless in accordance with the plan devised by Zeus. We boast ourselves to be the men of Agamemnon son of Atreus, who now has the greatest glory under heaven, for sacking such a great city and destroying a mighty army. And now we have come searching out your hills, on the chance that you will offer us hospitality or bestow on us such gifts as are right among strangers. But show your respect for the gods, good sir, for we are truly suppliants. And Zeus the Protector watches over suppliants and foreigners, and he attends helpless strangers."

Thus I spoke, and he answered me at once in this heartless fashion: "Stranger, you are a fool to have come such a long distance only to bid me fear the gods or avert them. The Cyclopes pay no heed to aegis-bearing Zeus or the blessed gods because we are better than they. I will not spare you or your companions to avert the wrath of Zeus, but only if it is my own wish to do so. But tell me where you left your well-built ship when you came here. Is it in some remote spot, or near at hand? For I would know."

He spoke to test me, but his purpose did not go unnoticed for I was very clever. Accordingly, I answered him in these deceptive words: "Poseidon the earth-shaker shattered my ship, hurling it against the jagged rocks of your island and grounding it on the promontory. Then a wind blew up from the sea, but I escaped utter destruction with these my companions."

When I had concluded he answered not a word from his savage heart, but sprang up and laid hands on my comrades. Snatching two of them at once he dashed them on the ground like two puppies, and their brains spilled out making the floor wet. Cutting them up, limb by limb, he prepared his supper. And he devoured them like a lion of the hills, leaving nothing — entrails, flesh, bones or marrow. Weeping, we could only raise our hands to Zeus when we saw this grisly deed, and we despaired in our hearts. But when the Cyclops had filled his great belly, eating human flesh and drinking raw milk then he lay down inside the cave, stretching himself out among the sheep. At first my proud heart bade me come close to him, draw my sharp dagger from my thigh and stab him through the chest. But a second thought prevented me: we would all have perished miserably in our inability to push aside the huge stone with our hands that he had set in the lofty doorway. So we waited there weeping until bright day. When early morning and rosy-fingered dawn appeared, then he kindled a fire and milked his fine animals in regular order, putting a young lamb under each. After finishing his hurried chores he again laid hold of two men at once and prepared his meal. When he had dined he drove his fat flock out of the cave, easily removing the huge door stone, which he replaced as one might put the top back on a quiver. Thereupon the Cyclops led his sleek charges up the mountain, whistling loudly, while I remained behind brooding darkly on vengeance, if Athena gave me the upper hand. The Cyclops had a cudgel of green olive wood lying beside the pens, fresh cut, which he meant to carry after it had dried out. Looking at it we judged it to be about the size of the mast of a capacious black merchant ship of twenty oars crossing the sea, for it appeared to be every bit as long and as thick as that. Drawing near it I cut off about six feet, and gave it to my comrades, bidding them make it smooth. They did so. Then I drew near again, sharpening the end to a sharp point, which I proceeded to heat in the fire until it glowed. Then I removed it and hid it away in the dung, with which the cave was abundantly provided. Next I commanded the others to draw lots to decide who would help me raise the pikestaff and plunge it in his eye when sweet sleep overtook him. And they selected four men, the very ones I would have chosen, while I was picked as the fifth along with them. In the evening he returned with his fair fleeced sheep. Straightway he drove them into the cave, every single one, for not one was left outside in the high-walled courtyard, either because he suspected something or because god so ordered. But when he had lifted the great stone into place in the doorway he seated himself, milking the ewes and the bleating she goats, each in order, and under each he placed a young lamb. When he had completed his hurried chores then, once more, he seized two men to prepare for his supper. Drawing near I addressed the Cyclops, holding a cup of dark wine in my hands. "Here, Cyclops, drink this wine now that you have eaten human flesh. In this way you will discover the kind of liquor our ship carried. For I was bringing you a drink offering that you might pity us and send us home. But you fell into an unbearable rage. Wretch, how can anyone later visit you from the cities of men? You have acted abominably."

When I had spoken he took the cup and drank. He was simply delighted with the sweet-tasting drink and immediately demanded another. "Kindly give me more, and tell me at once your name so I can give you a present, one that it will rejoice you to receive. Assuredly the barley-rich land of the Cyclopes yields a fine grape nourished by the rain of Zeus, but your wine is pure nectar and ambrosia." Thus he spoke and once more I gave him sparkling wine. Three times I gave him to drink, and three times in his folly he drank it. When the wine began to overpower his senses then I addressed the Cyclops with honeyed words. "Cyclops, you ask what is my illustrious name, and I will reveal it to you, but do you give me the gift you promised. No One is my name, and No One I am called by my mother, my father and all the rest of my friends." When I had finished he answered me from his cruel heart. "No One, I will eat you after your companions, for they shall all precede you. That is my gift." Then he bent himself down till he lay prone, turning his thick neck sideways, overcome by all-powerful sleep. And from his throat he belched forth wine and gobbets of human flesh. He roared in his drunken slumber. Then did I poke the pikestaff deep into the ashes to make it hot, exhorting my companions lest any draw back from helping me out of fright. But when the stake, green though it was, seemed ready to burn, for it was glowing throughout, then quickly I withdrew it from the flames while my comrades stood by. A god gave us great courage. Seizing the sharp-pointed olive staff the men thrust it at his eye. Meanwhile I stood over it twisting the pole around, like a man drilling a hole in the planking of a ship while others below turn the drill this way and that with a thong, so that the drill keeps on turning without pause. Thus did we revolve the fire-tipped stake in his eye, and the hot blood gushed around it. His lids and eyebrows were singed all around and the pupil of his eye was burned out. The innermost parts of the eyeball sizzled in the fire, just as when a bronze smith, tempering an adze or a great axe-head, plunges it into cold water with a loud hiss. And this also is what gives strength to iron. Thus did his eyeball hiss around the olive staff. He roared aloud in his pain and the cave resounded with his screams, while we scurried out of the way in terror. Then he plucked the staff, all wet with blood, from his eye and hurled it out of his hands in agony. And he called out in a loud voice to the Cyclopes who lived in the vicinity in their airy hilltop caves. Hearing his voice they came down, one from one direction, one from another. Standing before the cave they asked what was troubling him. "Pray what has come over you, Polyphemus, shouting this way in the divine darkness and depriving all of us of our sleep? Has some mortal driven away your sheep against your will, or is someone murdering you, by fraud or by force?"

Then mighty Polyphemus answered those outside the cave. "Friends, No One is murdering me by fraud or by force." Then they answered again, replying with winged words. "Since there is not anyone overpowering you alone by force, and since it is impossible to escape illness sent by Zeus, you must call on Lord Poseidon, your father."

Thus speaking they departed, while I laughed in my heart that my clever trick about my name had deceived them. But the Cyclops, groaning and twisted with pain, groped around with his hands and pulled the stone away from the doorway, seating himself in the entrance. He spread out his hands hoping to catch anyone who approached the door along with the sheep. In this way, no doubt, he thought I would be helpless. So I took thought how it might turn out for the best, trying to discover some escape from death for myself and my comrades. I considered every wile and stratagem, for life itself was at stake, and the danger was near at hand. Finally the following suggested itself to me as the most feasible plan. There were some fine big well-fed wooly rams with dark fleece. These I silently fastened together with twisted willow withes on which the Cyclops had been in the habit of reposing his foul monstrous shape. I tied them together in groups of three: the one in the middle would bear a man, while the other two would flank my comrades. Each third sheep transported a man. But there was one ram by far the largest of all the animals, and I seized him by the back and curled myself into the fleece under his belly. Then I gripped his wondrous wool with my hands, twisting myself around into the wool, with a steadfast heart. Thus we remained, sighing for divine day.

When morning first appeared and rosy-fingered dawn, then the male sheep hurried out to pasture, while the unmilked ewes waited in their pens, for their udders were filled to bursting. Their master, in great pain, felt over the backs of all the sheep as they stood upright, but the fool did not notice that the wooly sheep were tied around the chest. Last of all to reach the entrance was the ram with me, sagacious in counsel, weighing down his fleece. Feeling him over, mighty Polyphemus said: "My pet ram, why have you come to me the last of the flock to leave the cave? Never before have you lagged behind the other sheep in going out, but you were easily the first to crop the tender blades of grass, walking with great strides, and in the evening you were also first, eager for home and your stall. But now you are the very last. Surely you miss the eye of your master which an evil man and his miserable associates have completely blinded, overpowering my senses with wine, No One, a man whom I assert has not yet escaped destruction. And if you agree, I wish you had the power of speech to tell me where the wretch has gone, trying to escape my wrath. Then would he be caught, from one place or another in the cave, and his brains dashed out on the ground relieving my heart from the woes heaped on it by that good-for-nothing No One."

Having spoken he let the ram through the door. Proceeding a little way from the cave and the courtyard I first freed myself from the animal, then released my comrades. With all speed we drove the sleek long-legged flock through the countryside, turning them many times, until we reached our ship. Those of us who had escaped death were a welcome sight for our dear companions, but they wailed in lamentation for the others. But I put a stop to this, forbidding them to mourn. Instead, after we had loaded a goodly number of sheep on board, I gave orders to set sail at once over the salt sea. They embarked forthwith, taking their places at the oarlocks, and sitting in regular order they smote the gray sea with their oars. But while we were still within hailing distance, I taunted the Cyclops in this fashion: "Cyclops, you were not supposed to use brute force and devour the comrades of a helpless man in your hollow cave. But assuredly your evil deeds might be expected to overtake you, wretch, when you did not fear to devour guests in your own home. But Zeus and the other gods have punished you."

Thus I spoke, but his heart was moved to even greater anger. Breaking off the top of a lofty hill he hurled it, sending it in front of the dark-prowed ship. The ocean rose high under the impact of the rock, and a wave coming from the sea rolled the ship back shoreward, pushing it towards the land. However I seized a long pole in my hands and pushed the ship away, urgently bidding my comrades with a nod of my head, to lay on with the oars so we might escape his malevolence. And they bent themselves rowing. But when we had crossed twice as much ocean as before, I was about to accost the Cyclops, but my comrades opposed me with soothing words, one from one side one from another: "Obstinate man, pray why do you wish to provoke this savage? Only now he threw a rock into the sea which forced our boat back to the mainland, and we say he can still destroy us. For if he hears anyone making a noise or shouting, he will smash our heads and our wooden ship with a jagged piece of rock, he can throw such a great distance."

Thus they pleaded, but they did not persuade my proud spirit. Once more I accosted him angrily: "Cyclops, if you are asked what

mortal it was who shamefully blinded your eye, say that it was
Odysseus, sacker of cities, the son of Laertes, who lives in Ithaca."
Thus I spoke. With a groan he answered me: "Alas, a long time ago
a prediction was made to me. There used to be a seer here, a good
man and a great one, Telemus son of Eurymus, who excelled in
prophecy and who grew old as the soothsayer of the Cyclopes. He
told me all the things that would happen in the future, and that I
would lose my sight at the hands of Odysseus. But I expected the
arrival of some fine big man clothed in great power. But now, a
worthless little fellow, a weakling has destroyed my eye after first
overpowering me with wine. But come, now, Odysseus, that I may
give you a hospitable gift. I urge the earth-shaker to give you a fine
escort. For I am his son, and he boasts that he is my father. And he
if he chooses will heal, and no one else whether a man or an immortal god."

Thus he spoke. But I answered him again: "If I were able to deprive you of life and soul I would send you to the house of Hades
where no one would heal your eye, not even the earth-shaker." Thus
I replied, and then he prayed to Lord Poseidon, raising his arms to
the starry heavens. "Earth-shaker, dark-haired Poseidon, hear me!
If I am really your son and you claim to be my father, grant that
Odysseus the sacker of cities never get home again. But if he is fated
to see his dear ones and to reach his well-appointed home in the land
of his fathers, then let him arrive late after losing all his companions;
and let him arrive in the ship of a stranger, and let him find trouble
in his household."

Thus he prayed, and the dark-haired god heeded him. Then once
more he picked up a much larger stone and sent it spinning a tre-
mendous distance. It struck a little behind the dark-prowed ship just
missing the tip of the steering oar. The sea was churned up by the
rock, but the wave carried the ship forward and urged it towards the
shore.

Note

1. I.e., from the Land of the Lotus Eaters.

2

Hesiod: Farmer, Moralist, Poet

THE Works and Days *is a rambling poem written in verse simply because* *prose was not yet recognized as a vehicle for literature. The dactyllic* *hexameter of the epic was the obvious verse form for Hesiod as it was for* *Apollo at Delphi. The tone differs as much from the Iliad as Piers the* *Ploughman from the Beowulf. The episode of the Hawk and the Night-* *ingale is our earliest Greek fable.*

Works and Days, 1-382, 479-536

MUSES OF Pieria, come speak, celebrating with songs of praise your father, through whom mortal men are named or nameless, for whether they are spoken of or not depends on great Zeus. He easily strengthens the weak and crushes the strong, humbles the fa-mous and raises up the unknown. For it is easy for thunder-bearing Zeus, whose abode is on high, to straighten the crooked and to wither the proud in heart. Do thou, seeing all and understanding all, correct judgments with justice, but I will reveal the truth to Perses.

But there is not only one kind of strife on earth, but two. And one the thoughtful man would praise, the other is blameworthy, for they are widely separated in spirit. The first is cruel, fostering evil war and battle. Nor does anyone love this one, but only from necessity and because the immortals have so decreed do men honor this bane-ful strife. Dark night bore the other earlier one, and Cronus' son on his lofty throne in heaven placed it in the roots of the earth, much more beneficial to man. For this strife urges on to toil even the idle man. For when, not working himself, he sees another become rich then is he eager to plough, to plant and improve his property. Neigh-bor emulates neighbor desirous of wealth. This strife is good for mortals, and potter vies with potter, carpenter with carpenter, beggar with beggar and bard with bard.

O Perses, do you lay these things up in your heart, lest the strife that rejoices in evil keep your thoughts from work, to fasten your eyes on the quarrels and disputes of the market place. But there is little time for disputes and arguments unless one has an ample store of the season's produce laid away inside, produce which the earth bears, the grain of Demeter. You ought to provide yourself with this before contending and fighting over the possessions of others. You will have no second chance to accomplish this. Come, let us settle our quarrel forthwith by a swift decision in the name of Zeus, for that is the best way. When we divided our inheritance before you seized and pillaged what was not yours, by fawning on gift-devouring kings, always ready to give judgment on such a basis. Wretches! They do not know how much a half is better than the whole, nor what wealth there is in mallow and in asphodel.[1] For the gods have concealed from man the means of livelihood. Otherwise you could easily gain in a single day enough to live in idleness for a year. Then could you straightway hang your steering oar over the hearth and be rid of the work of the oxen and the patient mules.

But Zeus has kept this secret[2] angry in his heart because Prometheus of crooked counsel deceived him. That is why he devised woeful miseries for mankind. For he withheld fire, but the noble son of Iapetus stole it from all-wise Zeus in a hollow reed, eluding the Thunderer. In his anger cloud-gathering Zeus addressed him as follows:

"Son of Iapetus, master of all tricks, you are delighted at stealing fire and cheating me — a great scourge to yourself in the future, and to mankind. As the price of fire I will give you evil, yet all will welcome it with glad hearts, evil though it will be."

Thus he spoke, and the father of gods and men laughed out loud. Then he ordered renowned Hephaestus to mix earth with water, to endow the mixture with human speech and to shape it like a beautiful maiden, delightful as an immortal goddess. And he ordered Athena to teach her the arts, how to weave an intricate web; and golden Aphrodite he ordered to shed grace on her head, and also painful desire and devouring care. He bade Argus-slaying Hermes, the messenger, to bestow on her a shameless spirit and a thievish disposition.

Such were his orders, and they obeyed their ruler, Cronian Zeus. Straightway the famous lame god moulded the clay in the likeness of a bashful maiden, in accord with the instructions of Cronus' son, and Athena of the gleaming eyes dressed and adorned her. The divine

Graces and revered Persuasion placed golden bracelets on her body, while the Hours with beautiful hair crowned her with a chaplet of spring flowers. Pallas Athena fitted her with every ornament. Then the Argus-slaying messenger god filled her breast with false deceiving words, and implanted in her a thievish disposition in accord with the instructions of loud-thundering Zeus. The herald of the gods gave her speech. He called the woman Pandora[3] because all the dwellers on Olympus had given her gifts, a woe to breadwinning men.

Now when he had completed his dire irresistible plan then the father of the famous Argus-slayer sent the swift messenger of the gods to carry his gift to Epimetheus. Epimetheus paid no heed to Prometheus' warning never to accept a gift from Olympian Zeus, but to send it back, lest it prove an evil thing for mortals. But later, after he had accepted it, then he came to know it as evil.

Before this human beings lived on earth untroubled with unpleasant work, or with painful sicknesses that bring their dooms to mankind. For in their miserable state mortals rapidly grow old. Then the woman removed the great lid from the cask with her hands, and scattered the contents, loosing baneful miseries on mankind. Only Hope remained there inside an unbreakable home, below the rim of the cask. And she did not fly out the door; before this could happen Pandora replaced the lid on the cask in accord with the counsels of Zeus the cloud-gatherer. But the others, a legion of troubles, wandered about among mankind. The land was filled with evils and likewise the sea. Diseases sought men out by day and by night, bringing evil to mortals silently, since Zeus in his wisdom deprived them of speech. Thus it is not by any means possible to thwart the designs of Zeus.

But if you like I will outline another tale for you, very skillfully. And do you impress it on your mind, how men and the immortal gods have sprung from the same roots.

The immortals dwelling on Olympus first fashioned a golden race of speaking men. This was in the time when Cronus ruled in heaven, and men lived as free from care as the gods, without sorrow or hardship. Nor did the miseries of old age touch them. They remained unchanged, and sound of limb, rejoicing in plenty and removed from all hardship and grief; and when they died it was as though they were overcome by sleep. They had every good thing. The soil of its own accord yielded an inexhaustible supply of fruits. Willingly they lived in peace on the land, with an abundance of good things, wealthy in their flocks and friends of the blessed immortal gods. But when the earth covered them this race became pure earth spirits, benevolent averters of evil and guardians of mortal men. Therefore they are always watching judgments and evil deeds. Enveloped in mist they wander over the world bestowing riches, for this royal prerogative belongs to them.

And then the gods who live on Olympus made a second, much meaner race, of silver, not like the gold either in noble stature or in understanding. For one hundred years the child remained skipping about at home with his dear mother, a great baby. But when he grew up and reached man's estate he lived foolishly and painfully for a short time. For they could not refrain from reckless acts of violence against one another; they had no wish to honor the immortals by tending the sacred altars of the blessed gods, as is right and customary among men. Then Cronian Zeus buried them in his wrath, because they refused to give honor to the blessed gods who dwell on Olympus. But when the earth had concealed this race they came to be called blessed underworld spirits by mortals, of the second rank to be sure, but still honor is given them.

Then Zeus made a third race of speaking men, the bronze race, not at all like the silver one but of ash wood, strong and terrible, devoted to the violent and baleful deeds of Ares. They were a monstrous race, eating no bread: unyielding, hard of heart, invincible. Irresistible arms grew from their mighty shoulders on a powerful frame. Their weapons were of bronze, they had bronze houses and they worked in bronze, for there was no black iron. At last, overpowering one another by force they entered the cold broad house of Hades, unhonored. Black Death seized them, terrible though they were, and they left the bright light of the sun.

Now when earth had also buried this race then once more Zeus fashioned another, the fourth race on the much-nourishing earth. And these were far superior and more righteous, the divine race of heroes called demigods in the age just before our own, on the boundless earth. And these fell war and the terrible din of battle destroyed: some by seven-gated Thebes contending for the flocks of Oedipus in the Cadmeian land, and others who had crossed the vast gulfs of ocean to Troy for the sake of lovely-haired Helen. And when death finally enfolded them, Father Zeus the Cronian gave them a place to live apart from mankind at the ends of the earth. And there they live without sorrow, joyful heroes, on the Islands of the Blessed which yield sweet fruits beside deep-eddying ocean. Three times each year the grain land bears an abundant crop, and Cronus rules over them — for the father of gods and men loosed his bonds. Honor and fame attend these likewise.

Then once more thundering Zeus fashioned another race of men, the fifth on the all-nourishing earth. Would that I were not living during the fifth age of man, but that I had either died earlier or been born later. For now we have the iron race. Neither by day nor by night is there any release from devastating sorrow and suffering, for the gods will give harsh cares, though some good things will be mixed in with the bad. But Zeus will destroy this race of speaking men also. For when men are born with gray heads then will the race come to an end. Nor will a father be in any way of like mind with his children nor his children with him; nor guests with their host, nor a friend with a friend; nor will a brother be dear as in days gone by. But straightway they will dishonor their aging parents. Finding fault the wretches will speak to them roughly, not regarding the vengeance of the gods. Nor will they make any return to their old parents for their upbringing, following the law of the fist. Nor will there be any thanks for the man who keeps his oath, for the just and good man. Instead they will honor evil doers and men of violence. Judgment will be based on force, and there will be no shame. The evil man will entangle his better with crooked words, then swear to it with an oath. And Envy with malicious tongue, rejoicing in abominable wickedness will walk beside all miserable men. And then Shame and Nemesis, their fair skin wrapped in snow-white robes will leave the spacious earth for Olympus and the race of the immortals, abandoning mankind. But painful sorrows will remain for mortal men, and there will be no defense against evil.

And now I will recount a fable for kings who understand themselves. Thus did the hawk address himself to the nightingale of many songs, carrying her high up in the clouds held fast in his claws. And the nightingale was weeping piteously, impaled on his crooked talons. And the hawk spoke to her, in his might, as follows:

"Wretch, what are you screaming about? For now you are held by one who is far superior to you. And I will carry you off anywhere I like, singer though you may be. And I will make a meal of you or let you go, just as I please. Only a fool tries to contend with his betters. Not only will he be vanquished, but also suffer the additional agony of being shamed."

Thus spoke the swift-flying hawk with outspread wings. And you, Perses, do you pay attention to justice and avoid false pride. For pride is harmful to the man of low degree. Not even the wellborn can manage it with any ease, it weighs him down when crossed by fate. There is a better way than that, which leads to appropriate deeds. Right conduct comes out ahead of pride in the end. The fool learns this only from experience. Oath keeps pace with crooked judgments for the moment. There is confusion when Justice is manhandled by bribe-devouring men who pervert the law with crooked judgments. But Justice pursues covered with mist, complaining about the city and the behavior of the people, and bringing evil to men who drive her away and deal unfairly. But for those who give righteous judgments to strangers and to natives and do not turn aside from the right, their city flourishes and their people prosper. Fostering peace is in their land, nor does Zeus the Thunderer ordain troublesome war for them. Nor does famine ever attend men of upright judgments, or any other disaster, but the possessions they care for yield abundantly. The land furnishes them a good living. In the mountains the tall oak bears acorns and is crowded with bees. Their fleecy sheep are heavy with wool. Their wives bear children like their parents. They are provided with all good things. They do not go to the sea in ships, but the life-giving land furnishes its fruits. But those whom evil arrogance leads on to evil deeds, on them Cronian Zeus, the Thunderer, has pronounced judgment. Frequently a whole city suffers for an evil man, who is an offense, doing wicked deeds. On such men the Cronian has sent great woe from heaven, both famine and pestilence at the same time. The people wither away and their wives do not give birth. Their households decrease through the cunning of Olympian Zeus. At one time he destroys their great army or their wall, or else Cronus' son takes vengeance on their ships on the ocean.

O Kings, do you yourselves reflect on this punishment! For the immortals are present among men and they take note of those who grind one another with crooked judgments, disregarding the gods. Three times ten thousand of Zeus' immortals on the all-nourishing earth watch out for mortal man. They easily keep track of judgments and evil deeds; wrapped in mist they wander through the land. Justice is a maiden born of Zeus, held in high honor by the gods who inhabit Olympus. And when anyone harms her with unjust accusations then straightway she seats herself beside her father Cronian Zeus and tells of the wicked minds of men, until the people atone for the wickedness of their kings, who with evil intent turn Justice from her path with crooked statements. Guard against these things, Kings, make your words straight, you bribe-swallowers; avoid all kinds of crooked judgments. The man who harms another also harms himself, and an evil plot damages most the one who concocts it. The eyes of Zeus are everywhere and he knows everything. And if it be his wish he sees this too, nor does it escape his notice what kind of justice any city contains inside itself. Now may I not be a righteous man among men, nor my son either, for it is pointless to be just if the unjust man is to prevail. But I cannot believe that all-wise Zeus will ever permit that!

Perses, do you store these things up in your mind, and from now on pay attention to justice, shunning every sort of insolence. The Cronian has laid this down as the law for mankind, but the birds in the sky, and the beasts and the fish devour one another, because there is no justice among them. But he has given justice to man, and justice is far the best thing. When anyone is willing to speak out what he knows is right, then Zeus the Thunderer gives happiness to that man. But when anyone intentionally violates his sworn oath in giving testimony, thus doing justice irreparable harm, then the generation he leaves after him will be dimmed, while the descendants of the man who keeps his oath will be better off.

But I will tell you what I know will be to your advantage, Perses, great fool though you are. Evil is easy to find and in abundance, for that path is smooth and lies ready of access. But the deathless gods have made the road to Virtue a hard road. It is long and uphill, and at first the going is rough. But when you reach the top it is easy to find her, however difficult it may have been before.

Best by far is the man who knows and reflects on all these things, things which are better at once and also in the long run. But good also is the man who is persuaded by words of wisdom. But a man who is ignorant himself and who also fails to store up in his heart what he has been told, is good for nothing. Now always remember my behests, noble Perses, and toil, so hunger will hate you and bounteous Demeter will hold you in esteem, filling your life with abundance. For hunger is always the companion of the man who does not work. Both gods and men are angry with a man who lives in idleness, like the stingless drones who eat what the bees have produced without working themselves. May you delight in regulating your tasks properly, so good things will abound in their season. By work men become rich in flocks, and also by work they become much dearer to the immortals. There is no shame in work, but idleness is a reproach. But if you labor the shiftless man will soon envy your wealth, for virtue and honor accompany riches. And however well off you may be, it is still best for you to work.

If you will only turn your foolish thoughts away from the possessions of others and devote your life to work as I enjoin you to do! The needy man has an unpleasant feeling of shame, shame which is sometimes a great evil to a man and sometimes a blessing. Shame goes with misfortune, confidence with well-being. Goods should not be acquired by violence, it is better when they are bestowed by the gods. If anyone gains great wealth by using force, or gets hold of it by talk — as usually happens when men's understanding is blinded by greed and when rapacity tramples down all sense of shame — the gods easily humble that man; his house declines and his wealth remains with him a short time only. Likewise when anyone wrongs a suppliant or a guest, or when a man enters his brother's bed stealthily to do what he should not do with his brother's wife, or when someone senselessly commits a crime against orphaned children, or quarrels with his venerable father on the threshold of old age and abuses him with harsh words. Then Zeus himself becomes angry, and in the end punishes him severely for his wickedness. But do you thrust such thoughts entirely out of your heart, and sacrifice what you can to the immortal gods in a pure and holy spirit, burning the thigh bones. Then again entreat them with libations and incense when you go to bed and also when the sacred daylight returns, so that they will have kind and friendly feelings towards you. And invite your friend to dinner, but leave your enemy alone, and be sure to invite the man who lives near you. Whenever anything untoward occurs the neighbor comes though half-dressed, but relatives arrive at their leisure. A bad neighbor is an affliction just as a good neighbor is a blessing. He who has a good neighbor has something of a great value; his ox will not die unless he has a bad neighbor. It is well to give and receive good measure from a neighbor; if you can, give him even better measure. Then when you are in need you will be sure of having enough. Do not make a dishonest profit, as a dishonest gain is a curse. Be a friend to the man who is friendly, ask favors of one who asks for them, give to the man who gives to you, but not to the man who does not. One gives to the generous but no one gives to the mean. Giving is good but rapine is an evil that causes death. When a man gives of his own free will, even a large gift, he is pleased with giving and rejoices in his heart. But when a man takes something by force, even though it is a small thing, his heart is cold and stiff. He who adds to what he has will escape sharp hunger. If you add a little often enough to the little you have it will soon become great. Nor is a man troubled by what is laid up in his own house, for it is safer at home and riskier abroad. It is good to take from what you have, but it depresses the spirits to be in need of what you do not have.

Do not stint yourself when the cask is broached or when it is nearly used up, but be sparing in between. It is a mean thing to husband the dregs. Even for a friend let a fixed price be set. When you settle with your neighbor, laugh, but have a witness. Either trust or distrust can ruin a man. Let not your wife deceive you, flaunting her buttocks, and coaxing you slyly for some choice thing. He who trusts his wife also trusts thieves. An only son will preserve the heritable property; thus wealth will increase in your house. But if you leave a second son you should not die until you are old. Yet it is easy for Zeus to bestow vast wealth on a larger number. The more the care that is bestowed on more things the greater will be the increase. And you, if your heart yearns for wealth, then learn how this can be accomplished: by work, and work and more work.

*   *   *

If you wait for the turning of the sun[4] to plough the divine soil, you will reap a meager harvest, sitting down in order to reach it with your hands. Binding the grain with the ears turned both ways, covered with dust, you will carry it off in a basket[5] by no means rejoicing. Few will be those who watch you admiringly. Now strangely varied are the purposes of aegis-bearing Zeus, difficult for mortal man to understand. But this can be your remedy if you plough late. When the cuckoo first sings "cuckoo!" in the leaves of the oak, bringing joy to mortals on the boundless earth, then on the third day may Zeus not fail to bring rain, enough to cover the hoofs of the oxen but no more. For then the late plougher will rival the man who ploughs early. Keep all these things well in mind, and do not be caught unawares either by clear spring or by the season of rains.

Pass by the smithy without taking a seat there to warm yourself and gossip in the winter time. For though the cold keeps him from the fields a resolute man can greatly improve his property in that season. So do not let the hardships of evil winter reduce you to ruin, your feet swollen with frostbite and your hands shriveled up with cold. The man who idly waits in reliance on false hopes, reproaches himself cruelly when he has no food. No cheering thoughts console the poor man sitting in a public place, when his livelihood is uncertain. Warn your servants while it is still mid-summer: "It will not always be summer, build your sheds!"

When the month Lenaeon comes with his evil days, each one of which galls the cattle, be on the watch against him and against the cruel frosts that afflict the land when Boreas blows, Boreas with his blasts driving across horse-breeding Thrace and over the broad sea; and the land and the woods are bellowing. And many a towering oak and many a sturdy pine Boreas, hurling himself into the mountain glens, brings down to the nourishing earth so that the whole forest groans aloud. And the animals shiver, putting their tails inside their legs, even those whose flanks are covered with fur, for the icy cold also pierces their hairy breasts; and it penetrates the hide of the ox which cannot stop it; and it also reaches the shaggy goat. But the force of Boreas' blast fails only to penetrate the sheep thanks to their fleecy wool. Yet it makes even the old men run fast. But it does not pierce the tender skin of the young maiden who remains at home with her dear mother, as yet unacquainted with the work of Aphrodite the Golden. And she bathes her youthful body and anoints herself with olive oil before going to bed in an inner chamber — in the winter time when the boneless fish[6] devours his own arms in his fireless home, a wretched abode. Nor does the sun show him where to feed, for he is wandering above the city and the land of black men, and delays showing his light to all the Greeks. And then do the animals with horns and those without grind their teeth woefully, and flee through the wooded glens. Then is each concerned with obtaining shelter, a snug retreat or a hollow cave. Men in that time have the appearance of three-footed beasts; with broken backs and heads bent towards the ground, they wander in this fashion to escape the white snow.

Notes

1. I.e., the poor man's fare.
2. I.e., how to make a living without hard work.
3. I.e., "all gifts" (*pan + dora*).
4. I.e., the winter solstice.
5. I.e., too little for a wagon load.
6. I.e., the cuttle fish or polyp.

3

The Father of History
Looks at Egypt

HERODOTUS was probably born in Halicarnassus early in the fifth century. The epic tradition was still strong, but the first logographers had shown prose to be a more flexible instrument for presenting factual material and drawing conclusions from it. Specifically this had been done in describing strange peoples, their customs and the natural features of the lands in which they lived. Most famous of these early writers was Hecataeus of Miletus. He visited Egypt, and his Description of the World was well known to Herodotus. When Herodotus left Halicarnassus and why he remained in exile we do not know, but he travelled widely gathering information for his work. His History was probably begun before its ultimate purpose, to explain the causes and describe the events of the Persian War, had become clear to the author. He spent some time in Athens, and is reliably thought to have joined the colony at Thurii in South Italy sponsored by Pericles (444 B.C.). He lived at least until 430 B.C.

The present passage deals with Egyptian geography and the controversy about the Nile. Here Herodotus pits himself against earlier writers, notably Hecataeus, but he includes their views however little he agreed with them, and this gives us a better perspective.

Herodotus, Histories, ii, 17-34

17] DISREGARDING the views of the Ionians on the subject, this is what we think about it: that Egypt is the entire country inhabited by the Egyptians, just as Cilicia is the land of the Cilicians and Assyria that of the Assyrians. Also we do not see how the boundary between Asia and Libya can properly be defined except as the boundaries of Egypt. Now if we were to follow Greek practice we would divide the whole of Egypt into two parts, beginning with Catadupa and the city of Elephantine and claiming separate names for them, one part being in Libya and the other in Asia. For the Nile splits Egypt right down the middle, starting with Catadupa and flowing on to the sea. Until it reaches the city of Circasorus the Nile proceeds as a single stream, but beyond that city it divides into three channels: the one to the east is called the Pelusiac branch, while a second one which inclines to the west has come to be known as the Canopic branch. And finally, the Nile has a direct channel which carries it down to the apex of the Delta, then through the middle of the Delta until it flows into the sea. This channel, which is called the Sebennytic branch, is not the least renowned nor does it carry the smallest amount of water. There are also two other streams that break off from the Sebennytic branch and reach the sea separately, being called the Saitic and the Mendesian mouths, respectively. The Boltinic and the Bucolic branches have been dug artificially, they are not true mouths.

18] Now the oracle of Ammon confirms my opinion that Egypt is such as I have described it, though I learned this after I had already made up my own mind on the subject. The inhabitants of the cities of Marea and Apis on the border of Egypt and Libya used to regard themselves as Libyans rather than as Egyptians. Being vexed at the religious restrictions which prevented them from eating the flesh of cows they sent word to Ammon, claiming that they were not Egyptians and that they had nothing in common with the Egyptians; that they lived outside of the Delta and had no obligations towards them; and finally that they wished to be allowed to eat anything they liked. But the god would not give them permission, asserting that whatever is watered by the Nile is Egypt, and that those who dwell below Elephantine and drink the waters of that river are Egyptians. Such was the pronouncement of the oracle.

19] In flood time the Nile inundates not merely the Delta, but also the so-called Libyan and Arabian lands for as much as a two days' journey on either side, sometimes more, sometimes less. But I was unable to find out anything about the nature of the Nile, from the priests or from anyone else. I was eager to learn from them why the Nile rises for one hundred days beginning with the summer solstice, and then recedes during approximately the same number of days, abandoning its bed so that it remains low all winter long until the summer solstice comes around again. But I was unable to learn anything from any of the Egyptians about this, though I questioned them about the peculiar nature of the Nile which behaves in a way opposite to other rivers. Wishing to learn about these things, and also why this is the only river which has no breezes blowing from it, I kept on making inquiries.

20] But some of the Greeks who want to impress us with their wisdom offer three explanations about the water, two of which I do not think worth refuting, so I will merely point out what they are. Now one of these views is that the etesian winds are responsible for the river's rising, by preventing it from flowing into the sea. But frequently the Nile acts in the same way when the etesian winds are not blowing; also if these winds were the cause then other rivers that flow against the etesian winds ought to be affected in the same way as the Nile, and to an even greater degree, since they have a weaker current corresponding to their much smaller size. But there are many rivers in Syria, and many others in Libya which do not show the slightest resemblance to the Nile in their behavior.

21] The second view, even less intelligent than the first, is the wild notion that the Nile behaves this way because it flows from Ocean, and that Ocean flows around the entire earth.

22] The third explanation, despite the fact that it is easily the most plausible, is even farther from the truth. For it too resolves nothing, asserting that the Nile, which empties itself into Egypt after flowing from Libya through the heart of Ethiopia, comes from melted snow! For how, pray, can it come from snow when for most of its course it flows from a very hot region to a cooler one? In the first place the hot winds that blow from these regions offer the most convincing evidence, to anyone capable of thinking about it, that the river is not at all likely to come from snow. Secondly, the whole region is rainless and free of ice, while it is absolutely necessary for rain to follow snow within five days, so that if it did snow there this region would also have rain. Thirdly, the inhabitants are black from the heat. Kites and swallows stay the year around, but cranes escape the winters of the Scythian land by migrating to these regions during that season. But if it actually snowed so much in the country traversed by the Nile and where the Nile begins, none of these things would happen, so this explanation is necessarily refuted.

23] But the writer who talks about Ocean, appealing to a dubious legend, cannot be refuted. But I am not aware of the existence of any river "Ocean", and I think Homer or one of the other early poets invented the name and introduced it in his work.

24] But since one who finds fault with prevailing opinions ought to offer his own view on these obscure matters, I will relate why I think the Nile rises in the summer. During the winter, blown off his former course by storm winds, the sun reaches the upper parts of Libya. Thus the whole matter is explained in a few words. For where the god comes nearest to the land it is likely that that land especially will be thirsty for water, and the streams of the local rivers will be dried up.

25] Or, to elaborate, this is what happens: In traversing the upper parts of Libya the sun brings about certain results. For while the air in these parts is always clear and the land is always warm — there being no cold winds — when the sun goes there it has the same effects we are accustomed to when it crosses the center of the heavens in summer. It sucks up water to itself, and in doing so thrusts it back into the upper regions, where the winds take hold of the water, disperse it and dry it up. Now the winds that blow from this quarter, the south and the southwest winds, are probably much the rainiest winds of all. But I do not think the sun gets rid of all the annual Nile water each time, but that it retains some water around itself. When the winter moderates then the sun returns to the middle of the heavens, and from then on it sucks up water equally from all rivers. During the time when quantities of rain water are added to them and the land is broken up into gullies, then the rivers are large; but in summer when the rain fails and water is sucked up by the sun, then they are meager. But the Nile, being rainless, is still sucked up by the sun, so that it is probably the only river which flows more feebly in winter than in summer: for then it is drawn up by the sun on an equal basis with all the other rivers, but in winter the sun draws on it alone. That is why I regard the sun as the cause of these phenomena.

26] And in my opinion the sun is also responsible for the dryness of the air, burning it to excess during its transit, so that it is always summer in the upper parts of Libya. But if the climatic conditions in the heavens were changed, and if where the north wind and winter now are, there the south and the south wind should be, then under those conditions the sun would be blown from the midst of the heavens by the northern winter wind to the regions of upper Europe, just as now it goes to Libya. Traversing all of Europe I imagine it would have the same effects on the Ister that it now has on the Nile.

27] And for the breezes not blowing off the river I offer this explanation: that it is unlikely for a breeze to blow from a river that comes from a hot region, for breezes are wont to blow from something cold.

28] But let this be as it is and as it was before. There was not a single Egyptian, or Libyan or Greek with whom I talked who professed to know about the source of the Nile except for the Clerk of the Sacred Property of Athena in the Egyptian city of Sais, and I thought he was joking when he claimed to have accurate information. Nevertheless he told me that there are two mountains, each rising to a sharp peak, between Syene in the Thebaid and Elephantine; and the names of these mountains are Crophi and Mophi. Now according to him the source of the Nile, which is bottomless, rises between these mountains, and half of the water flows towards Egypt and the north while the other half flows to Ethiopia and the south. He also said that the Egyptian monarch Psammetichus went there to find out whether the source really was bottomless, and that after letting down a twisted rope many thousands of fathoms long he failed to reach the bottom. Now if what the priest told me actually happened, then in my judgment there are strong eddies forming a back current at the place where the stream dashes against the mountains, and this would not allow the sounding line to touch bottom.

29] I was not able to learn anything more about this from anyone else, but I did find out something more about the upper reaches of the Nile, going on as far as Elephantine myself, and hearing reports on what lies beyond. Above Elephantine the land rises so steeply that it is necessary for the boat to proceed ox-fashion, harnessed with a tow rope to each side of the stream. If the towline broke the boat would be carried down by the powerful current. This section lasts for four days by boat, and the Nile there twists and turns like the Maeander River. It is necessary to navigate for about eighty miles in this way, and then one comes to a smooth flat stretch where the Nile forms an island. The name of the island is Tachompso. Above Elephantine there are already Ethiopians living, and Ethiopians occupy half of this island, Egyptians the other half. Next to the island there is a large lake, around which the Ethiopian herdsmen pasture their animals. Sailing through the lake you will rejoin the Nile, which empties into this lake. Disembarking at this point, you continue for forty days by road, because the Nile is full of low-lying flat boulders and jagged rocks that protrude. After crossing this region in forty days you board a vessel again for a twelve days' sail which brings you to a sizeable town called Meroe.

This city is said to be the chief city of the rest of the Ethiopians. The inhabitants worship only the gods Zeus and Dionysus, but they hold them in very high esteem. An oracle of Zeus has been established there, and the people go to war only where and when the god orders them to do so.

30] Sailing from this city you reach the Deserters in the same amount of time it took to reach the chief city of the Ethiopians from Elephantine. These "deserters" are called *Ascham,* a word which may be translated into the Greek tongue as "those who stand at the left hand of the king". Now some 240,000 Egyptian soldiers deserted to the Ethiopians for the following reason: In the reign of Psammetichus troops were stationed in Elephantine to guard against the Ethiopians, others in Daphnae near Pelusium against the Arabs and Assyrians, and still others in Marea against the Libyans. In my day the Persians still maintained forces where they used to be under Psammetichus, at least there are Persian garrisons in Elephantine and in Daphnae. Now when after three years of guard duty no replacements were sent out, they consulted together and resolved on a common plan of action. Accordingly they all revolted from Psammetichus and headed for Ethiopia. As soon as he learned this the king set out in pursuit, and finally caught up with them. He pleaded with them at length, imploring them not to renounce their ancestral gods or to abandon their wives and children. But one of the deserters is said to have answered him, at the same time exposing his private parts, to the effect that as long as these remained in their possession they would not have any lack of wives, or children either. Accordingly they continued on to Ethiopia and offered themselves to the Ethiopian king, who gave them a gift in return. There were some Ethiopians at variance with him whom he told them to drive out, taking over their lands. As a result of the settlement of these men among them, the Ethiopians became more civilized, adopting the customs of the Egyptians.

31] Beyond Egypt the Nile is known for forty days' journey by boat and by road, for this is the total amount of time used in travelling from Elephantine to the Deserters. The river flows from the west and the setting sun. Beyond this point no one can speak with any certainty, because the intense heat has made it a desert.

32] However I did obtain the following account from some Cyrenaeans who said they had visited the oracle of Ammon and conversed with the ruler of the Ammonians, Etearchus. After various other matters had been discussed the talk came around to the Nile and how no one knew where it began. In this connection Etearchus mentioned some Nasamonians who had come to see him. The Nasamonians are a Libyan people who live along the Gulf of Syrtis and for a short stretch to the east of it. When they arrived and were asked whether they had anything new to relate about the Libyan wastes, they replied that there were some harebrained young sons of their chiefs who, when they reached the age of manhood, did many strange things. They selected five of their number by lot to explore the Libyan desert in an effort to find out more than had been learned by those who had travelled it for the farthest distance. The part of Libya along the northern sea,[1] beginning with Egypt and ending where Libya ends at the promontory of Soli, is all inhabited by a multitude of Libyan tribes, except for the part held by the Greeks and the Phoenicians. But beyond the sea and the men who inhabit the coast comes the wild beast part of Libya, and beyond the wild beast country it is terribly dry and sandy, a total desert. Now they said that these young men were sent out by their comrades well supplied with food and water. First they crossed the inhabited region, then the region of wild beasts, following which they made their way through the desert in a westerly direction. After many days spent in crossing a vast expanse of sand they caught sight of trees standing in a plain. They drew near in order to pluck the fruit that was growing on them, but while they were helping themselves some little men appeared, smaller in stature than ordinary men, who arrested them and carried them away. The Nasamonians could not understand their speech, nor could they understand the Nasamonians. They led them through enormous swamps beyond which they reached a town, where all the inhabitants were black and of the same stature as their captors. The town stood beside a great river which flowed from the west towards the rising sun, and in that river crocodiles could be seen.

33] This was the substance of the story of Etearchus the Ammonian as it was told to me, except that the Cyrenaeans said he reported that the Nasamonians returned home, and that the men they had seen were all sorcerers. Also Etearchus conjectured that the river flowing by was the Nile, a plausible conclusion since the Nile flows from Libya, cutting through the heart of the country. Now it is my belief, inferring what is not known from what is known, that the Nile starts out like the Ister.[2] For the Ister River rises among the Celts in the city of Pyrene, then flows through Europe, dividing it down the middle. The Celts live beyond the Pillars of Heracles and they border on the Cynesians, who live farthest west of the inhabitants of Europe. Now the Ister ends in the Euxine Sea, which it enters near the Milesian colony of Istria.

34] Since the Ister flows through a populated region many people know about it, but no one can tell about the source of the Nile because the part of Libya through which it flows is a wilderness. Whatever can be learned about this river as far up as it has been explored has already been told, and how it discharges itself into Egypt. Now Egypt lies very nearly opposite to the mountains of Cilicia. From these mountains to Sinope on the Euxine Sea is a five days' journey for a well-girdled man. And Sinope lies right across from where the Ister empties into the sea. Therefore I believe the Nile, which crosses the whole of Libya, is co-extensive with the Ister. Let this be sufficient on the subject of the Nile.

Notes

1. I.e., the Mediterranean.
2. I.e., the Danube.

4

The Legend of
Western Colonization

ALTHOUGH the following passage comes from Diodorus Siculus, his chief source was Timaeus. Timaeus composed a general history while an exile in Athens over a period of fifty years, and added to it on his return to Sicily, where he lived to record the Roman invasion of Sicily (264 B.C.). Immensely learned and obviously having access to the extant literature, he wrote a very detailed history, emphasizing Sicily and the West, which now survives only in fragments, frequently citations made to refute him by later detractors such as Polybius. In the present selection we can see his views on heroic chronology, with the legendary period sliding down into clearly historical times. It was Timaeus who put chronology on a firm basis by the use of the Olympic Era (776 B.C.) as a fixed point.

Diodorus Siculus, from Agyrium in Sicily, lived in the first century B.C. Not a historian but a compiler, we owe him, reluctantly, a great debt, because many of the sources he used were excellent and sometimes it is only through Diodorus that any part of their contents has been preserved. The extent of our obligation becomes apparent when, with Book XXI of his forty-book Historical Library, Diodorus, too, becomes a series of fragments.

Diodorus Siculus, v, 2-23 (Timaeus)

2] APPROPRIATELY to our subject, for we have called this the Island Book, we shall speak first of Sicily, since it is the mightiest of the islands, and has also won first place by the antiquity of its legends.

In antiquity the island was called Trinacria because of its shape, but was renamed Sicania by the Sicans who settled there, and last of all it was denominated Sicelia from the Sicels who crossed over from Italy in a body. The distance around it is 4360 stades, and of the three sides the one from Peloris to Lilybaeum is of 1700 stades, that from Lilybaeum to Pachynus in the Syracusan land of 1500 stades, and the remaining side of 1140 (1160?) stades.

Now the Sicilians (Siceliotes) have an ancestral tradition which has been handed down from generation to generation that the island is sacred to Demeter and Corē. Some of the poets relate that this island was bestowed as a bridal gift by Zeus at the wedding of Pluto and Persephone. The most reliable historians say that the ancient inhabitants, the Sicans, are autochthonous, and that the deities just mentioned first showed themselves in this island, and that it was the first to produce ears of grain, thanks to the excellence of its soil. For the most illustrious of poets testifies to this when he says: "Everything was unsown and untilled; /wheat, barley and the vine are bourne/ and wine from large grapes, and God's rain fosters them."[1] For in the Leontine plain, and in many other parts of Sicily, the so-called wild wheat grows up to the present day. In general, when inquiring where in the world the crops mentioned first appeared, it is probable that the primacy should be given to the best soil; also, and this fits in with what has been said, the pioneer goddesses are seen to have been held in special esteem by the Sicilians.

3] Also they say there is the plainest evidence for the rape of Corē having occurred here, since the goddesses sojourned in the island because they were particularly fond of it. The mythologers say that the rape of Corē occurred in the meadows of Enna. And this is a plain near the city, famed for its violets and all sorts of other flowers, and worthy of the goddess. And it is said that trained hunting dogs cannot follow a trail because of the fragrance given off by the flowers, their natural perception being impeded. Now the meadow mentioned before lies above, perfectly smooth and well-watered, it is lofty and circular, cut off on all sides by cliffs. It seems to lie in the center of the whole island, and therefore, by some, it is called the navel of Sicily. It has groves and meadows with ponds nearby, and in the neighborhood is a very large cave with a subterranean gulf inclined to the north, through which, according to legend Pluto drove his chariot to snatch Corē away. The violets and the other sweet-smelling flowers amazingly continue to bloom the year round, offering a thoroughly charming flowery prospect. And they relate that Athena and Artemis, equally esteemed for their virginity with Corē, lived there, and that along with her they gathered flowers and made a robe for Father Zeus. Because of their sojourn together, and all their meetings with one another, they grew very fond of this island, and each of them obtained a district. Athena's district was in the area near Himera, where the nymphs sent forth springs of hot water to please Athena during the time Heracles was there, and where the natives dedicated a place to her which was still called Athenaeum up to the present day. And Artemis obtained the Syracusan isle from the gods, the one called by her Ortygia, as it was by oracles and by men. Likewise, to please Artemis, the nymphs sent forth a very large spring on this island, the one named Arethusa. And this spring not only in the ancient days had many large fish. But it happens that they remain in our day, being sacred and not to be touched by man. And frequently when some have been eaten during the circumstances of war, the divinity has given wondrous signs, and has inflicted great misfortune on those who dared touch them. But we will give an exact account of this in the appropriate periods.

4] Like the two goddesses mentioned Corē obtained the meadows, near Enna, and then a great spring in Syracuse was dedicated to her, the one called Cyanē. They relate that Pluto, snatching up Corē, carried her off in his chariot near Syracuse, and that, opening up the earth, he plunged down with her to Hades, but that a spring gushed forth — the one called Cyanē — near which the Syracusans hold a splendid festival every year. Private citizens sacrifice the smaller sacred victims, but the state immerses a bull in the lake, this being the sacrifice inaugurated by Heracles at the time he traversed all Sicily, driving the cattle of Geryon. After the rape of Core they relate that Demeter, being unable to find her daughter, snatched brands from the Aetna craters and travelled over a great part of the world, and that she conferred benefits on men who received her hospitably, recompensing them with cereal grains. The Athenians received the goddess very graciously so she gave them the cereal grains first, after the Sicilians. In return, this people honored the goddess more than others, with splendid sacrifices and the Eleusinian mysteries, which became known to all men for their great antiquity and their sanctity. And many acquired the blessing of grain from the Athenians and then passed seed along to their neighbors until the whole world was supplied. The Sicilians, being first to participate in the discovery of grain thanks to the partiality shown them by Demeter and Corē, established sacrifices and festivals to each goddess, calling them after their names, and indicating the time when the gifts were made. For they made the return of Corē about the time when the grain happens to reach maturity, and they celebrate this sacrifice and festival with much reverence and feeling, as it is only right for those who have been chosen before all other men for the finest gift, to give thanks in return. For the rites of Demeter they chose the time when the sowing of the grain first takes place. They celebrate a festival named after this goddess for ten days, a festival magnificent for the splendor with which it is conducted, and for the arrangements imitating the ancient way of life. It is customary during those days to use foul language when they meet one another, so that the goddess, grieved over the rape of Corē, may laugh at their abusive talk.

5] Many old historians and poets testify to what we have said above about the rape of Corē. And Carcinus the tragic poet, who often lived in Syracuse as a foreigner, and who observed the enthusiasm of the inhabitants for the sacrifices and festivals of Demeter and Corē inserted the following lines in his poem: "They say the mysterious maiden of Demeter's, /Pluto seized by secret guile,/ Then plunged into the black recesses of the earth./ The mother in longing for her vanished maiden/ Went a searcher over the whole earth circuit./ And the land of Sicily, and the hills of Aetna/ Filled with fiery streams hard to traverse,/ All sighed with sorrow for the maid/ And the whole noble race wasted away, deprived of food./ Therefore they honor the goddess even now." It is not right to omit the great benefactions of the goddess to men. For in addition to the use of grain, she also taught men how to cultivate it, and she introduced laws which accustomed men to deal honestly, and for that reason they say she was called Thesmophorus. One can find no other benefit greater than these discoveries; for they comprehend both living, and living well. We will content ourselves with what we have said about the myths handed down among the Sicilians.

6] About the first Sicans who lived here it is necessary to speak briefly since some of the historians disagree. Philistus in fact says they settled in the island as emigrants from Iberia, and that they got this name from a certain Sicanus river in Iberia. But TIMAEUS, refuting the ignorance of that historian, shows conclusively that they were autochthonous. While he offers many proofs of their antiquity, we do not think it necessary to discuss them. Now in ancient times the Sicani lived in villages, and built their towns on the most defensible hills because of freebooters; for they were not organized in one dominion under one king, but had separate rulers over each town. At first they occupied the whole island and obtained a living by tilling the soil. Later, however, Aetna emitted blasts of fire in many places, and a quantity of lava poured out over the land so that the country came to be destroyed for a long distance. As the fire continued to spread year after year over a large area, they became alarmed and abandoned the eastern part of Sicily, moving into the west. Eventually, many generations later, the Sicel people crossed over in a body from Italy, and settled the land abandoned by the Sicans. The Sicels continued to push forward greedily, ravaging the territory of their neighbors; wars frequently took place between them and the Sicans until they concluded a satisfactory treaty establishing the boundaries between their countries, and we will describe this in detail at the proper time. The last colonies in Sicily worth mentioning were those of the Greeks, who founded their cities by the sea. They mingled with one another, and also, since so many Greeks sailed over, they learned their speech. Finally, sharing their way of life, they rid themselves of their barbarous speech and even of their name, being called Sicilians (Siceliotes).

7] Having said enough about these matters we will turn to an account of the so-called Aeolian islands. They are seven in number and have the following names: Strongylē and Euonymus and also Didymē, Phoenicodes and Ericodes, and in addition to these, Hiera Hephaestou and Lipara — which has a city of the same name. They lie between Sicily and Italy due west of the Straits. They are 150 stades away from Sicily and are all comparable in size, the largest having a perimeter of 150 stades. They have all experienced great blasts of fire, whose craters and chasms are still visible. And even now there is a rush of wind from the chasms and a loud crackling noise, on Strongylē and Hiera. Also sand is blown out and red hot stones such as are seen in the neighborhood of Aetna. Some say there are underground passages from the islands all the way to Aetna, with the outlets connected at either end; consequently the craters on the islands burn alternately with those on Aetna.

They say that in ancient times the Aeolian islands were deserted, but that later a man named Liparus, who was the son of King Auson and who had been worsted by the faction of his brothers, got hold of warships and soldiers and fled from Italy to the island named after him, Lipara. That there he founded the city of his name, and cultivated the soil in the other islands mentioned above. When he grew old, they say Aeolus the son of Hippotus, with others, put

in to Lipara, and that he married Liparus' daughter Cyanē, and that
he ruled over the island, combining his own subjects and the inhabitants into a common state. But since Liparus had a longing for
Italy, he helped him establish his rule over the region near Sur-
rentum, where he reigned with great satisfaction, and then died. He
was buried magnificently and obtained heroic honors from the inhabitants. Now this Aeolus is the one mythologers say Odysseus
visited during his wanderings. They say he was pious and upright,
and also that he was kind to strangers; also that he introduced
the use of sails for ships; and that by observing the indications of
the fires he could accurately predict the local winds — which is the
reason for the tale that he was the custodian of the winds. They
say that he was called the friend of the gods because of his great
piety.

8] Aeolus' sons were six in number: Astyochus, Xuthus and Androcles, and in addition to these Pheraemon, Iocastes and Agathyrnus. All of them obtained a great reputation, both because of their
famous father and for their own virtues. Of these, Iocastes, clinging
to Italy, ruled the coast as far as the area of Rhegium; Pheraemon
and Androcles ruled Sicily from the Straits to the area of Lilybaeum.
Of this land the Sicels inhabited the eastern part and the Sicans the
western. These peoples disputed with one another, but they willingly
obeyed the aforementioned sons of Aeolus because of Aeolus' well-
known piety and because of the son's mildness. Xuthus ruled the
country around Leontini which is even now called Xuthia after him;
Agathyrnus, ruling the land now called the Agathyrnitis, founded
a city named Agathyrnus after himself. Astyochus retained the rule
over Lipara. All of these men obtained great honor, imitating the
piety and uprightness of their father. For many generations their
descendants succeeded to these kingdoms, but finally the kings of
Aeolus' line were eliminated in Sicily.

9] After this the Sicels entrusted the rule to the best men, and the
Sicans, disputing about the rule with one another, waged war for a
long time. Many years after this, when the islands were becoming
more and more deserted, some Cnidians and Rhodians, vexed by the
harshness of the Asiatic rulers, decided to send out a colony. Therefore, choosing as leader one of their number, Pentathlus the Cnidian
who traced his ancestry back to Hippotes the descendant of Heracles,
in the 50th Olympiad[2] when Epitelides won the footrace — Pentathlus
and his men sailed to the part of Sicily near Lilybaeum. They found

the Egestaeans and the Selinuntines fighting one another. Persuaded to ally themselves with the Selinuntines they suffered heavy losses in battle, including Pentathlus himself. Therefore, the survivors decided to return home, since the Selinuntines had been conquered. Choosing Pentathlus' kinsmen as their leaders, viz. Gorgus, Thestor and Epithersides, they sailed off through the Tyrrhenian Sea. When they reached Lipara they met with a friendly reception, and were persuaded to live in Lipara along with the inhabitants, of whom about 500 descendants of Aeolus' expedition remained. Later, because of Etruscan piracy on the sea they went to war and built a fleet. Then they divided themselves up, some farming their common islands, others arraying themselves against the pirates. Making their property common property, and grouping themselves in eating clubs (syssitia) they continued for some time, leading a communal life. Finally, they would divide all the islands up for twenty years, and when that period had elapsed they would divide them into allotments again. Subsequently they defeated the Etruscans in numerous naval battles and often dedicated considerable tithes in Delphi from the booty.

10] While speaking of the Liparian state it remains to give an account of the reasons why in later days it grew, not only in prosperity but also in reputation. For it is graced by nature with fine harbors and with famous hot springs. Not only is bathing in them conducive to health for the ailing, but the warm temperature of the water offers no slight pleasure and enjoyment. Therefore, many in Sicily troubled by strange disorders, arrive there, and after making use of these baths are unexpectedly restored to health. This island also has the famous mines of STYPTERIA[3] from which the Liparaeans and Romans derive great revenues. For STYPTERIA is not found anywhere else in the world, and it is very useful. Naturally, having a monopoly, they raise the price, and make an incredible amount of money. Only on the island of Melos is a small amount of STYPTERIA produced, but not enough for many cities. While the Liparaean island is small, it produces enough crops, particularly those that make for luxury. Then, too, an abundance of all kinds of fish is offered to the inhabitants, and there are those fruit trees that particularly minister to the pleasures of taste. We will content ourselves with what has been said about Lipara and the other Aeolian islands.

11] Beyond Lipara towards the west there is an island of the sea, small in size and deserted, and called Osteodes[4] because of a particular circumstance. In the days when the Carthaginians and the Syracusans used to wage many great wars with large land and sea forces, in those days they had many mercenaries of many different races; and they were a rough lot, accustomed to stir up many serious rebellions, particularly when they failed to receive their pay on time; then they would display their natural meanness and daring. There were once about 6000 in number who did not receive their pay, and so they rushed off in a body shouting at the generals. When the latter were at a loss what to do, and they had already yelled many times for their pay, they then threatened that they would help the Carthaginians with their arms, and they also began to lay hands on their leaders. When the Council of Elders had brought charges and the dispute continued to become more and more heated, the Council secretly told the generals to get rid of all the culprits. The generals, accepting these orders, put the mercenaries on board ship and sailed off as though on some warlike mission. Reaching the island mentioned, they landed all the mercenaries on it, and then sailed away, abandoning the culprits. The mercenaries were very disheartened at this circumstance, and being now unable to aid the Carthaginians they perished of hunger. There were so many prisoners who died on such a small island that the tiny area was filled with their bones, and that is how the island got its name. Thus it was that, acting in this outrageous fashion, the mercenaries were overtaken by the greatest misfortune, perishing for lack of food.

12] Since we have told about the Aeolian islands we think best to make some mention of those lying near another part of Sicily; for there are three maritime islands off the southern coast, each of which has a city and harbors capable of offering a refuge to boats driven by storm. First is the one named Melite, 800 stades away from Syracuse. It has many harbors with excellent accommodations, and the people who live there are well-to-do. And there are all types of craftsmen in their shops, the best making linens of exquisite softness and fineness. Their dwellings are worth remarking, magnificently built with elaborate cornices, foundations and stuccoed. This island was a colony of the Phoenicians who, extending their commerce as far as the western ocean, kept this as a haven, for it is well provided with harbors, and lies on the open sea. For this reason those who lived there benefitted greatly from the merchants, and rapidly raised their standard of living, and grew in reputation. Beyond that island is another one, bearing the name of Gaulus, a Phoenician colony on the open sea graced with convenient harbors. And next comes Cercina, pointing to Libya, with a moderate-sized city and harbors, not only serviceable for merchants but also convenient for warships. Now that we have spoken of the islands to the south we will turn back to the islands next to Lipara which lie on the so-called Tyrrhenian Sea.

13] Opposite the Etruscan city of Poplonium there is an island they call Aethaleia. It is 100 stades from the coast, and got its name from the amount of soot (AITHALOS) on it. It contains a large amount of ferrous rock which they crush, for the smelting and manufacture of iron; for they have a copious supply of that metal. Sitting in their workshops they break the rocks, and then heat the crushed stone in certain ingeniously contrived furnaces. There, melting the stone under great heat, they separate it into appropriate sizes shaped like sponges. The merchants bid for them, and then take them off to trade in Dicaearchia and other centers. Those who buy these ingots collect a number of metal workers, and mould the material into all sorts of iron shapes; some they turn into impressions of birds (?), and others into useful shapes of picks, sickles and other tools. Then these are carried everywhere by merchants until a large part of the world benefits from them.

Three hundred stades beyond Aethaleia is an island the Greeks call Cyrnus, but the Romans and the inhabitants call Corsica. This is a convenient place to land, and it has a fine harbor, Syracosium. There are two sizeable cities, one of which is called Calaris, the other Nicaea. And of these, the Phoenicians founded Calaris, which they occupied for some time until driven out by the Etruscans. Controlling the sea, the Etruscans founded Nicaea and appropriated the islands lying off Etruria. Ruling the Corsican cities for a considerable period they levied tribute from the natives in the form of resin, wax and honey which the island furnishes in large quantities. The Corsican slaves seem to be different from other slaves so far as the necessities of life are concerned, a difference corresponding with their nature. The whole island is very large, and much of the land is wooded, covered with a succession of oak groves and watered by small rivers.

14] The natives subsist on milk, honey and meat, all of which this land furnishes in abundance, and they live on good terms with one another, and deal fairly more than almost any other barbarians. The honeycombs found in trees in the mountains belong to whoever first discovers them, and no one disputes his claim. The cattle are distinguished by brands and even if unguarded they are kept for the owners. Also in managing other matters they show a surprising preference for honesty. But they have an extraordinary custom connected with the birth of children. When the woman brings forth, no attention is paid to her child-bed, but her husband falls down as though ill, and is brought to bed for a set number of days, just as if he were in great bodily pain. In this island there grow many excellent boxwood trees, and that is why the honey produced there always has a bitter taste. Barbarians inhabit it, and they speak a strange difficult tongue. Their numbers amount to upwards of 30,000.

15] Next to this is the island named Sardinia, comparable in size with Sicily, and inhabited by barbarians called Iolaeis, thought to be descended from the Thespiaeans who settled there with Iolaus. In the period when Heracles was accomplishing his celebrated labors he had many children by the daughters of Thespius, and in accordance with an oracle Heracles sent them off to Sardinia, along with a considerable force of Greeks and barbarians, to establish a colony. Iolaus, Heracles' nephew, was in charge; he seized the island and built worthy cities on it. Portioning out the land he called the people Iolaeis, after himself, and he built gymnasiums, temples to the gods and everything else to make life agreeable — indications of which remain to our time. For the fairest plains are called Iolaëia, getting their name from him, and the people, even now, keep its name derived from Iolaus. The oracle concerning this colony promised those who participated that the colony would preserve its independence forever, and it is remarkable that up to now the oracle has guaranteed unbroken self-government for the inhabitants. For the Carthaginians, growing powerful and ruling the island, were unable to enslave those who first possessed it, for the Iolaeis fled to the mountains and built underground houses. They raised many herds of cattle, for which there is abundant pasturage, and lived on milk, cheese and meat. Withdrawing from the lowlands they abandoned the unpleasantness of hard work, living an agreeable life in the mountains, and subsisting on the foods mentioned above. Although the Carthaginians often marched against them with considerable forces, they remained free, thanks to the rough terrain and the difficulties of getting at them underground. Finally, when the Romans took over and frequently marched against them, they remained unconquered by a hostile army, for the same reasons. Nevertheless, in the early days Iolaus returned to Greece after arranging matters in the colony, and the Thespiaeans, after governing the island for many generations were finally driven out to Italy, where they settled down in the region near Cyme. The rest of the population, being entirely barbarian, chose the best men from among the inhabitants as their leaders, and kept their independence up to our own times.

16] Having said enough about Sardinia we will turn to the islands that come next in order. Beyond those already mentioned is an island called Pityussa, which gets its name from the numbers of pine trees (PITYS) growing there. Being on the open sea, it lies three days and three nights away from the Pillars of Heracles, one day and a night from Libya and one day's sail from Spain. It is about the same size as Corcyra. Its virtues are moderate; it has a small acreage of vineyards, and olive trees have been grafted on to the wild olives. Of the products raised there they say the wool is beautifully soft. The island is cut up into noteworthy plains and hills, and it has a city called Eresus (?), a Carthaginian colony. It has considerable meadows, and walls built on a large scale, and a great number of well-built houses. Various barbarians inhabit it, but particularly the Phoenicians. The colonization took place 160 years after the founding of Carthage.

17] Then there are other islands opposite Spain called the Gymnesiae by the Greeks because the natives go about naked during the summer season, but called the Baliarides by the inhabitants and by the Romans because of their excelling all men in casting great stones with their slings. The larger of these islands is also the largest of all the islands except for the seven — Sicily, Sardinia, Cyprus, Crete, Euboea, Cyrnus and Lesbos — and it is one day's sail from Spain. The smaller island lies to the east and nourishes many varieties of livestock, particularly very tall mules of surpassing strength. Both islands have excellent fertile soil, and there are over 30,000 inhabitants. Among nourishing products they yield no wine at all, and therefore everyone is greatly addicted to wine because of its scarcity among them. Since olive oil is very rare, they prepare oil from the mastich tree; mixing this with lard, they use it to anoint their bodies. But above all they dote on women, whom they prize so highly that whenever women are carried off by pirates coming ashore, they are ransomed, three or four men being exchanged for one woman. They live under cliffs, and make excavations beyond the cliffs, generally tunnelling out many areas underground where they live, seeking both shelter and security in them. They make no use of silver or gold currency, and forbid their being brought into the country at all. They give the following reason for this: Of old, Heracles marched against Geryon, son of Chrysaor, who possessed a vast amount of silver and gold. In order to have possessions which will not lead to plotting, they have set up a wealth not tinged with silver or gold. Consequently and in accord with this decision, in the Carthaginian expeditions which took place long ago they did not bring back their pay to their own country but bought women and wine instead, spending all their pay on such commodities.

18] There is a strange custom of theirs about weddings. At the wedding feasts the kinsmen and friends on the basis of their age — first, second, and so on — all have intercourse with the bride in turn, an honor enjoyed last of all by the bridegroom. They also have a peculiar and very extraordinary custom about burying the dead. Smashing the limbs of the body with clubs, they throw it into a receptacle, and place a quantity of stones on top. Their military equipment consists of three slings. One they wear around the head, one around the belly, while they carry the third in their hands. In waging war they throw much larger stones than others, and with such violence that whatever is hit appears to have been struck by a catapult. Therefore, during attacks in siege warfare they strike men standing on the battlements and disable them, while in battle they smash through shield, helmet and all protective armor. Their aim is so accurate that usually they do not miss the target offered. The reason for this is their continued practise from childhood on, for as children they are forced to use the sling unceasingly by their mothers. For a loaf of bread is fastened to a beam as a target, and it is not given to the novice to eat until he hits the bread, and obtains permission from his mother to eat it.

19] Since we have described the islands lying inside of the Pillars of Heracles, we will speak of those on Ocean. Off Libya there is an island on the open sea which is large enough to be worth mentioning. It lies many days' sail west of Libya. It is a productive land, much of it mountainous, but with a sizeable plain of surpassing beauty. Traversed by navigable rivers which irrigate it, there are many parks planted with all sorts of trees, and there are numerous gardens intersected by sweet running waters. This land offers its abundance for enjoyment and for luxury. The mountains have many large oak groves, and all sorts of fruit-bearing trees, and for living in the mountains there are many gullies and springs. The island as a whole is watered by sweet streams which not only give great pleasure to those who live there, but also contribute to their health and strength of limb. There is much hunting of game and animals of all kinds, and since they are so well supplied with game from these beasts they lack nothing in reaching the height of luxury and magnificence. Also, the sea which washes that island has quantities of fish, because Ocean by its very nature everywhere teems with all kinds of fish. And, in general, this island is surrounded by a benign atmosphere; most of the year it yields many nuts and other seasonal fruits, so that it seems the abode of gods rather than of men, so exceedingly prosperous is it.

20] In ancient times this place was not discovered because of its remoteness from the inhabited world, but it was discovered later in this way. The Phoenicians, who were always making trading voyages from earliest times, planted many colonies in Libya, and no small number in the western regions of Europe. Their revenues increasing to their satisfaction they accumulated great wealth, and took a notion to sail the sea called Ocean, outside the Pillars of Heracles. First they founded a city on the Straits itself, by the Pillars and on the European side, which they named Gadira, being a peninsula; and then they built other structures suitable for the area and also a splendid temple to Heracles, and gave magnificent sacrifices regulated in accordance with Phoenician usage. This temple was highly regarded then, and even more so in later times down to our day. For many famous Romans, men of great deeds, made vows to this god and fulfilled them after achieving success. Now the Phoenicians, for the reasons given, explored the coast outside the Pillars, and sailing along by Libya they were carried out by heavy winds on a long voyage through Ocean. Driven by the storm many days they reached the island mentioned. Observing its characteristics and its prosperity, they made it known to everyone. Then, when the Etruscans gained control of the sea and planned to colonize there, the Carthaginians prevented them. They also took good care lest many emigrate there from Carthage, attracted by the virtues of the island. They planned at some future time to make it their refuge from the uncertainties of Fortune, if an appalling disaster should ever come upon Carthage. For as masters of the sea they would be able to sail off to this island with all their goods, unknown to their conquerors.

21] Since we have described the ocean opposite Libya and the islands on it, we will turn our attention to Europe. Off the coast of Gaul right opposite the so-called Hercynian forest — and we have heard that here are the largest mountains in Europe — there are many islands on the ocean, the largest of which is called Prettanice. In early times it was not frequented by foreign powers, for we have not heard of Dionysus or Heracles or any other heroes or princes who campaigned against it. In our day C. Caesar, who was denominated a god for his deeds, was the first to attempt the island. Defeating the Britons, he forced them to pay a fixed tribute. But now we will describe the island, and the tin that is found there. The island is triangular in shape, and resembles Sicily in that the sides are unequal. Extending at an angle from Europe, the point which is the shortest distance from Europe they call Cantium, which they say is about 100 stades away from the continent, and here it is that the sea has its outlet. Another point, called Belerium, is said to be four days' sail from the mainland. The remaining point, which they say projects out into the sea, is called Orcas (?). The smallest side is 7500 stades, extending alongside Europe; the second side, that from the channel to the apex, is 15,000 stades; and the remaining side is 20,000 stades, so that altogether the island has a circumference of 42,500 stades. They say an autochthonous people live in Prettanice, who inculcate the old way of life in their upbringing. For example, they use chariots in warfare, such as the old Greek heroes are held to have used in the Trojan war. They have shabby houses, mostly built of reeds or out of wood. They gather up the ripe grain, and cutting off the ears they store them in roofed structures, from which they take the old ears day by day to be ground up for their food. In their habits they are simple and far removed from the sharpness and skulduggery of men today. Their diet is sparing and very different from the luxury that goes with wealth. The island is well populated, but the atmosphere is very cold, lying as it does beneath the Bear itself. There are many kings and potentates, but for the most part they get along peacefully with one another.

22] But about the customs there and other particulars we will write separately when we come to Caesar's expedition to Britain, but now we will tell about the tin which occurs there. Now the inhabitants of Prettanice who dwell by the so-called Point Belerium are very hospitable to strangers, and as a result of their relations with foreign merchants their way of life has become civilized. For they prepare the tin, skillfully working the ground which yields it. Now being like rock, it has strata, which they channel out, melting and purifying it afterwards. Then, striking off pieces the size of knuckle bones, they carry them off to an island which lies near Prettanice and is called Ictis. During the ebb tides the area between dries up, and they transport an abundance of tin to this island on wagons. A strange thing happens with reference to the nearby islands, the ones between Europe and Prettanice. During the flood tide the channel between is flooded and islands are seen, but during the ebb the sea goes off drying up a large area so that what had been islands appear as peninsulas. There the merchants buy from the natives and carry their cargoes to Gaul. Finally, travelling overland through Gaul for about thirty days, they bring their goods by horse to the mouth of the Rhone River.

23] Contenting ourselves with what has been said about tin we will now give an account of the so-called electrum.[5] There is a Scythian island above and opposite Gaul, a marine island on Ocean, and it is named Basileia. There the waves cast forth great quantities of so-called electrum, which is not found in the inhabited world. Many of the ancients have written completely incredible myths about it which have been disproved by events. For many of the poets and the historians say that Phaethon the son of Helios, being yet a boy, persuaded his father one day to give up his chariot, but that Phaethon, driving the chariot, was unable to manage the reins, so that the horses, despising the lad, rushed off away from their usual course. At first, wandering about in the sky, they set it ablaze, creating the so-called Milky Way, and afterwards they set fire to a great part of the world and burned no small amount of land. Zeus, accordingly, angry over what had happened, struck Phaethon with a thunderbolt and restored Helios to his usual rounds. Phaethon fell by the mouth of the river now called the Po, but formerly known as the Eridanus. His sisters wept extravagantly in their great sorrow over his death, and were transformed into black poplars. And they said that each year they weep at the same time, and their tears harden to form what is called electrum, excelling in splendor those of similar origin usual at the death of young persons, in a way corresponding to their sorrow. But all those who have shaped this myth are in error, and they have been refuted by the achievements of later times. One must attend to the true account. For electrum is gathered on the island mentioned, and it is brought over to the opposite continent by the inhabitants, and from there to our regions, just as has been described.

Notes

1. *Od.*, IX. 109/11.
2. 580 B.C.
3. Alum?
4. I.e., "Bone Island."
5. I.e., amber.

5

The Greek Tyrants

AFTER the great period of colonization (750–550 B.C.) in which Greeks from the mainland of Greece, the coast of Asia Minor and the Cyclades established themselves with varying degrees of success around the Black Sea, along the coast of Thrace and Macedonia, in North Africa, in Sicily and South Italy, at Marseilles, along the French Riviera and on Spain's Mediterranean shore, there followed a period of rapid economic change which was reflected by political upheavals even before the safety valve of migration had been closed. Frequently the landed gentry were superseded for a time by the strong rule of one man, the tyrant. The old tyrants have been given and no doubt often deserved to be given a bad name, but without them the fifth century Greek city-state resting firmly on the sturdy shoulders of the citizen hoplite would never have developed as it did. Aristotle, who died in 322 B.C., looked back over Greek political developments with the eye of a political scientist and the ardor of a philosopher who wished to reduce all phenomena to a rational explanation, a pattern of cause and effect. The passage here, short as it is, may suggest why Machiavelli and earlier writers like Marsiglio of Padua found him so useful.

The longer passages are again from Herodotus and give us the tradition of the more celebrated tyrants as they were remembered in the fifth century.

a Aristotle, Politics, *1313a.34-1313b.29, 1315b.11-39*

NOW TYRANNIES are maintained by two diametrically opposed methods, the first of which is the traditional one by which most tyrants have carried on the government. Many devices of this sort were invented by Periander of Corinth and many more have been borrowed from the Persian rule. Some effective ways of preserving tyranny are reported from ancient times, such as: putting down the outstanding persons and eliminating men of independent spirit; forbidding common meals, education and things of that kind, thus taking precautions against whatever might have the double effect of engendering self-confidence and mutual trust; not permitting schools or meetings of scholars, but doing everything possible to prevent anyone from knowing anyone else (for knowledge tends to give men confidence in one another); and keeping those who are not abroad in plain view, dangling about the court (for in this way they are not apt to do anything without being detected, and their constant servitude will make them timid). Other such Persian and barbarous practices are tyrannical, for they are all the same. Also the trying not to miss anything said or done by their subjects, but making use of spies like those so-called "Talebearers" in Syracuse and the eavesdroppers Hiero sent out whenever there was a social gathering (for men are less apt to talk frankly for fear of such spies, and even if they do talk are more likely to be found out), is tyrannical; so is the practice of promoting mutual suspicion, stirring up friend against friend, the common people against their betters and the rich against one another. Then too it is customary for tyrants to impoverish their subjects, both to obtain pay for their guards and also to keep the people so busy that they will have no time to conspire against them. Examples of this are the pyramids of Egypt, the temple of Olympian Zeus built by the Pisistratids and the constructions of Polycrates in Samos (for all lead to the same result, keeping their subjects busy and impoverished). Then, too, there is the imposition of confiscatory taxes like the one in Syracuse (for under Dionysius they were required to give up all their property over a five-year period). Tyrants also make war to keep their subjects occupied and to force them to feel the need for a ruler.

*   *   *

Now the most short-lived governments are oligarchy and tyranny. The most enduring tyranny was that of Orthagoras and his sons in Sicyon, which lasted for one hundred years. The reason for this is that they treated their subjects with moderation and frequently put themselves below the law. Then, too, Clisthenes was too warlike to be despised with impunity, and they all devoted a great deal of attention to the interests of the common people. Clisthenes is even said to have presented the judge who decided a case against him with a crown. Reputedly there is a seated statue of this judge in the market place. (Pisistratus is also credited with allowing himself to be haled before the Areopagus for judgment.) The next longest tyranny was that of the Cypselids in Corinth, which lasted for seventy-three years and six months: for Cypselus was tyrant for thirty years, Periander for forty and one half years, and Psammetichus the son of Gorgus three years. And the reasons are the same: Cypselus was a popular leader who ruled without a bodyguard, while Periander, though despotic, was also warlike. Third in length was that of the Pisistratids in Athens. But it was not continuous, for Pisistratus was driven out of his tyranny twice. Thus in a period of thirty-three years he was tyrant for only seventeen, while his sons held the tyranny for eighteen years, the whole period of rule amounting to thirty-five years. Of the others the longest was that of Hieron and Gelon in Syracuse, though it was not very enduring, amounting altogether to only eighteen years: Gelon died after being tyrant for seven years, Hieron ruled ten years and Thrasybulus was driven out after eleven months * * But the majority of tyrannies have only lasted a short time.

b Herodotus, Histories, *v, 92; vi, 126-131; i, 59-64; iii, 39, 44-48, 54-56, 60*

v

92] IN Corinth the city used to be governed as follows: there was an oligarchy, and those who were called the Bacchiads administered the affairs of the city, marrying and giving in marriage only among themselves. Now Amphion, who was one of this group, had a lame daughter named Labda. Since none of the Bacchiads wanted to marry her, Aëtion the son of Echecrates obtained her hand; he came from the district of Petra and traced his descent back to Caenides the Lapith. When he had no children by this wife or any other he went to Delphi to get advice about offspring. As soon as he went in the Pythia addressed him in these words:

> Aëtion, no one honors you, though you are worthy of honor.
> Labda is pregnant, she will bear a great stone which will fall
> on the rulers and bring justice to Corinth.

Now it happened that the oracle given to Aëtion was reported back to the Bacchiads, who had received an oracle about Corinth earlier which seemed obscure, but which had the same meaning as that of Aëtion. It reads as follows:

> An eagle[1] is impregnated in the rocks, and will bring forth a lion, a mighty devourer of raw meat. Many will he loosen at the knees. Ponder this well, Corinthians who dwell by fair Peirene and beetling Corinth.

Now at first this puzzled the Bacchiads, but when they learned of the oracle given to Aëtion they connected the two as being in agreement. When they realized this they kept quiet about it in the hope of destroying Aëtion's expected offspring. As soon as his wife gave birth they sent ten of their number to the neighborhood where Aëtion lived to slay the infant. When they reached Petra they entered the hall and asked for Aëtion's child. Labda, not knowing why they had come, but assuming that it was out of friendship for the father that they were asking to see the infant, brought him out and handed him to one of their number. Now on the way over they had decided that the first man to get hold of the child would dash it on the ground, but by a stroke of luck the baby happened to smile at the man who took him, who was overwhelmed with pity when he saw it. Unable to kill the baby he passed it on to the second man, and he to the third until the infant had been handed around by all ten, not one of them being willing to do the deed. Restoring the child to his mother they went outside and stood beside the gate upbraiding one another, especially blaming the first one for failing to carry out their agreement. After some time had gone by they decided to go back again and accomplish the murder collectively. But Corinth was fated to come to grief through the seed of Aëtion. Waiting inside near the door Labda had heard everything they said. Fearing they would slay the child if they got their hands on him again, she carried him off and hid him in what seemed to her the least likely place for him to be found, in a chest[2] — for she knew that if they came back to look they would search everywhere. And that is just what happened. They returned, but when after searching they were unable to find him they decided to go away, telling those who sent them that they had carried out their orders. So they went away and made their report. But later on when Aëtion's son was older and had outlived this danger he was given the name of Cypselus after the chest.

When as a full grown man Cypselus went to Delphi to consult

the oracle, he received an ambiguous reply which induced him to seize and to hold Corinth. This was the oracle:

> Happy is this man who enters my house, Cypselus the son of Aëtion, for he shall be king of Corinth the famed, he and his sons, but not the sons of his sons.

Such was the oracle, and this is the kind of man Cypselus was: he drove many Corinthians into exile, many others he deprived of their possessions and still more of their lives. After ruling for thirty years and finishing the web of his life he was succeeded as tyrant by his son Periander.

Now at first Periander was milder than his father, but after an exchange of messages with Thrasybulus of Miletus he became more savage than Cypselus had ever been. For he sent a herald to ask Thrasybulus how to put his affairs on the safest basis, and how he might best rule over Corinth. Thrasybulus took the man who had come from Periander outside the city into a cultivated field. Then he led him through the standing grain, and while questioning the herald and examining him on the reasons for his coming out from Corinth, he kept on cutting off the heads of grain that stood highest, then threw them down. In this way he destroyed the best and tallest part of the crop. After traversing the field he dismissed the herald without making any reply. When the herald returned home to Corinth Periander was eager to find out Thrasybulus' advice. But the man told him that Thrasybulus had given him no message, and that he was surprised at being sent to see anyone mad enough to destroy his own property. And then he told him what he had seen Thrasybulus doing. But Periander understood his meaning. He decided to take Thrasybulus' advice and put the leading men to death. After that he treated the citizens with extreme cruelty. Whatever Cypselus had failed to do in the way of killing or banishing was completed by Periander. . . . That is tyranny for you, Lacedaemonians, and such are its deeds.

* * *

vi

So it was that the Alcmaeonid house became very wealthy, and the Alcmaeon in question won the victory in the Olympic Games with his four-horse chariot.

126] In the second generation after him Clisthenes the tyrant of Sicyon raised the dignity of the house so that it became much more renowned among the Greeks than it had been before. Now Clisthenes, the son of Myron and the grandson of Andreas, had a daughter whose name was Agaristē. He wanted to search out the best man in all Greece and to give him his daughter in marriage. At the Olympics in which he won the four-horse chariot race Clisthenes issued a proclamation inviting any Greek who thought himself worthy of being Clisthenes' son-in-law to come to Sicyon on or before the sixtieth day, for Clisthenes would celebrate the wedding one year from the sixtieth day. Then all Greeks who were distinguished, either for deeds of their own or because of the cities from which they came, arrived as suitors. Clisthenes had made preparations for them to compete with one another in the footrace and in wrestling.

127] From Italy came Hippocrates' son Smindyridas of Sybaris, the most luxurious suitor to apply (that was when Sybaris was in its prime), and from Siris came Damasus, said to be the son of Amyris the wise. These were the candidates from Italy, and from the Ionian Gulf came Amphinestus the son of Epistrophus the Epidamnian. He came from the Ionian Gulf. Now there came Males the Aetolian, the brother of that Titormus, renowned throughout Greece for his strength, who fled to the remotest parts of Aetolia to get away from mankind. And from the Peloponnese there was Leocedes the son of Phidon, the Argive tyrant who introduced his system of measures into the Peloponnese and who was also the most insolent man in Greece: he even drove out the Elean officials in charge of the Olympics and ran the games himself. This man's son came and also Amiantus the son of Lycurgus from Trapezus in Arcadia; also Laphanes came from Paeus in the Azanian district of Arcadia, who was the son of that Euphorion who, as the story is told in Arcadia, once entertained the Dioscuri in his house and afterwards offered hospitality to all men; and Onomastus the son of Agaeus came from Elis. Now these were the suitors from the Peloponnese, but from Athens there came Megacles the son of this Alcmaeon who had come back from seeing Croesus, and another man, Hippoclides the son of Tisander, distinguished in Athens for wealth and good looks. From Eretria, which was flourishing at that time, came Lysanias, the only Euboean representative. From Thessaly there was

Diactorides of the family of the Scopidae in Crannon; and from the Molossians came Alcon. These were the suitors.

128] When they arrived on the day appointed Clisthenes first inquired closely into the nationality and lineage of each, then he kept them there for a year testing their bravery, disposition, education and manners, seeing them individually and as a group. He tried out the younger ones in gymnastic competition, but above all he tested them on their social behavior. For as long as he detained them he continued all these contests, but he also entertained them lavishly. Of all the suitors the Athenians pleased him best, and of these he rather preferred Hippoclides the son of Tisander, both on account of his bravery and because he was related by birth to the Cypselids of Corinth.

129] When the day came for settling the marriage, and the man chosen from among them all was to be revealed, Clisthenes sacrificed one hundred oxen and gave a banquet for the suitors and all the people of Sicyon. After they had dined the suitors vied with one another, capping verses and telling stories for all to hear. As the drinking proceeded Hippoclides, who easily outdid all the others, asked the fluteplayer to play a dance tune for him. The fluteplayer obliged and Hippoclides began to dance. Although he danced quite to his own satisfaction Clisthenes, who was watching, disapproved of the whole thing. But Hippoclides persisted, and after a while he asked to have a table brought in. When this was done he performed a series of figures on it, first in the Laconian style and then Attic figures; but finally he stood on his head and gesticulated with his hands and feet. Even during the first and second demonstrations Clisthenes became disgusted at the very idea of having Hippoclides for a son-in-law, because of his dancing and shameless behavior, though he managed to contain himself, not wanting to break out at him. But when he saw him waving his arms and legs around he lost all control, calling out: "Son of Tisander, you have danced away your marriage!" And the young man replied: "Hippoclides couldn't care less!" — which is how the saying originated.

130] Then, calling for silence, Clisthenes addressed them as follows: "Gentlemen, suitors for the hand of my child I commend you all, and if it were possible I would gratify you all, rather than by selecting one of your number to reject the others. But since there is only one girl for whom I have to decide it becomes impossible to treat all of you as I would like. But to each of you who is deprived of this wedding I am giving a talent of silver, both because you are worthy to marry into my family and also to make up to you for your long absence from home. My daughter Agaristē I betroth to Megacles son of Alcmaeon, in accordance with the laws of Athens." When Megacles accepted the proposal the marriage was celebrated by Clisthenes.

131] This is what happened in the choice of a suitor, and this is how the Alcmaeonids became famous throughout Greece. As a result of this marriage Clisthenes was born, the man who established the tribes and a democratic constitution in Athens, for he was named after his maternal grandfather from Sicyon. This man and also Hippocrates were born to Megacles, and Hippocrates had another Megacles and another Agaristē, named for the daughter of Clisthenes. She married Xanthippus the son of Ariphron, and while she was pregnant she had a dream in which she thought she gave birth to a lion. A few days later she bore Pericles to Xanthippus.

*　　*　　*

i

59] Thus Croesus learned that at this time[3] the Athenian people were both held down and distracted by Pisistratus the son of Hippocrates, the tyrant of Athens. While Hippocrates was attending the Olympic festival as a private citizen a marvellous thing happened. As he was sacrificing, the cauldrons standing nearby filled with meat and water became very hot and boiled over, though there was no fire. When Chilon the Lacedaemonian, who happened to be on the spot, saw this marvel he advised Hippocrates, first not to take a wife into his house for the sake of children, or secondly to send her away, and if he happened to have a son to disown him. But Hippocrates did not choose to follow Chilon's advice, so afterwards this Pisistratus was born to him. When the Athenian factions of the Coast and the Plain fell into dispute with one another, the former led by Megacles son of Alcmaeon, and the Plain under the leadership of Lycurgus son of Aristolaïdes, Pisistratus formed a third party with his eye on the tyranny. He collected a following by championing the interests of the men of the upland districts, and then resorted to the following stratagem. Wounding himself he drove his span of mules into the market place pretending to be fleeing from his enemies who, according to him, tried to kill him as he was driving through a field. He begged the people to grant him some sort of a guard. He had won popularity earlier as a general against Megara, by capturing Nisaea and other great achievements. The Athenians were deceived by him, so they voted Pisistratus the right to pick out some of the citizens to act as club-bearers, but not as spearbearers; for they followed along behind him carrying wooden staffs. But these men joined Pisistratus in a revolt and seized the acropolis. Then Pisistratus ruled over Athens without disturbing the existing magistracies or changing the constitution. He administered the city in accordance with the established laws, governing it extremely well.

60] Not long afterwards the partisans of Megacles and Lycurgus came to an understanding and drove him out. So the first time Pisistratus held the tyranny in Athens he was driven out before it was firmly established, but it was not long before the men who drove him out quarreled again. Being pretty roughly handled in the struggle that followed Megacles sent a messenger to Pisistratus, asking him whether he would marry his daughter to recover the tyranny. When Pisistratus received his offer and agreed to the terms, then in order to expedite his return they employed by far the most preposterous trick I have ever encountered, especially since Greeks have long been regarded as much sharper than barbarian peoples and much freer from downright stupidity, and also considering that the men who perpetrated this fraud were Athenians, felt to be the most intelligent people in Greece. There was a woman of Paeania named Phyē, who was six feet tall and very good looking. Equipping her with armor they placed her on a chariot and decked her out in such a way as to make her look most attractive, then drove on towards the city, sending heralds on ahead to make a special announcement when they came into town. And this is what they said: "Oh Athenians, receive Pisistratus with a good will. Athena honors him above all men, and she is personally bringing him back to her acropolis." While they were making the rounds with this announcement the rumor spread throughout the countryside that Athena was bringing Pisistratus back. Thereupon the townspeople adored that woman as a goddess and welcomed Pisistratus.

61] After he had recovered the tyranny in this fashion Pisistratus carried out his pledge by marrying Megacles' daughter. However, since he already had sons of his own and also since the Alcmaeonids were held to be under a curse,[4] he did not wish to have any children by his new wife. Accordingly he did not have intercourse with her in the legal way. At first his wife kept quiet about this, but later, either voluntarily or in answer to a question, she told her mother, who in turn told her husband. In the heat of his resentment Megacles came to terms with the rival factions, feeling that he had been treated with the utmost contempt. When Pisistratus learned what had been contrived against him he got right out of the country. Arriving in Eretria he took counsel with his sons, where Hippias' advice to win back the tyranny was adopted. Accordingly they collected gifts from the cities that were in any way obligated to them, and while there were many that gave substantial support the Thebans surpassed them all in the extent of their contributions. When some time had passed, not to make a long story of it, they completed their preparations to return. Argive mercenaries joined them from the Peloponnese, and a Naxian volunteer named Lygdamis showed the greatest enthusiasm, furnishing both men and money.

62] Starting out from Eretria they headed for home in the eleventh year, first occupying Marathon on Attic soil. While they were camped there partisans came out to join them from the city and still others poured in from the country districts, preferring tyranny to freedom. And they united their forces. But all the time Pisistratus was raising money, and even when he seized Marathon the men of Athens paid no attention, but when they learned he was on the march from Marathon against the city then they went out against him. So they marched in full force against their enemies, while Pisistratus and his army started out for the city from Marathon. They converged on the same spot, reaching the temple of Pallas Athena. There the two armies drew up opposite one another. Then, under divine inspiration, the Acarnanian soothsayer, Amphilytus, came up to Pisistratus and addressed the following hexameter to him:

Hurled is the mesh of the net, its encompassing folds are wide-stretched. Under the rays of the moon will the tunnies rush in in the night.

63] That was what he was inspired to say, and when he heard the oracle Pisistratus accepted it and attacked with his army. But the Athenians from the city had had their dinner at the time, and some of them were playing dice while the rest were asleep. Falling on the Athenians Pisistratus routed them. While they were fleeing Pisistratus devised a very clever plan to prevent the Athenians who were now scattered from coming together again. Putting his sons on horseback he sent them on ahead. Whenever they caught up with any of the fugitives they said what Pisistratus had ordered them to say, urging them not to be afraid but to return each to his own home.

64] The Athenians obeyed, and so Pisistratus became tyrant for the third time. He strengthened the tyranny with large numbers of mercenaries, and he increased his revenues at home, also collecting money from the Strymon valley. He took their children as hostages from those Athenians who did not immediately go into exile but remained at home, and he settled the affairs of Naxos (for Pisistratus took the city by force and put it in the hands of Lygdamis). Also he purified the island of Delos in accordance with an oracle. He exhumed the bodies of the dead from the whole area within view of the temple, and moved them to another part of Delos. So it was that Pisistratus became tyrant of Athens, and some Athenians fell in battle while others fled from their native land with the Alcmaeonids.

*   *   *

iii

39] While Cambyses was marching against Egypt the Lacedaemonians made an expedition against Samos, against Polycrates the son of Aeaces who held Samos as the result of a revolution. At first he ruled the island in conjunction with his brothers Pantagnotus and Syloson, but later after he killed the former and drove Syloson, the younger one, into exile he ruled Samos by himself. As ruler he established guest friendship with Amasis the king of Egypt. After that Polycrates' affairs prospered rapidly and his fame spread to Ionia and the rest of Greece. Whenever he decided to march he was uniformly successful. He had one hundred fifty-oared ships and one thousand bowmen. He attacked everyone and carried off their goods, sparing none, for he said friends were more grateful to him for returning their property than if he had never taken it. He controlled many islands and also many cities on the mainland. In a naval battle he captured the Lesbians who were on their way in full force to help the men of Miletus. The captives, bound together, dug a trench all around the walls of Samos.

*   *   *

44] Now it was this same Polycrates, prosperous in all his undertakings, against whom the Lacedaemonians made war at the request of the Samian exiles who later founded Cydonia in Crete. Meanwhile, unknown to the people in Samos, Polycrates had sent a herald to Cambyses the son of Cyrus, who was assembling his forces against Egypt, begging him to send someone to Samos to ask for military aid. Cambyses was pleased at this suggestion so he did send someone to Samos asking Polycrates for a naval force to accompany him to Egypt. Choosing those citizens he suspected of planning to revolt Polycrates sent them off with forty triremes, telling Cambyses not to send them back again.

45] Now some say the Samians sent by Polycrates never reached Egypt, but that when they had sailed to Carpathus they conferred together and decided not to go on any further. Others say that they did go to Egypt but watched for a chance to escape. While they were sailing back to Samos Polycrates met them with his ships and offered battle. Winning the victory the returning Samians landed on the island, but after that, being defeated in a land battle, they sailed off for Lacedaemon. There are also those who say that the Samians returning from Egypt conquered Polycrates, but I think they must be wrong. For if they were strong enough to dispose of Polycrates there would have been no reason for them to call on the Lacedaemonians. Furthermore it is unlikely that when he had large numbers of mercenary bowmen as well as native troops he would have been defeated by such a small number of returning Samians.

46] Now when the Samians who had been driven out by Polycrates arrived in Sparta, they appeared before the magistrates and pleaded with them long and earnestly. But the first time they held forth the magistrates said they had forgotten the earlier part of their speech and did not understand the later part. So at their second hearing the Samians brought a sack and said nothing except that the sack needed meal. The Spartans answered that the word "sack" was superfluous, but they did agree to help them.

47] After making preparations the Lacedaemonians went out against Samos, as the Samians say to repay them for the time they had helped them with their ships against the Messenians, but according to the Lacedaemonians they did not go to help the Samians so much as to avenge themselves for the theft of the bowl they sent to Croesus, and that of the corslet Amasis the king of Egypt had sent them as a gift. The Samians had seized the corslet the year before they took Croesus' bowl, and it was of linen, embroidered with many ornamental figures in gold and in "tree wool." What made it so remarkable was the yarn used in the corslet, which was so fine that each strand had 360 threads, all distinguishable. There is another one like it dedicated by Amasis in the temple of Athena at Lindus.

48] Now the Corinthians were also eager to take part in the Samian expedition.

* * *

54] Arriving with a large force the Lacedaemonians laid siege to Samos. Attacking the wall they penetrated the suburban area by scaling the tower by the sea, but when Polycrates came to the rescue with a strong force they were driven out. Then the mercenaries and many of the Samians themselves made a sally down from the tower that stood on the brow of the hill, but after a brief engagement they fled back again, pursued by the Lacedaemonians, slaying as they came.

55] Now if all the Lacedaemonians who were there had been like Archias and Lycopas, Samos would have been taken. For these men followed the fleeing Samians inside the walls and died in the city when the way out was barred against them. Now I met an Archias, third in descent from this Archias and himself the son of Samius, in the Pitanē district,[5] for that was where he lived. He made himself responsible for visitors from Samos, and he told me his father had been named Samius because his father's father had died heroically in Samos. He also said that he looked after the Samian visitors because the Samians had given his father a state funeral.

56] Now after besieging Samos for forty days without making any headway the Lacedaemonians returned to the Peloponnese.

* * *

60] I have spent so much time on the Samians because they accomplished the three greatest engineering feats of all the Greeks: First there is a tunnel with two entrances dug down through a 900-foot mountain. The tunnel is over three quarters of a mile long, being eight feet high and eight feet wide. Through its entire length another tunnel has been cut twenty feet deep and three feet wide by which the water is conveyed in pipes from an abundant spring down into the city. The engineer of this tunnel was a Megarian,

88

Eupalinus the son of Naustrophus. So this is one of the three structures, and the second is a mole in the sea around the harbor, one hundred and twenty feet deep and a quarter of a mile long. The third work they built is the largest temple we have ever seen, the original architect of which was Rhoecus the son of Philes, a Samian. And that is why I have spent so much time on the Samians.

Notes

1. *Aëtos.*
2. *Cypselos.*
3. Ca. 550 B.C.
4. See V, 71.
5. Of Sparta.

6

Before Salamis

INEVITABLY Herodotus was influenced by the Periclean "party-line" in interpreting the past, and though he was too shrewd to accept it blindly, he had difficulty in sorting out the facts. That he tried to do so is shown in his account of Marathon, where he does mention—though with disapproval—the view that the Alcmaeonidae (a family closely allied with Pericles) attempted to betray Athens to the Persians (VI, 115). But his account of Themistocles, probably the greatest statesman Athens produced, bears clear traces of the malice of his political rivals and heirs. Nor had the first Atthis, that is the first local chronicle of Athens, yet been written, though Herodotus' contemporary, Hellanicus of Lesbos, was soon to fill this gap. Herodotus' account of the appeal to Gelon should dispose of the idea popularized by Ephorus in the fourth century, that Persia and Carthage synchronized their attacks on the Greeks, east and west. It came to be believed that Salamis and Himera were fought on the same day, a fiction encouraged by Syracusan writers in search of an iron-clad alibi for the failure of Syracuse to help in the great cause. Everyone not at Salamis needed an explanation: the Corcyraeans said they were held back by heavy winds (Herodotus, VII, 168); the Cretans, not famed for veracity, said their archers were there (Ctesias, Persica 26).

Herodotus, Histories, vii, 138-145, 157-162, 175-176; viii, 1-10, 40, 75-76, 78-83

vii

138] OSTENSIBLY the king's expedition was directed against Athens, but actually it was aimed at the whole of Greece. Although they learned this a long time in advance not all Greeks acted in the same way: for some gave land and water to the Persian confident they would suffer nothing unpleasant at barbarian hands; others, while they did not give land and water, remained badly frightened because the ships in Greece were inadequate in numbers or in strength to meet the invader, and because many of the Greeks who were unwilling to take part in the war would gladly go over to the Persian side.

139] And now I feel obliged to state my own opinion, one which will be invidious to many people. Nevertheless I shall not hold back from saying what I think is the truth. If the Athenians had abandoned their country for fear of the threatening danger, or even if they had stayed and surrendered themselves to Xerxes then no one would have attempted to oppose the king on the sea. Yet if no one had opposed Xerxes on the sea this would have been the result on the land: Even though there had been a plurality of walls through the isthmus guarding the Peloponnese, the Lacedaemonians would have been betrayed by their allies, not voluntarily but of necessity, as the barbarian took city after city with his fleet, until they stood alone. After accomplishing great feats the Lacedaemonians would have perished bravely fighting by themselves. This would have been their fate unless they came to an understanding with Xerxes earlier, when they saw the other Greeks going over to Persia. Thus the Persians would have controlled Greece on both elements, for I cannot understand what advantage there would be in having a wall across the isthmus if the king controlled the sea. And if anyone should call the Athenians the saviors of Greece he would not be wrong, because whichever side they supported was the side destined to prevail. By choosing the side of Greek freedom they were responsible for arousing all of Greece that had not yet gone over to Persia and, next to the gods, for driving off the king. Not even the threatening oracles from Delphi, terrifying as they were, persuaded them to abandon Greece, but they remained and dared to meet the invader of their country.

140] When the Athenian envoys sent to Delphi had gone through the usual formalities at the temple, they entered the hall and seated themselves, preparing to consult the oracle. Then the Pythia,[1] whose name was Aristonicē, addressed them as follows:

Wretches why are you sitting there? Fly to the ends of the earth, leaving your houses and the lofty peaks of your wheel-shaped city. For the head will not remain in its place, nor the body, nor the ends of the feet or the hands, nor will anything be left in between, but all will be in evil plight. Fire and angry Ares pursuing in his Syrian war chariot will bring thee down. He will destroy many other fortified places, not yours alone. And he will give over many temples of the immortals to destroying fire, temples that even now stand dripping with sweat, shaking with fear. And black blood pours down from the rooftops, portending evil violence. But leave this sanctuary, and cover your ills with a brave heart.

141] When the Athenian messengers heard this they were deeply troubled. While they were mulling over the evil prophecy, Timon the son of Androbulus, a man second to none in influence at Delphi, advised them to consult the oracle a second time carrying branches as suppliants. The Athenians were persuaded to do so, and they said: "O ruler, grant us a more propitious oracle about our native land, honoring these suppliant boughs with which we have come. Otherwise we will not depart from this shrine but stay here until we die." When they had spoken the prophetess proclaimed a second oracle as follows:

Not even Pallas can propitiate Olympian Zeus, entreating him with many words of deep cunning. But this word I will say to you again, unutterable. Although everything else will be seized that lies between Cecrops' hill and the deep clefts of the divine Cithaeron, Thunderer Zeus grants the Trito-born goddess the Wooden Wall alone, unravaged, to preserve you and your children. But do not quietly wait for the horsemen and the infantry, the vast host coming from the mainland, but turn your backs in retreat. The time will come when you will stand. O divine Salamis, you will lose the sons of your women, whether at the time of planting or of gathering in.

142] Deciding this was more encouraging than the earlier oracle, as it was, they wrote it down and went back to Athens. When the sacred messengers returned and reported to the people, many different opinions were expressed as to the meaning of the oracle, but especially these two opposite views: Some of the older men thought the god meant that the acropolis would be saved, for in former times the Athenian acropolis was protected by a wattled fence, and they argued that this was the Wooden Wall; but the others said the god was referring to their ships, and that he ordered them to rely on them, letting everything else go. But those who held that the ships were the Wooden Wall were tripped up by the last two verses of the Pythian oracle: "O divine Salamis, you will lose the sons of your women, whether at the time of planting or of gathering in." For the view of those who regarded the ships as the Wooden Wall was controverted by those lines. The soothsayers interpreted this as meaning they ought to prepare themselves for a naval defeat near Salamis.

143] Now there was in Athens a man who had recently risen into prominence, Themistocles, known as the son of Neocles. Now this man said the soothsayers had not given the correct interpretation. For if the phrase had been meant to apply to the Athenians the language would not have been so soothing. Instead of "O divine Salamis," it would have said "O cruel Salamis," if the inhabitants were to perish around it. But rightly interpreted the response of the god referred to the enemy, not to the Athenians. And it advised them to prepare for a naval battle, their ships being the Wooden Wall. After Themistocles had given his explanation the Athenians preferred it to that of the soothsayers which would not allow them to prepare for a naval engagement, and forbade them to make any resistance but urged them abandon their Attic land and colonize some other region.

144] Earlier another proposal of Themistocles won the day. The Athenians had accumulated a large sum of money in the public treasury from the mines at Laurium, which they intended to divide up among themselves, each receiving ten drachmas. But Themistocles persuaded the Athenians to forego this dividend in order to spend the money to build two hundred warships, allegedly for the war against Aegina. The outbreak of that war saved Greece by forcing Athens to become a naval power. The ships were not used for the purpose for which they were built, but they were available when Greece had such desperate need for them. These ships had already been constructed by the Athenians and now it was only necessary to build more of them. After debating the oracle they decided to meet the barbarian with their entire fleet when he came against Greece, in obedience to the god, together with those Greeks who so desired.

145] Now these were the oracles given the Athenians. When those who were right-minded about Greece assembled in one place to make plans and to pledge loyalty to one another they decided, after debate, to reconcile all enmities and end all wars against one another: for some of them were embroiled together, notably the Athenians and the Aeginetans. Then, learning that Xerxes was in Sardis with his army they decided to send spies to Asia to find out what the king was doing, and also to send envoys to Argos to make an alliance against Persia, and to send others to Sicily to Gelon son of Deinomenes and to Corcyra, summoning them to the aid of Greece; still others were sent to Crete with the object of uniting all the Greeks, if that were possible, so they might combine their efforts in the face of a danger that threatened everyone alike.

*   *   *

157] Now when the messengers from Greece reached Syracuse they approached him[2] and spoke as follows: "The Lacedaemonians and their allies have sent us to ask you to join us against the barbarian. No doubt you have heard that he is threatening Greece, that he has bridged the Hellespont and that he is bringing the whole army of the East out of Asia, intending to march against Greece. While he pretends to be attacking Athens alone, he really means to subject all of Greece to his rule. You have attained great power and no small part of Greece belongs to you, the ruler of Sicily. Therefore help those who are freeing Greece, and yourself be a fellow liberator. The whole of Greece united would be a powerful force, a match for the invaders. But if some of us are arrant traitors, and others do not care to take vengeance then there is little hope for the Greek cause, and there is grave danger that all of Greece will fall. Do not think that if the Persian conquers us by defeat in battle he will fail to move against you, but guard yourself against this. By helping us you will also be protecting yourself. For on the whole, the final result is apt to be for the best when a plan has been well thought out in advance."

158] That is what they said, but Gelon answered them violently as follows: "Greeks, you do not hesitate to summon me in arrogant language to come as an ally against the barbarian, yet earlier I asked you to join me in attacking a barbarian army at the time when I was embroiled with Carthage. I was planning to exact vengeance for the murder of Dorieus the son of Anaxandrides by the Egestaeans, and I urged you to help me free the trading stations, from which you would have derived great benefits and profit, but you were unwilling to give aid either for my sake or for the sake of avenging the murder of Dorieus. For all you cared the whole region[3] would have been divided up by the barbarians. But now that our affairs have taken a favorable turn and war has come your way, you remember Gelon! However, though you have treated me shabbily I will not pay you back in kind, but I am ready to help you with 200 warships, 20,000 hoplites, 2,000 heavy cavalry, 2,000 bowmen, 2,000 slingers and 2,000 light cavalry. Also I will undertake to provide food for the whole Greek army as long as we are at war. But I make this promise on condition that I am to be the leader and general of the Greeks against the barbarian. On no other conditions would I take part myself or send others to participate."

159] Unable to contain himself when he heard this Syagrus replied as follows: "Truly if Pelopid Agamemnon were to hear that the Spartans had been deprived of their leadership by Gelon of Syracuse he would groan aloud! But do not say any more about our turning over the command to you. If you are willing to help Greece then know that you will do so under Lacedaemonian command. If it is unlawful for you to take orders then do not help."

160] Then after he had taken note of Syagrus' unfriendly words, Gelon made a final proposal, as follows: "Spartan guest, abusive speeches usually arouse a man to anger, but though your remarks are arrogant you will not persuade me to act boorishly in return. While you insist so much on retaining the leadership, it would be more appropriate for me to claim it than for you, since I command a much larger army and far more ships. However, since this suggestion is so repugnant to you I will yield a part of my original proposal. If you command the land forces then I will lead the fleet; if it is your pleasure to command at sea, then I am willing to take over the army. But you must content yourself with these terms or else depart without this large force of allies."

161] This was Gelon's proposal. Then the Athenian envoy, getting in ahead of the Spartan, replied as follows: "O King of Syracuse, Greece did not send us to you because of a lack of leaders, but for an army. Now you say you will not send an army unless you are to lead Greece, for you are desirous to have the command. Now when it was a matter of the leadership of all the Greek forces we Athenians remained silent, knowing that the Spartan would be quite capable of answering you for us both, but now that you relinquish the overall command and ask to lead the naval forces, this is the situation: If the Spartans do not desire it then it belongs to us. And while we will raise no objection if they wish to command we will not yield the control of the fleet to any other power. It would be pointless for us to have acquired the largest naval force in Greece if, being Athenians, we should give up the command to

Syracuse! For we are the oldest nation, the only Greeks who are not immigrants. And the epic poet Homer says that the man who led them against Troy was the leader best able to control and draw up the army. So there is nothing boastful in our talking this way."

162] Gelon answered as follows: "Athenian guest, it looks as though you would have a great sufficiency of leaders but no followers! Therefore, since you will make no concessions but insist on having everything, lose no time in returning by the shortest route, and tell Greece the spring has been taken out of the year."

*   *   *

175] When the Greeks arrived at the isthmus they discussed . . . what their strategy would be and where they ought to fight. The plan adopted was that of guarding the pass at Thermopylae, because it seemed to be narrower than the entrance into Thessaly, being a single pass, and also because it was nearer their own homes. As for the path by which the Greek defenders were cut off at Thermopylae, they knew nothing about it until they learned of it from the Trachinians after reaching Thermopylae. Their plan was to guard this pass to prevent the barbarian from going on into Greece, while the fleet was to sail to Artemisium in the territory of Histiaea. These positions were close enough together for each to know what was going on at the other station, and the location of each was as follows:

176] Now Artemisium is a narrow strait separated off from the open Thracian Sea, between the island of Sciathus and the mainland of Magnesia; and beyond the strait is the coast of Euboea where there is a temple of Artemis. The pass into Greece through Trachis is fifty feet where it is narrowest, not that this is actually the narrowest point, because both before Thermopylae and behind it, near Alpeni to the rear, there is room for only one wagon; and in front, beside the Phoenix River near the town of Anthela, it is also only one wagon wide. West of Thermopylae lies Mt. Oeta, steep, lofty and inaccessible, while to the east of the road there are swamps and the sea. In the pass itself there is a hot springs which the natives call Chytri, above which an altar has been erected to Heracles. A wall was built at the pass which had a gate in the old days. The Phocians built the wall for fear of the Thessalians, when they came in from Thesprotis to take over the Aeolian territory they now occupy. When the Thessalians were trying to conquer them the Phocians kept on guard: they diverted the water from the hot springs into the pass so that the surface was broken up into gullies, doing everything they could to stop the Thessalians from invading their country. This wall was built a long time ago and most of it had already fallen at that time, so they decided to raise it again to keep the barbarian out of Greece. Very close to the road is a village called Alpeni, and that is said to be where the Greeks obtained their supplies. Now the Greeks picked these two sites as suitable. After examining every possible position ahead of time to find a place where the barbarian would be unable to make use of his great numbers of cavalry they chose this as the spot to meet the invader of Greece. When they heard the Persians were in Pieria they moved out from the isthmus, their land forces advancing overland to Thermopylae, the fleet proceeding by sea to Artemisium.

*   *   *

viii

1] The Greek contingents in the fleet were the following: the Athenians furnished 127 ships (the Plataeans, making up in valor and spirit for their inexperience in naval matters, helped man the Athenian ships); the Corinthians brought 40 ships and the Megarians 20; the Chalcidians also manned 20 ships furnished them by Athens; the Aeginetans 18, the Sicyonians 12, the Lacedaemonians 10, the Epidaurians 8, the Eretrians 7, the Troezenians 5, the Styrenses 2; the Ceians 2 ships[4] and 2 penteconters; and the Opuntian Locrians came to help with 7 penteconters.

2] Now these were the forces at Artemisium, and they have been named in order of the number of ships furnished by each. The total number of ships gathered together at Artemisium, not counting the penteconters, was 271. But the commander with the highest authority was provided by Sparta, Eurybiades the son of Eurycleides, because the allies refused to follow the Athenian leaders unless a Spartan was at the head, otherwise the fleet might have been disbanded.

3] In fact, before sending to Sicily for help the suggestion had been made that Athens should be given the command of the fleet. When the allies protested Athens yielded, because they felt the real issue was the survival of Greece, and that if they quarreled over the leadership Greece might be destroyed. They were right in thinking so, since internal conflict is as much worse than a war in a common cause as war is worse than peace. Realizing this they did not insist but yielded, and as long as they had a great need of the allies they continued this policy. But when Persia had been pushed back and was now defending its own territory then, using Pausanias' insolent behavior as an excuse, they took over the leadership from the Lacedaemonians. But that happened later on.

4] At that time when the Greeks who had come to Artemisium saw the large number of ships that had reached Aphetae, and saw the whole region swarming with soldiers they were afraid, because the strength of the barbarian had grown alarmingly beyond what they had expected; they were about to flee from Artemisium back to Greece. Learning that this was their intention the Euboeans begged Eurybiades to stay for a little while so they could evacuate their children and the rest of the households. Failing to convince him they approached the Athenian general Themistocles. They won him over with 30 talents, in return for which the Greeks were to stay and fight a naval battle off Euboea.

5] Themistocles kept the Greeks there in this way. He gave Eurybiades five talents as though it were his own money, but when he had accepted, Adeimantus the son of Ocytus, a Corinthian, still held out, saying he would not stay but would sail away from Artemisium. But Themistocles addressed him with an oath, as follows: "You will not abandon us, not when I give you a greater gift than the king of the Medes would give you for deserting the allies!" And as he spoke he sent a present of three silver talents to Adeimantus' ship. Thus these men were won over by bribes to humor the Euboeans, but Themistocles profited personally, quietly pocketing the rest. Those who took the money assumed that Athens had provided it for this purpose.

6] So it came about that they waited in Euboea and fought a naval battle. It happened in this way. The barbarians reached Aphetae early in the afternoon, and when they saw the small Greek force, of which they had had advance reports, drawn up in battle position off Artemisium they were eager to attack, hoping to capture them. However they decided against an immediate frontal assault for fear that when they saw them coming the Greeks would turn to flight, and that with darkness to cover their retreat they might well get away. But according to them not even the torchbearer ought to escape with his life.

7] Therefore they resorted to a stratagem. Picking 200 ships out of the entire fleet they sent them off outside Sciathus (to avoid their being seen by the enemy) to sail around Euboea, past Caphareum and past Geraestus to the Euripus, so that when they got there they could cut off the line of retreat of the Greeks when the others attacked them from the front. With this in mind they sent off the chosen ships, not intending to attack the Greeks that day, or until they got the signal indicating that the ships sailing around had arrived. After sending them off they held a review of the rest of the fleet off Aphytae.

8] At the time of the review there happened to be with the fleet Scyllias of Scione, the best diver of his day, a man who had salvaged many valuable things for the Persians from the wreckage off Pelium[5] at no small profit to himself. This man Scyllias had been planning for some time to desert to the Greeks, but the opportunity had not arisen before. Now I cannot truthfully say how he reached the Greeks, but I would be surprised if the story that is told is accurate. He is said to have dived into the sea at Aphytae without emerging before he came up at Artemisium, after crossing almost ten miles of ocean! Other seemingly incredible stories are told about this man, but some of them are true. As for this particular tale, my own opinion is that he went to Artemisium in a boat. As soon as he arrived he informed the generals about the wreck and how it happened, and about the ships sent around Euboea.

9] When they heard this the Greeks held a Council. After many proposals had been made they finally adopted the plan of staying where they were that day, and making camp; then in the middle of the night they would move forward and meet the ships sailing around. Afterwards, when no one sailed against them, they waited until late in the afternoon, then attacked the barbarians, wishing to test them in battle and in the manoeuvre of cutting through the line.

10] When Xerxes with the rest of his generals and soldiers saw them advancing with a few ships they thought they were mad. Still they brought up their own ships expecting to capture them with ease. They probably had strong hopes when they saw the Greeks with a small number of ships, while their own were both faster and more numerous.

*   *   *

40] After Artemisium the Greek fleet headed for Salamis at the request of the Athenians. The Athenians had asked them to go to Salamis so they could transport their wives and children to safety away from Attica, and also to discuss what they ought to do next. They needed to make plans to meet the existing situation, since they had been deceived in their hopes; for though they had counted on finding the full Peloponnesian levy in Boeotia waiting for the barbarian, they found no one there. Then they heard they were building a wall across the isthmus, devoting their efforts to preserving the Peloponnese, and once it was secure letting everything else go. When they heard this they requested them to head for Salamis.

*   *   *

75] And when Themistocles' plan was overruled by the Peloponnesians he slipped away from the Council, and when he came out he sent a man to the Persian camp in a boat, telling him what to say. The man's name was Sicinnus, a slave and the tutor of Themistocles' sons. After these events Themistocles made him a Thespian when Thespiaea was enrolling new citizens, and also made him a rich man. When he arrived in his boat he spoke to the barbarian generals in these words: "The Athenian general sent me without the knowledge of the other Greeks (he happens to favor the king and would rather see your affairs prosper than those of the Greeks), to say that the Greeks are terrified and wish to flee. Now the best possible thing you can do is not to stand by and let them get away. They do not agree among themselves, so they will not stand against you. You will see them fighting one another in the naval battle, since some favor your side while others do not." When he had given them this intimation he went away.

76] Since they believed what he said they first landed a large number of Persians on the island that lies between Salamis and the mainland; then, at midnight they brought up the western arm of the fleet in a circular movement towards Salamis; then those stationed near Ceos and Cynosura came up and covered the whole of the narrows as far as Munychia with their ships. The reason for bringing up these ships was to make it impossible for the Greeks to escape: they would be penned up at Salamis in revenge for their success at Artemisium. And they landed the Persians on the small island of Psyttaleia for this reason: when the naval battle occurred both men and wrecks would be very apt to be swept there, since the islet lies in the channel where the battle was to take place, and thus they could save their own men and destroy the enemy. All this was done silently to prevent the enemy from finding out. The men were occupied in this way all night long, not getting any sleep.

*   *   *

78] There was a great dispute among the generals at Salamis. They did not yet realize that the barbarian fleet had surrounded them, but assumed them to be drawn up in the same positions they had seen them in during the day.

79] While the generals were arguing Aristides the son of Lysima-chus, an Athenian who had been ostracized by the Assembly, crossed over from Aegina. I believe, after making inquiries about his char-acter, that he was the best man in Athens and the most honorable. When this man stood outside the Council, he sent in word asking to speak to Themistocles—not that he was his friend, but rather his enemy—but he called him because he was prepared to overlook the past in view of the great dangers in the present, and he wanted to talk to him. He had already heard the Peloponnesians were eager to draw their ships back to the isthmus. When Themistocles came out Aristides spoke to him as follows: "We must find some other time for quarreling and argue then about which one of us has accom-plished the most for his country. Now I tell you it makes no differ-ence whether we say much or little about leaving here with the Peloponnesians. For I can say on the basis of what I have seen personally, that even if the Corinthians and Eurybiades himself want to do so, they cannot sail away. We are encircled by the enemy. But go inside and tell them."

80] And Themistocles replied: "Your advice is very much to the point and your news is welcome, for you have just observed what I have been praying would happen. Know then that I am responsible for the action of the Medes. Since the Greeks would not fight volun-tarily they had to be forced to fight against their will. But since you are the one who brings this salutary news, do make the announce-ment yourself. If I make it they will think I invented it, and I will never get them to believe the barbarians have really done this. But you go in and tell them what the situation is. Once you have told them it makes no difference whether they are convinced or not convinced, since they cannot escape if we are hemmed in on all sides as you report."

81] So Aristides went in and spoke, explaining he had come from Aegina and barely managed to slip past the blockade, and that the whole Greek fleet was surrounded by Xerxes' ships. He urged them to prepare to defend themselves. After imparting this information he left, and the controversy broke out again, most of the generals not accepting his report.

82] While they were still unconvinced a trireme manned by a crew from Tenos under the command of Panaetius the son of Sosimenes, a Tenian, deserted to them from the enemy, and confirmed the whole story. For this deed the Tenians are inscribed on the tripod in Delphi in the list of those who defeated the barbarian. Including this ship which came over at Salamis, and the ship that deserted earlier at Artemisium from Lemnos, the numbers of the Greek fleet were raised to 380 ships, for previously they had just lacked two of that number.

83] Since the Greeks believed the Tenian report they prepared for a naval battle.

Notes

1. I.e., the priestess of Apollo.
2. I.e., Gelon.
3. I.e, the Greek West.
4. I.e., triremes.
5. See VII, 190.

7

The Founding of the Athenian Empire

IN A SENSE this passage is a compliment to Herodotus, since Thucydides joins his own history to that of his genial predecessor, finding the work of Hellanicus inadequate to bridge the gap. Thucydides firmly established the view that the historian ought to concern himself primarily with contemporary events. His subject is the Peloponnesian War (431–404 B.C.). Herodotus was the first ancient historian, Thucydides is the founder of modern history. Nevertheless his sketch of the period between the wars, the Pentecontaëtia (Fifty Years) as it is called, is the best evidence we have for the time of Athens' greatness. The author was one of the board of ten generals annually elected in Athens, and his failure to prevent the Spartans from taking Amphipolis (422 B.C.) forced him into exile for the duration of the war. His political views must be inferred from the history itself. His admiration for Pericles is evident, as is his distrust of Cleon. No one, however, set higher standards of accuracy and impartiality, and few historians have equalled his ability to eliminate unessentials. Unlike Herodotus he carefully selects what seems to him the correct explanation, seldom leaving the reader any alternative. Contemporaries, with a wealth of information at their disposal, were not deceived, but we find it difficult to judge his work since we have chiefly the facts he decided were significant. His history breaks off in 411 B.C., but we still have Xenophon's continuation (the Hellenica, 411–362 B.C.), which enhances our admiration for Thucydides.

Thucydides, i, 89-118 (The Pentecontaëtia)

89] NOW THIS is how the Athenians came to attain the power that they held. After the Medes had been driven out of Europe by Greek victories on land and sea, and after those who fled had been destroyed together with their ships at Mycale, then the Spartan king, Leotychides, who commanded the Greeks at Mycale, returned home with the Peloponnesian allies. But the Athenians and the allies from Ionia and the Hellespont who had now revolted from the king, stayed on to besiege Sestos, which the Medes held. Wintering there, and taking Sestos when the barbarians abandoned it, they sailed out of the Hellespont, each returning to his own city. As soon as the barbarians had evacuated their country the Athenian government conveyed back their women and children and the rest of their possessions from where they had been left,[1] preparing to rebuild the city and its defenses. Little of the wall was still standing and most of the buildings had fallen, though a few which the ranking Persians had occupied still remained.

90] When they saw what was planned the Lacedaemonians sent an embassy, partly because they preferred that neither they nor anyone else should have a wall, but chiefly because the allies were disturbed, being alarmed at the size of the Athenian fleet, such as had not existed before, and the audacity they had shown in the Median war. They requested them not to build a wall but rather to join them in levelling whatever city walls there were outside the Peloponnese. Without disclosing the suspicions that motivated this proposal, they argued that if the barbarian came again in the future he would find no secure base of operations such as Thebes had recently offered him, while the Peloponnese would meet their own needs both for attack or for retreat. On the advice of Themistocles the Athenians immediately dismissed the Lacedaemonian spokesmen after promising that they would send envoys to discuss their proposals. Then Themistocles bade them send him to Sparta as soon as possible, but not to despatch the other envoys they had selected right away, but instead to keep them back until they had raised the wall high enough so that it could be defended. Also everyone in the city, men, women and children, were to work on the wall, without sparing any building, private or public, that might be of use in the work, but to confiscate them all. After giving these instructions and promising that he would take care of everything else, he departed. When he arrived in Sparta he did not go near the authorities, but continued to delay and make excuses. And when one of the magistrates asked him why he did not approach the government he explained that he was waiting for his fellow envoys, and that some business must have kept them back; however, he expected them very shortly and was surprised that they had not yet arrived.

91] Because of their friendship for Themistocles they believed him, until others arrived stating categorically that they had seen the wall being built and that it had already reached a considerable height, so that it was impossible to discredit them. Learning this Themistocles begged them not to be governed by words, but to send some of their own men to see for themselves, men who could be relied on to make an honest report. Accordingly men were despatched, but Themistocles secretly sent word to the Athenians to detain the men as inconspicuously as possible and not release them until they themselves returned — for in the meantime his fellow envoys, Habronichus the son of Lysicles and Aristides the son of Lysimachus, had joined him with the news that the wall was now adequate — and he was afraid that when the Spartans learned the truth they would not let them go. Then, while the Athenians detained the envoys in accordance with his instructions, Themistocles approached the Spartans and announced that his city now possessed walls quite sufficient to protect the inhabitants, and that if the Spartans or their allies wished anything they should send envoys to Athens, and that in the future they would be dealing with men who were quite capable of discerning both their own interests and those of the alliance. When they decided it was advisable to abandon their city they had gone on board their ships, and they had made this bold decision without Spartan advice, yet their proposals had proved inferior to none when they consulted together. But now they had decided that it would be preferable for the city to have a wall, a particular advantage for their own citizens but also as a common benefit for all the allies. For unless she were strong in her own right she could not give the same advice or carry equal weight in the common cause. Therefore he said that either all the allies ought to be without walls, or they ought to agree that the present arrangement was right.

92] When the Lacedaemonians heard this they did not display any open animosity towards the Athenians, for they had not sent the envoys to stop the government from carrying out its plan but only to advise them against it. Also at that time they were on particularly good terms with the Athenians because of their zeal against the Mede. But underneath they were chagrined that their plan had failed. The envoys on each side returned home without incident.

93] This was the way in a short period of time the Athenians walled the city, and even now there is visible evidence that the construction was carried out in a hurry. The foundations are built of a great variety of stones which are not always fitted together, each having been laid in as it was brought, and many grave markers and carved stones were worked into it. The wall was enlarged on all sides of the city, and that is why they used everything in their haste. Themistocles also induced them to complete the Piraeus wall — he had begun this earlier during the magistracy he held for a year in Athens[2] — which he thought to have an ideal location. It had three natural harbors, and when Athens became a naval power he thought it would be of great service in strengthening her position — he was the first who dared to suggest they ought to move the city to the coast — and at the same time in establishing her empire. On his advice they built the wall around the Piraeus to its present thickness. Two wagons travelling in opposite directions brought the stones along the wall, nor was any rubble or earth placed in the center but large stone blocks were squared off, bound together on the outside with iron clamps set in lead. But when it was finished the height was only half what he had intended. Planning to frustrate enemy attacks by its very height and thickness, he thought a few physically unfit men would be adequate for defense, allowing the others to man the ships. He put chief reliance on the fleet because, as it seems to me, he perceived that the king's naval expedition was easier to attack than his land force. Also, thinking the Piraeus was better situated than an inland city, he frequently admonished the Athenians if they should ever be overpowered on the land to go down to the Piraeus, and defy everyone with their fleet. This is how the Athenians built their walls and made other preparations after the retreat of the Mede.

94] Pausanias, the son of Cleombrotus of Sparta, was sent from the Peloponnese with twenty ships as general of the Greeks; with him sailed the Athenians with thirty ships and a number of the other allies. They headed for Cyprus, reducing the greater part of it, and later went on to take Byzantium by siege from the Medes who held it.

95] Pausanias had already shown himself to be so violent in his rule that the other Greeks were incensed, especially the Ionians and those who had recently been liberated from the king. Approaching the Athenians they requested them to be their leaders on the basis of kinship, and not to give in to Pausanias even if he resorted to force. The Athenians received their proposal, and decided not to ignore it, but to consider how it would be advisable for them to implement it. Meanwhile the Lacedaemonians sent for Pausanias to question him about reports they had heard. In fact he had been charged by the Greeks present with frequent acts of injustice which bore more resemblance to the behavior of a would-be tyrant than that of a general. It happened that when he was recalled the allies, out of hatred for him, attached themselves to the Athenians, except for the soldiers from the Peloponnese. When he returned to Sparta he was convicted of some offenses against private individuals, but he was acquitted on the major charges. Not the least of these was the accusation of siding with the Mede, though it seemed quite clear that he had. They did not send him out again as a commander, but they did send Dorcis along with one or two others and a small force, but the allies no longer entrusted them with the command. When they saw this they went away, and the Lacedaemonians sent no one afterwards to take their place for fear the men who went out would deteriorate, as they had seen happen with Pausanias. So they withdrew from the Median war, thinking the Athenians capable of leadership, and also thinking at that time that they were their friends.

96] Obtaining the leadership in this way and, thanks to the hatred of Pausanias, with the approval of the allies, the Athenians prescribed which cities were to furnish money and which ships against the barbarian, with a view to plundering the king's dominions in retaliation for what they had endured. It was at this time that the office of the Hellenotamiae[3] was first established in Athens to receive the "tribute", as the money collected was called. The first tribute assessed was for 460 talents, the treasury was in Delos, and the meetings took place in the temple.

97] Beginning as the leaders of autonomous allies taking advice together in a common council, they raised their power to this great height by war, and by their management of affairs during the period between this war and the Median war, which included warfare against the barbarians, against their own rebellious allies and against the Peloponnesians whenever they happened to encounter them. I have included these events as a digression in my own account because this period has been neglected by all my predecessors, who have either written about Greek history before the Median war or else about that war itself. And one of them, Hellanicus, who touched on this period in his Athenian History is very sketchy and inaccurate in his chronology. Then too, this period explains the Athenian empire and the way it was established.

98] First, under the generalship of Cimon they captured Eion on the Strymon River from the Medes in a siege, and enslaved the inhabitants; next they took the Aegean island of Scyros, a Dolopian settlement, and colonized it themselves. Then there was a war against Carystus, unsupported by the other Euboeans, which ultimately submitted on terms. Later on they made war on Naxos, which had revolted, and captured it after a siege. This was the first allied city which was enslaved in violation of the charter,[4] but afterwards it happened to others as the occasion arose.

99] While there were other causes for revolt the most important were derelictions in sending tribute or ships, and desertion when it occurred. For the Athenians were harsh and exacting, using punitive measures against men who were not accustomed to making great exertions and who resented it. And the Athenians were no longer satisfied with governing equitably and they did not carry on campaigns on an equal basis, it being easy to coerce those who resisted them. The allies themselves were to blame for this: through the reluctance of most of them to go on campaign that would take them away from home, they had assessed themselves to furnish an equivalent sum of money instead of ships, thus increasing the Athenian naval force by the expenditures they had agreed to make, so that whenever they revolted they were unprepared, and inexperienced in war.

100] After that came a double land and sea battle on the Eurymedon River, between the Athenians and their allies and the Medes, both of which were won by the Athenians on the same day under the generalship of Cimon the son of Miltiades, who captured and destroyed all two hundred of the Phoenician triremes. Somewhat later it happened that the Thasians revolted from them in a dispute over trade and over the mines which they held on the opposite Thracian coast. Sailing to Thasos with a fleet the Athenians won a naval victory and made a landing. About this time they sent 10,000 settlers from their own number and from the allies to the Strymon to colonize what was then called Ennea Hodoi,[5] but now Amphipolis. After conquering Ennea Hodoi from the Edonians and advancing into the interior of Thrace they were destroyed by the united Thracians at Edonian Drabescus, since the Thracians were hostile to the establishment of the colony.

101] Defeated in battle and pressed by siege the Thasians appealed to Sparta to help them by invading Attica. They gave secret assurances that they would and they intended to do so, but they were prevented by the occurrence of an earthquake, as a result of which the helots and also the Thuriatae and the Aethaeënses, who were perioeci, revolted and went off to Ithomē. Most of the helots were descended from the ancient Messenians who had been enslaved, and so all of them were called Messenians. Therefore war broke out between those on Ithomē and the Lacedaemonians. In the third year of the siege Thasos capitulated to the Athenians. They were required to level their walls and give up their ships; also to pay a certain sum of money on the spot and tribute in the future; and to yield their land and the mines on the mainland.

102] As the war against Ithomē went on and on the Lacedaemonians called on their other allies, including the Athenians, who arrived in considerable numbers under the command of Cimon. They had been specially invited because they were regarded as experts in siege warfare, so when the siege dragged on it was blamed on them, otherwise they would surely have taken the place by assault. It was this that caused the first open breach between the Athenians and the Lacedaemonians. For when they failed to take the stronghold the Lacedaemonians, dreading the audacity of the Athenians as well as their propensity for stirring up trouble, regarding them also as foreigners,[6] dismissed them only of all their allies, fearing also they might be persuaded to join in the rebellion by the men on Ithomē. They did not mention this, however, but merely said they no longer needed their services. But the Athenians, knowing very well they had not been dismissed for this convenient reason but because of some suspicion, took it very hard. Resenting the way the Lacedaemonians had treated them, the Athenians, as soon as they got home, broke off their alliance with Sparta against the Mede, and allied themselves with Sparta's enemies the Argives, and with the Thessalians, establishing alliances with both with the same oaths and on the same terms.

103] In the tenth year the men in Ithomē, unable to hold out any longer, surrendered to the Lacedaemonians on condition that they were to leave the Peloponnese under a truce, never to return. If anyone were caught doing so he was to become the slave of his captor. The Lacedaemonians had previously received a Delphic oracle to release the suppliant of Zeau at Ithomē. So they moved away with their wives and children, but out of hostility to Sparta the Athenians received them and settled them in Naupactus which they happened recently to have seized from the Ozolian Locrians. Then, hard pressed by Corinth in a war over boundaries, Megara revolted from the Spartan alliance and joined Athens. Having control of Megara and Pegae the Athenians built long walls for the Megarians extending from the city to Nisaea, which they guarded themselves. This was not the least important reason for the beginning of Corinth's intense hatred of Athens.

104] Inarus the son of Psammetichus, a Libyan and the king of the Libyans in Egypt, stirred up most of Egypt into revolt from King Artoxerxes, starting out from Mareia above the city of Pharos. Obtaining the rule, he called in the Athenians. And they responded, leaving Cyprus where they happened to be campaigning, with two hundred ships of their own and of their allies. Sailing up the Nile from the sea they got control of the river and even captured two parts of Memphis; they attacked the third, which is called the White Wall, inside which were the Medes and Persians who had escaped and the Egyptians who had not joined the revolt.

105] After landing at Haliae the Athenians fought a battle with the Corinthians and the Epidaurians in which the Corinthians were victorious. Later on the Athenians engaged a Peloponnesian fleet near Cecryphaleia and the Athenians won. After these events when war broke out between Athens and Aegina there was a great naval battle with the allies participating on both sides, which was won by the Athenians, who landed after capturing seventy ships, and began siege operations under the generalship of Leocrates the son of Stroebus. Thereupon, desirous of helping the Aeginetans, the Peloponnesians transported three hundred mercenary hoplites who had been in the service of Corinth and Epidaurus to Aegina, and also the Corinthians occupied the heights of Gerania. From there they went on down into the Megarid with their allies, thinking the Athenians would be unable to help the Megarians in the absence of large forces in Aegina and Egypt, and that if they did help they would have to withdraw from Aegina. The Athenians, however, did not move their army from Aegina, but the over-age men and the very young men who had remained in the city, went to Megara with Myronides as their general. After a battle had been fought on fairly even terms they disengaged their forces, each feeling that they had not been worsted in the encounter. Still the Athenians really did win, so when the Corinthians withdrew they set up a trophy. But the Corinthians, after being mocked by their elders in the city, formed ranks about twelve days afterwards and marched back to set up a trophy as though they had been victorious. The Athenians coming from Megara to the rescue, destroyed those who were setting up the trophy and then attacked and defeated the rest.

106] The vanquished withdrew, but no small number of them were hard pressed so that they missed the road and got into some private estate which happened to be surrounded by a deep ditch with no way out. When they saw this the Athenians held them back by confronting them with their hoplites. Then they stationed the light armed troops in a circle around them and stoned to death all who had gone inside. And that was a very sad thing for Corinth, but the main body of the retreating army reached home.

107] The Athenians at this time had begun to build their long walls to the sea, one to Phalerum and one to the Piraeus. When the Phocians invaded Doris the mother land of the Lacedaemonians which consists of Boeum, Cytinium and Erineus, they captured one of these towns, but then the Lacedaemonians came to aid the Dorians with 1,500 of their own and 20,000 allied heavy infantry, led by Nicomedes the son of Cleombrotus — taking the place of King Pleistoanax the son of Pausanias who was still a boy — and having forced the Phocians to yield the city by agreement, they were on their way home. Now if they decided to return by way of the Crisaean Gulf and the sea the Athenians planned to sail around with their fleet and stop them. Also it seemed unsafe for them to march by way of Gerania with the Athenians holding Megara and Pegae, for the Geranian road was a difficult one and under constant surveillance by the Athenians who, as they then realized, intended to block them at this point. Therefore they decided to wait in Boeotia and find out how they might return with the greatest safety. And there were some Athenians who secretly encouraged them, hoping they would overthrow the democracy and put a stop to the construction of the long walls. But the Athenians came against them in full force, while the Argives and the other allies also arrived, the Argives with 1,000 men. Altogether there were 14,000 soldiers. Perceiving the Spartans hesitating which way to go, and also suspicious of any move to upset the democracy they marched against them. Thessalian cavalry came in to help Athens in accordance with their alliance, but they went over to the Spartan side during the battle.

108] In this engagement, which took place at Tanagra in Boeotia, the Spartans and their allies were victorious though there were heavy casualties on both sides. The Lacedaemonians then entered the Megarid and laid waste the countryside, returning home by way of Gerania and the isthmus. But the Athenians, under the general-ship of Myronides, marched out against the Boeotians on the sixty-second day after the battle. Defeating them in battle at Oenophyta, they conquered Boeotia and Phocis, razed the walls of Tanagra, took one hundred of the richest men of the Opuntian Locrians as hostages and then finished their own long walls. After these events the Aeginetans capitulated to the Athenians, tearing down their walls, surrendering their ships and being required to pay tribute in the future. And the Athenians with Tolmides the son of Tolmaeus as general sailed around the Peloponnese. They burned the Lacedae-monian docks,[7] took Chalcis away from Corinth[8] and, making a landing in Sicyonian territory, defeated them in battle.

109] Now the Athenians and their allies remained in Egypt, en-gaged in various types of warfare. At first the Athenians were vic-torious, so the king sent Megabazus, a Persian, to Sparta with money to persuade the Peloponnesians to invade Attica to force the Athe-nians to withdraw from Egypt. When he accomplished nothing despite Megabazus' munificence, he called him back to Asia with the money that remained, and sent a Persian, Megabyzus the son of Zopyrus, out to Egypt with a large army. Taking the overland route he defeated the Egyptians and their allies in battle, drove the Greeks out of Memphis and finally blockaded them on the island of Pro-sopitis. After besieging them there for a year and six months he diverted the water and dried up the canal, thus grounding their ships and joining most of the island on to the mainland. Then he crossed over on foot and seized the island.

110] So it was that after six years of warfare the Greek cause was ruined. A few were saved out of many by marching through Libya to Cyrene, but most of them perished. Egypt fell back under Persian rule except for Amyrtaeus the King of the Marshes, for him they failed to capture, both because of the extent of the marshes and because the swamp men are the most warlike of the Egyptians. But Inarus, the Libyan king who was responsible for all that had happened in Egypt, was taken by treachery and impaled. A supple-mentary squadron of fifty allied and Athenian triremes sailed out to Egypt, reaching the Mendesian mouth without any knowledge of what had happened. They were attacked by a land force, while most of their ships were destroyed at sea by a Phoenician fleet, though a small number of them escaped. This is what finally became of the great Egyptian expedition of Athens and her allies.

111} Orestes the son of Echecratidas, the Thessalian king, fled from Thessaly to Athens and persuaded the Athenians to restore him. The Athenians, together with their Boeotian and Phocian allies, marched against Pharsalus in Thessaly. Although they controlled the country for a short distance around the camp, beyond that the Thessalian cavalry kept them in check, so they failed to take the city or accomplish any of the objectives of the campaign, and returned, unsuccessful, with Orestes. Not very long after that 1,000 Athenians went on board the fleet at Pegae, for they held Pegae themselves, and sailed for Sicyon under the command of Pericles the son of Xanthippus, where they landed and engaged the Sicyonians, defeating them in battle. Then, picking up the Achaeans, they sailed across to Oeniadae in Acarnania. They made an attack and besieged the city, but returned home after failing to capture it.

112} Later, after an interval of three years, a truce for five years was established between the Peloponnesians and the Athenians. The latter, avoiding war with the Greeks, sent an expedition to Cyprus with 200 ships of their own and their allies under the command of Cimon. Of these, sixty ships sailed off to Egypt at the request of Amyrtaeus, King of the Marshes, while the rest invested Citium. Following Cimon's death and the outbreak of famine[9] the Athenians withdrew from Citium. Sailing past Salamis in Cyprus they fought a naval battle and a land battle against the Phoenicians, the Cypriotes and the Cilicians. After being victorious in both they went home, the ships that had gone to Egypt returning with them. After this the Lacedaemonians engaged in the so-called Sacred War, turning over the Temple of Delphi to the Delphians after they were victorious. But later, when they left, the Athenians gave it back to the Phocians after a victorious military campaign.

113} When some time had elapsed after these events and Boeotian exiles were in possession of Orchomenus, Chaeronea and other places in Boeotia, the Athenians marched out with 1,000 hoplites of their own and the contingents of their allies against these hostile places, under the generalship of Tolmides the son of Tolmaeus. Taking Chaeronea and enslaving the inhabitants they withdrew, leaving a garrison. While they were on the march the Boeotian exiles from Orchomenus together with the Locrian and Euboean exiles and others who shared their views, attacked them near Coronea. Being victorious in the battle they slew some of the Athenians and took others prisoner. Then the Athenians agreed to give up all of Boeotia, recovering their soldiers under a truce. The exiles returned and all the rest of Boeotia recovered its independence.

114] Not long after this Euboea revolted from Athens. Pericles had already crossed over when word came that Megara had revolted, that the Peloponnesians were about to invade Attica and that the Athenian garrison troops had been killed by the Megarians, except for a few of them who escaped to Nisaea. The rebellious Megarians were bringing in the Corinthians, the Sicyonians and the Epidaurians. Pericles hurriedly brought back his army from Euboea. After that the Peloponnesians plundered as far as Eleusis and Thria, being led by Pleistoanax, the son of Pausanias and King of the Lacedaemonians, but they returned home without advancing any further. Thereupon the Athenians crossed over once more into Euboea under the generalship of Pericles, subduing the whole island. They made treaties with everyone except the Histiaeans, whom they drove out, appropriating their territory.

115] Returning from Euboea they made a Thirty Years Peace with the Lacedaemonians and their allies not long afterwards, surrendering Pegae, Troezen and Achaea, Peloponnesian territory which the Athenians had held.

In the sixth year war broke out between the Samians and Miletus over Priene. After being defeated in battle the Milesians appealed to Athens, denouncing the Samians. Certain individuals from Samos itself lent their support, hoping to cause a revolution. As a result the Athenians sailed to Samos with forty ships, and then set up a democracy, taking fifty boys and an equal number of men as hostages. Leaving a garrison and depositing the hostages in Lemnos, they withdrew. There were some of the Samians who did not remain but fled over to the mainland. There they made an alliance between the leading men in the city and Pissuthnes the son of Hystaspes, who held Sardis at that time. Then they crossed over to Samos at night after collecting 700 mercenaries. First they attacked the democrats and got control of most of them, then after recovering their hostages from Lemnos they revolted. Turning over the Athenian garrison and the officers who were with them to Pissuthnes, they prepared for an immediate attack on Miletus. The Byzantines also joined them in revolt.

116] When the Athenians learned this they sailed to Samos with sixty ships, though they did not use sixteen of them, some being despatched to Caria to keep an eye on the Phoenicians and the others being sent to ask Chios and Lesbos for help. But with forty-four ships under Pericles as one of the ten generals, they fought a naval battle near the island of Tragia against seventy Samian vessels — twenty of them were transports, for they were all on their way from Miletus — and the Athenians were victorious. Later they were reinforced with forty ships from Athens and twenty-five from Chios and Lesbos. Landing and getting control of the land, they built siege walls and also blockaded the city from the sea. Then Pericles went off unexpectedly with sixty of the blockading ships towards Caunus and Caria. Phoenician ships had been reported to be sailing against them, for Stesagoras and others had left Samos with five ships seeking Phoenician aid.

117] Then suddenly the Samians sailed out, stormed the unprotected camp and destroyed the guard ships. After that they engaged the enemy fleet and were victorious, thus gaining control of their own waters for some fourteen days, during which they were able to transport whatever they wished in or out. When Pericles returned they were blockaded again by his fleet. Subsequently forty more ships came bringing help from Athens under Thucydides,[10] Hagnon and Phormio; twenty others under Tlepolemus and Anticles; and thirty more from Chios and Lesbos. The Samians made an abortive attempt to fight them at sea, but when they could not hold their own they capitulated in the ninth month of the siege, razing their walls, furnishing hostages, surrendering their fleet and agreeing to pay a stipulated sum of money to cover expenditures within a certain period of time. The Byzantines returned to their previous status of subject allies.

118] It was not many years after these events that the episodes occurred in Corcyra, Potidaea and elsewhere which served as the pretext for the war. All these actions of the Greeks against one another and against the barbarians took place in the space of approximately fifty years between the retreat of Xerxes and the beginning of the war. During this time the Athenians established their rule on a firmer basis and greatly increased their resources. The Lacedaemonians, though they perceived this did not prevent them, except for a short time, but usually remained inactive. Even before this they had not been prompt in attacking their enemies unless forced to do so. Later they had been occupied with war at home, until the power of Athens had obviously grown and threatened their own League. Then they felt it could no longer be tolerated, but decided to use force and to make every effort in prosecuting this war.

The Lacedaemonians themselves now decided that the treaty had been violated and that the Athenians were in the wrong. Sending to Delphi they asked the god whether it would be better for them to fight. The god is said to have replied that if they fought with all their might they would be victorious, and he said he would help, whether appealed to directly or not.

Notes

1. I.e., Troezen, Aegina, and Salamis.
2. I.e., probably as archon, though both the year and the specific magistracy are in dispute.
3. I.e., "Treasurers of the Greeks."
4. I.e., of the Delian League.
5. Or "Nine Ways."
6. I.e., not as Dorians but as Ionians.
7. I.e., in Gythium.
8. Not the famous Chalcis, but a town west of Naupactus.
9. The MS reading may be faulty and "plague" intended instead of "famine."
10. Otherwise unknown.

8

The Old Oligarch: An Unfriendly
View of the Athenian Democracy

ATTEMPTS to identify the "Old Oligarch" have failed. No one now believes this sardonic account of the Athenian democracy could have been written by Xenophon, though it has come down to us as a part of his corpus. Not only does the Constitution of Athens (given below in its entirety) reflect a different literary personality but it must have been written too early for Xenophon, at least before the Syracusan Expedition (415 B.C.), and probably before the Peloponnesian War. The writer was no professional, which would seem to rule out Antiphon, and he need not have been an Athenian. But the work is precious in that it adds an authentic contemporary voice where Thucydides so often speaks alone. Despite the hostile tone there is an evident respect for the efficiency of the Athenian government, in interesting contrast both with Thucydides and the later philosophic writers. We get a whiff of the salt breeze from the Piraeus, some sense of the role of the sea in the daily lives of the Athenian citizens.

The Athenian Constitution attributed
falsely to Xenophon

i

I DO NOT commend the Athenians for choosing the kind of government embodied in their constitution, because they have elected to give knaves the advantage over honest men, and for that I do not praise them. But given this decision, I will demonstrate that the rest of their measures, which strike the other Greeks as wrong, are well calculated to preserve the constitution.

2] First I will say this. They are right in deciding at the very beginning that the poor and the common people ought to prevail over the rich and the well born, because it is the common people who drive the ships that make the city strong. Pilots, boatswains, commanders of fifty, helmsmen and shipwrights: these are the men who strengthen the city far more than the heavy infantry and well-born gentlemen. This being so, it is right for everyone to share in the elective magistracies as well as in those chosen by lot, and every citizen who so desires has the right to be heard.

3] But there is no reason why they should participate in offices which, while necessary for their preservation, do not present any danger to the common people as a whole; therefore they do not believe that the generals or the cavalry leaders ought to be picked by lot. For the common people know that it is more to their advantage not to hold these offices but to reserve them for men of the highest ability. The people do insist, however, on holding any offices that are paid and will help meet household expenses.

4] Then some people are surprised that they give the lion's share of everything to brutish low-born persons rather than to men of consequence, but by doing so they apparently preserve the democracy. For if ordinary poor people of the inferior sort prosper this will strengthen the democracy, because there are so many of them; but if the rich and well born flourish then the common people will only be building up strong opposition for themselves.

5] In every country the better element is hostile to democracy. For in aristocratic states licentiousness and injustice are at a minimum, while discipline is prized highly; on the other hand, boorishness, disorder and roguery reach their height under a popular government. It is poverty that inclines men towards shameful acts, and the illiteracy and boorishness of some men is caused by lack of money.

6] Consequently, it might be urged that not everyone ought to be allowed to speak or to take his turn on the Council, but only the best and most capable persons. But here, too, they are well advised in allowing the very lowest persons to speak. If the speakers and Councillors were worthy men it would benefit men like themselves rather than the common people, but now when anyone may speak if he wishes, however low his birth, he will look out for what is good for him and others like him.

7] But someone might ask: "How can such a person understand what is good for him or good for the democracy?" But the people realize that the meanness and lack of cultivation of such a man when combined with good will are more advantageous than the virtue and wisdom of a worthy man when coupled with malice.

8] No city with such institutions can be the best city, but this is the most effective means of preserving a democracy. The common people have no desire for a city with good laws in which they would be enslaved, but wish to be free and to rule; so they are little concerned over bad laws. For the very thing in their laws that you call bad is what makes the common people free and powerful.

9] But if you are looking for law and order, you will provide first that the ablest men write the laws. Second, honest men will chastise the rogues, and honest men also will be the ones to give advice on matters of state. Nor will maniacs be allowed to become Councillors, to speak in or even to attend the assembly. The common people, to be sure, would immediately be subjected by the aristocrats.

10] In Athens slaves and metics[1] have the greatest license, for it is not permissible to beat a slave there, nor will he make way for you. Now I will tell you the reason for this custom: if it were legal for a free man to beat a slave, or a metic or a freedman, he would often beat an Athenian by mistake for a slave, because in Athens the common people dress no differently than slaves or metics, and they are not a bit better in appearance.

11] Although one is surprised at their letting slaves there live in comfort, sometimes in downright luxury, this too seems to be a part of their plan. Wherever there is a naval power it is necessary for slaves to work for hire, so we can receive their wages and let them go freely. When slaves are rich it is no longer profitable for my slave to fear you. Now in Sparta my slave is afraid of you. If your slave were afraid of me he would be apt to give up his money to save himself from danger.

12] For that reason we have established equal rights for slaves and free persons, and also for metics and citizens, because the city needs metics for the many trades and for the fleet; and probably that is why we have established equal rights for metics.

13] The common people banned the profession of gymnastics and music there, regarding them as immoral and knowing themselves incapable of practicing them. With regard to the offices of choregus, gymnasiarch and trierarch they know that rich men will act as choregi so the people will always be provided with choruses, and that the gymnasiarchs and trierarchs will also be rich men, so that the people will have these offices provided for them. The common people dearly love to be paid money for running, dancing or sailing their ships, in order to make the rich men poorer while they profit. And in the law courts they are not more concerned with justice than with profit to themselves.

14] With regard to the allies, they seem to sail around making accusations as they please and detesting men of merit, because they know that the ruler is certain to be hated by his subjects, and that if rich and deserving men controlled the cities the empire of the Athenian people would be of very brief duration. That is why they dishonor these, heaping indignities on the rich; they rob them of their money, drive them into exile or kill them, while they cultivate persons of the lowest sort. However, the rich Athenians protect the rich men in the allied cities, knowing that it is always to their advantage to look out for the best men in the cities.

15] One might think that Athens is strengthened when her allies are in a position to pay taxes, but the democrats believe that it is even better for each Athenian individually to have the possessions of the allies, while the latter keep just enough to enable them to continue living and working, but not enough to allow them to form a conspiracy.

16] The Athenian democrats are sometimes thought to be ill-advised in forcing their allies to sail to Athens for judgment. But on the other hand it is argued that there are advantages in this for the common people in Athens. First, they receive pay throughout the year from the fees. Then, too, they can sit down at home, without sailing off anywhere, and administer the allied cities. Also they protect the democrats and ruin their adversaries in the law courts, while if the allies decided their own cases at home then, out of hatred for Athens, they would ruin those who were the friends of the Athenian democrats.

17] Also, the Athenians derive a profit from having allied lawsuits decided in Athens. First, there is the one per cent. tax for sailing to the Piraeus.

18] Then, too, the renters of lodgings do better, as do those who have carriages or slaves for hire; public messengers also profit from the visits of our allies. In addition to these considerations, if the allies did not have to go away to settle their lawsuits then they would only need to show special attention to the envoys, generals, trierarchs and envoys sailing out from Athens, but now each of the allies is forced to pay court to the Athenian common people, knowing full well that when he comes to Athens in a lawsuit the case will be decided by the common people and no one else; for that is the law of Athens. And he will be forced to make supplication with outstretched hand when he enters the court. In this way the allies become more and more the slaves of the Athenian populace.

19] In addition to this, thanks to their overseas possessions and the posts they hold outside the country, they and their attendants learn how to handle an oar without giving it a thought. For often it is necessary for a man who sails to take an oar, as well as for his slave to do so. Good pilots are developed by experience with boats and by application. Some gain their experience piloting fishing boats, others with cargo ships, and from these they go on to triremes. Most of them are able to row as soon as they go on board ship, since their whole way of life has prepared them for it.

ii

The army, in which Athens is not nearly so well off, is regulated on the following principle: they expect to be inferior to the enemy and weaker, but they are superior to the tribute-paying allies on land and regard their army as sufficient so long as this superiority is maintained.

2] Chance has also played a part in arranging matters for them. The subjects of a land empire have the possibility of joining their small cities together into one unit and fighting as a single force, but islanders subject to rule from the sea cannot join their cities together in a single place, because the sea divides them and those who rule over them also rule the sea. Even if it were possible for the islanders to unite surreptitiously on one island they would succumb to hunger.

3] Of the cities ruled by Athens on the mainland the larger ones are held in subjection out of fear, the smaller ones by their needs, for there is no city that does not depend on imports or exports; yet these are denied any city not obedient to the rulers of the sea.

4] Then it is also possible for the rulers of the sea to behave like land powers on occasion, laying waste the territory of their betters. For they can proceed where there is no enemy force or only a small one, then, if the enemy approaches, go on board ship and sail away. And it is easier for them to do this than for the others to come to the rescue by land.

5] Further, the rulers of the sea can sail as far away from their own country as they wish to go, while land powers dare not march many days beyond their own territory; marches are slow, and it is impossible to carry enough food to maintain an army over a long period. Then, too, a land force must either march through friendly territory or win its passage by fighting, while a naval expedition can make a landing where it is superior, and where it is not, it can sail by that territory without going ashore until it reaches a friendly country or one whose strength is inferior to its own.

6] Furthermore, the very strongest land powers have a bad time of it when the crops are struck by some blight from Zeus, while the sea powers get off lightly. For not every land is afflicted at the same time so that produce comes in for the rulers of the sea from more abundant areas.

7] Then, to mention small matters after great, through control of the sea they have discovered new refinements in eating, preparing all sorts of concoctions: for whatever delicacies are to be found in Sicily, or in Italy, or in Cyprus, or in Egypt, or in Lydia, or in the Black Sea region, or in the Peloponnese or anywhere else are all brought together through the rule of the sea.

8] Likewise, hearing every language, they have borrowed a phrase here and another there, so that while Greeks in general employ their own distinctive speech, diet and way of life, the Athenians use a mixture of everything, both barbarian and Greek.

9] Realizing that the poor do not have the means, individually, to offer sacrifice, give sacred banquets, hold festivals and maintain temples, and live in a great and beautiful city, the democracy has found a way to make these things possible. Consequently the city sacrifices many victims out of the public funds, while the common people divide the offerings and feast on them.

10] There are some private gymnasiums and bathing places for the rich with dressing rooms, but the common people have erected many places of exercise for themselves with bathing and dressing rooms, and the riffraff get more enjoyment from them than the rich and prosperous.

11] Then, too, they alone are able to tap the resources of Greeks and barbarians. For if a city is rich in timber for shipbuilding, how will it market this without the consent of the rulers of the sea? And what if a city is rich in iron, or copper or flax, how will it sell them without permission from the rulers of the sea? But these are the very sources from which I obtain my ships: timber from one place, copper from another, flax and beeswax from others.

12] But more than this, they do not permit our rivals to carry off these materials on the threat of being denied access to the sea. But thanks to the sea I get these things from all the world without effort, while no other city possesses any two of them. Flax and timber are not found together, but where flax is most abundant the land is smooth and treeless; nor do copper and iron or any other two or three of these commodities come from a single city, but one from one city, one from another.

13] Now in addition to these things, every mainland area has a cape jutting out or else an island close by or some sort of narrows, where it is possible for the masters of the sea to drop anchor, and harass the inhabitants on the mainland.

14] But they have one weakness. If the Athenians ruled the sea while living on an island, it would be in their power to inflict harm whenever they wished without suffering anything in return, so long as they controlled the sea; their own land would not be laid waste nor would they expect the enemy. But as it is now the farmers and the rich men tend more to cultivate the good graces of the enemy, while the common people make no effort at conciliation but live free from worry, secure in the knowledge that nothing belonging to them will be burned or cut down.

15] And if they lived on an island they would also be rid of another cause for fear, since the city could never be betrayed by the rich, nor could the gates be opened to admit the enemy. For how could that happen if they lived on an island? No one would plot revolution against the people if they inhabited an island. But now revolution might be plotted in the hope that the enemy could be brought in to help them by land. If they lived on an island there would be no such danger.

16] However, since it was not their good fortune to live on an island in the beginning they do as follows: they deposit their wealth in the islands, relying on their control of the sea, while they disregard the devastation of Attic soil, knowing that if they gave way to compassion there, they would lose other greater benefits.

17] Then, too, oligarchies necessarily live up to their alliances and oaths, for if they did not abide by their agreements the exact nature of the violation would be known, thanks to the small numbers who made the agreement. But when the democracy makes an agreement, it is possible for anyone to put the responsibility on the speaker, and the man who put the proposal to a vote, while excusing the rest on the ground of absence, or because I am not pleased with what was agreed on in a full popular assembly. Even if this fails to work the democrats have devised ten thousand excuses for not doing whatever they wish not to do. And if anything bad results from a democratic scheme then the democrats charge the rich with working against them, and having caused the plan to fail; if, however, it leads to any good result, they take the credit for themselves.

18] They do not allow people to be made fun of or defamed in a comedy lest they hear ill of themselves, but privately they encourage anyone who wishes to do this, knowing very well that the person ridiculed is not ordinarily a democrat or one of the masses, but some rich, or well-born, or capable person. A few poor men on the popular side have been lampooned, but this would not have happened except that they were officious, or trying to take advantage of the people in some way. And that is why anger was not aroused against those who made fun of them.

19] Now I maintain that the common people in Athens know who the honest citizens are and who are the rogues. They also know and love the men who are convenient and useful to them, and if these men are knaves then they hate the honest men all the more. For they do not believe that virtue has been implanted in them for their own good but for evil. On the other hand there are some who truly belong to the common people, but whose nature is far from common.

20] But for my part I agree with the common people about democracy, for everyone may be excused for doing well by himself. But anyone who does not belong to the mob and yet chooses to live in a democratic city rather than in an oligarchical one, is ready to commit injustice, because he knows that it is easier for an evil doer to escape unnoticed in a democracy than in an oligarchy.

iii

Now while I do not approve of the type of government the Athenians have, I do think the democracy has been preserved by the means I have already indicated. But some people have also blamed the Athenians on the ground that sometimes a man cannot get a hearing in the Council or in the assembly, even if he waits a whole year.

2] But in Athens this only happens because the amount of business is so great that they are unable to hear everyone and dismiss them. How is it possible that they could, considering that, first, they have to conduct festivals such as no other Greek city has — and during these it is less possible to carry on the city's business — ; then, that they have private suits and public suits to settle and magistrates' accounts, so numerous that all the men in the world could not handle them; then, that the Council has to deliberate frequently about the war, financial questions, proposed legislation, about matters that continue to crop up in the city and among the allies; and that they have to receive the tribute, and pay attention to the dockyards and the temples? So is it surprising that with such an incredible amount to be done they find it impossible to take care of everyone? But some say:

3] "If anyone goes to the Council or the assembly with money, he will be heard." Now I am willing to grant that much can be accomplished in Athens with money, and that even more would be accomplished if more people offered money. But I also know very well that the city could not gratify every one of their petitioners no matter how much gold and silver they were offered.

4] They also settle matters connected with faulty ship repairs and public buildings. In addition they have to arrange the annual Dionysiac, Thargelian, Panathenaean, Promethean and Hephaestian festivals with the choregi. Also they approve and judge the candidates for office, examine the list of orphans and appoint guards over the prisoners.

5] Now these are things they do every year, but from time to time they must sit in judgment on military derelictions,[2] or when some other unexpected and serious offense has been committed, or unusual crimes of violence occur or some act of sacrilege. I have still left out a great deal, but the most important matters have been alluded to, except for the regulation of the tribute, which usually occurs every fifth year. But now do you not see that all these things must be dealt with?

6] Yet someone might reply that they need not be dealt with on the spot. But if it is admitted that all of them must be attended to, then this must be done within the year, but now even though they sit in judgment throughout the year they cannot check the flow of wrongdoing by virtue of the masses of persons involved.

7] True, but granting that these cases ought to be judged, someone might urge that they be tried by smaller panels. And in fact if the number of panels is increased there will necessarily be a smaller number on each panel. But then it would be easy to influence a small panel of judges by bribery, so they would give less equitable verdicts.

8] In addition to these things, it ought to be remembered that the Athenians are committed to holding festivals during which the courts are unable to function. And they hold twice as many festivals as anyone else, yet I put these festivals on a par with those of the city that holds the smallest number.

Considering all these things, I maintain that public affairs in Athens cannot be handled in any other way than they are at present, except perhaps for adding or taking away a little here and there. No drastic changes can be made without removing some portion of the democracy.

9] Many ways can be found to better the form of government, but the present system is adequate for preserving the democracy; nor would it be easy to improve on their methods of government except, as I have said, by adding or taking away a little here and there.

10] The Athenians are held to be ill advised, and here I agree, in taking the side of the lower classes in city revolutions. But they do this intentionally. For if they sided with the upper class they would be supporting men who do not think as they do. The upper class is not favorable to democracy in any city, but in each city it is the very worst element that favors democracy, like being attracted to like. That is why the Athenians side with the elements akin to themselves.

11] Whenever they have tried to side with the upper class it has worked out to their disadvantage: within a short space of time the common people in Boeotia were subjected. The same thing happened when they backed the upper class in Miletus, who shortly rebelled and butchered the democrats. And again, when they backed the Lacedaemonians instead of the Messenians it was not long before the Lacedaemonians made war on Athens, after defeating the Messenians.

12] Someone might suppose that no one in Athens was ever unjustly disfranchised. But I maintain that some have been unjustly deprived of their citizen rights, but certainly very few. But more than a few men are needed to attack the Athenian democracy.

13] And take note of this, also, that men who are justly dishonored are not enraged by it, but only those who are unjustly so. And how can anyone imagine that most people in Athens are unjustly dishonored when the people themselves rule over the magistrates? In Athens men are disfranchised for injustice in office, for speaking or doing something unjust and for similar reasons. Bearing this in mind one ought not to expect anything great from the disfranchised Athenians.

Notes

1. I.e., foreign residents.
2. Text corrupt here.

9

Aristotle's Views on Slavery

ARISTOTLE examines slavery just as he examines other established institutions, not with the zeal of a reformer but the critical eye of a scientist. He takes it for granted that slavery is as permanent as, let us say, the family. Yet Plato virtually abolishes the family in the Republic. That does not mean the Greek family was generally disapproved when he wrote or that those who criticized slavery in Aristotle's day were any more in earnest. There is no sign of moral indignation over the lot of the slave, the only concern about slavery being the bad effects it may have on the citizen.

Aristotle, Politics, *1253b1-1255b40, 1259b18-1260b7*

NOW THAT it is clear what are the parts that make up a city we must begin by speaking of household management, for every city is composed of households. And again the parts of household management are those of which the household is constituted, and a complete household consists of slaves and free persons. Since therefore, the minimum essentials for a household are: master and slave, husband and wife, father and children, therefore we must consider these three relationships — what each is and ought to be. They are respectively: despotic rule, "connubial" rule (for there is no term for the partnership of husband and wife), and thirdly "paternal" rule (for neither is this designated by a special term). Now let the parts I have mentioned be granted, but there is still another part which some identify with household management itself, while others regard it as its most important part. We must look into this. I am speaking of what is called money-making. But first we will discuss master and slave in order to explain this necessary relationship, and also with the hope that we may be able to add something to the understanding of this relationship that is preferable to current views on the subject.

There are some who regard despotic rule as a science, and who also regard household management, despotic rule, constitutional rule and royal rule as identical, a view I referred to at the outset (1252a); others maintain that despotic rule is unnatural. For while by law one man is a slave and the other free, they are not distinguished by nature. Therefore it is not a matter of right but of might.

Since the ownership of things pertains to the household, the acquisition of things pertains to household management (for without the necessities it is impossible to live let alone live well), just as the appropriate tools must be available for any particular craft if it is to accomplish its task. Of tools some are animate, others inanimate: the rudder, for example, is an inanimate tool of the pilot while the officer in the bow is an animate one. In the crafts the slave is a kind of tool, and in household management a possession is a tool for living. Assets are a multiplicity of tools and the slave is a kind of living asset; in fact the slave takes precedence over other tools. Now if it were possible for each tool to carry out its task on command or even to anticipate what is wanted, as the tripods of Daedalus or Hephaestus are reported to have done — which the poet says entered the assembly of the gods of their own accord[1] —, why then the shuttles would divide the web and the plectrum strum on the lyre, and there would be no need for builders to have workmen or for masters to have slaves. Now the tools referred to are instruments of production and the thing produced is of practical value: for the shuttle, when it is used, produces something else, but a garment or a bed is for use alone. Also, since producing and doing differ in kind and since both require instruments, then these instruments must have the same difference. Now life is doing rather than making, and therefore the slave is an instrument of those things that pertain to action. A possession is spoken of in the same way as a part, for a part is not merely a part of something else, but it is completely contained in that other thing. The same is true of a possession. Consequently the master is only the master of the slave, but he is not a part of the slave, while the slave is not merely the slave of the master but he belongs entirely to the master.

From this it is clear what the nature and the capacity of the slave are. For he who by nature belongs not to himself but to someone else, is by nature a slave. Furthermore, he is someone else's man who, if he is a possession, being a man, is an instrument possessed for action, and may be sold. Whether there is or is not anyone like this by nature, and whether it is or is not right and proper for any person to be a slave, must be examined next. It is not difficult to discover this and to learn by what has happened. Ruling and being ruled are not only necessary but advantageous. From their very birth some are marked out for subjection and others for rule. There are many types of rulers and of ruled, and the better those are who are ruled, the better the rule will be: for example, the rule over men is preferable to that over animals. For work done by better individuals is better work, and when one rules and the other is ruled they always have a task to perform.

For whenever a number of elements combine to form a common something, whether the elements are connected or separated, the ruling and the ruled always manifest themselves, and this universal natural characteristic is found in living creatures; in fact rule is even found in inanimate combinations such as a musical composition. But this is probably foreign to our investigation. Now an animal consists first of all of soul and body, the nature of the former being to rule and of the latter to obey. And we ought to look for natural rule in those whose nature is in a healthy state rather than in those where it is corrupt. Therefore we must examine a man with the best possible soul and body, for in him this will be evident, although in inferior persons or in those who are badly constituted the body often appears to rule over the soul because they are in an evil and unnatural state. Now as we said, despotic rule and constitutional rule are first observed in living beings, for the soul rules the body with an absolute rule, while the reason governs the appetites with a constitutional or royal rule. This shows that it is both natural and advantageous for the body to be governed by the soul, and for the emotional part to be governed by the mind and the reasoning part; the opposite arrangement or even their being on equal terms would be harmful to all the parts. This is equally true of man and of the other animals. Tame animals have better natures than wild ones and all of them benefit by the rule of man, for by that means they are preserved. Also the male has a different nature than the female, the one being superior and the ruler, the other inferior and the ruled. The same condition necessarily applies to all mankind. Those who are inferior to the same degree that the soul is superior to the body and man is superior to beast (and this is the condition of those whose proper function is to use their bodies which is what they do best), these men are slaves by nature who will be better off when subjected to rule, as in the cases mentioned above. He who potentially belongs to someone else and therefore is another's, and who has enough intelligence to understand what is wanted but not to reason is a natural slave. The other animals do not apprehend reason but obey their feelings. But in function there is very little difference between them, for both slaves and domestic animals help provide what is needed by the use of their bodies. Now nature intends to distinguish between the bodies of freemen and those of slaves, making the latter strong for menial tasks, the former upright, useless for work of that kind but adapted to the life of the citizen (and this is further divided into usefulness in war and in peace), but it often happens the other way around so that some have the bodies and others the souls of free men. For it is obvious that if they were distinguished in their physical appearance the way the statues of the gods are distinguished, everyone would agree that the rest ought to be their slaves. And if this is true of the body, then the distinction is even more valid when applied to the soul. But it is not so easy to perceive the beauty of the soul as it is that of the body. However it is clear that some men are free by nature and some are slaves, and that it is not only right for the latter to be slaves but also advantageous to them.

Still, it is not hard to see that those who maintain the opposite view are correct to a degree, because the terms slavery and slave are used in two different ways. Slave and slavery are recognized in law, and this law is a kind of convention by which those who are vanquished in war are said to belong to their conquerors. Now many of those skilled in legal matters attack this regulation on grounds of illegality, just as they invoke the charge of unconstitutionality in Athens against a speaker.[2] For they regard it as monstrous that those who resort to violence should, because of their superior strength, be able to subject and enslave those whom they have overpowered. Now there are wise men both for and against this view. The reason for their disagreement and also what confuses the discussion, is that ordinarily virtue when provided with the requisite means has the greatest capacity for exercising force, and that conquest always depends on superior excellence of some sort. Consequently the disagreement is really about justice, because some associate justice and good will, while others define justice itself as the rule of the stronger. But when these discrepancies have been removed there seems to be no cogent or compelling argument that superior excellence ought not to rule and to be master. Actually, imagining that they are arguing in behalf of justice — and the law is a kind of justice —, some regard enslavement in war as just at the same time they are denying it. For wars may have an unjust cause, and no one would maintain that the man who serves an unworthy person is a slave; if this were not so the very noblest persons might be slaves and the sons of slaves, if they happened to be captured and sold. Consequently they are unwilling to call these slaves, but only the barbarians. But when they say this they are really looking for the natural slave and nothing else, with whom our discussion began. For it needs to be pointed out that some persons are slaves everywhere, others nowhere. And the same holds for good birth, for such men regard themselves as noble, not merely at home but everywhere, but barbarians as noble at home, implying that the former represents nobility and free birth without qualification, the latter only in a limited sense, like Theodectes' Helen when she asks:

> Both sides alike from roots immortal sprung,
> Dare such a one be ever servant called?

When they say this they distinguish slavery and freedom, high birth and low, solely on the basis of virtue and vice. For they believe that just as a man comes from men and a beast from beasts, so a good man comes from good men. But while nature tries to bring this about she often fails. The dispute evidently has a logical basis, for it is clear that not all slaves and free men are naturally such; nor is there any doubt that when they are distinguished in this way the former benefit by being slaves and the latter by being masters. And it is both just and proper for the first to obey the command of the second and for the second to have the rule, a rule which obviously suits the nature of each, and the very reason he should be the master. The rule of the wrong man is useless and harmful to both. The advantage of the part is the same as that of the whole, and that of the body the same as that of the soul; but the slave is a part of the master, being distinguished as a kind of living part of the body. Therefore it is both expedient and kind for those to be slaves and masters whose natures respectively fit them to be such, but whenever this is not so and they are held in subjection by law, then the reverse is true.

The foregoing discussion shows that the rule of a master is not the same as the government of a city, and that all forms of rule are not identical as some maintain. For one is a rule over free men, the other over slaves. Now household management is royal since every household is ruled over by a single person, but civil government is rule over free men and equals. A master, moreover, is not defined by what he knows but by the kind of man he is, and this is likewise true of the slave and the free man. There does seem to be a kind of science for a master and another science for a slave, such as the training given slaves by the man in Syracuse, where he used to instruct slaves in their regular duties for a fee. This kind of instruction could be expanded to include the art of cooking and other menial services of that kind. For one task is distinguished from another as being more valuable or necessary, according to the saying: "Slave before slave and master before master." All such sciences are for slaves. The science of a master is that of using slaves, for it is not the possession but the use of slaves that makes him a master. And this science is nothing very great or formidable. What the slave knows how to do the master must know how to order him to do. But for those who do not have time to trouble themselves an overseer takes over the task, and they devote themselves to politics or philosophy. The science of acquiring property differs from both of them, though it is lawful, resembling the science of war or hunting. Now let master and slave be defined in this way.

*   *   *

Now it is obvious that household management takes more pains with human beings than with inanimate possessions, and with their excellence than it does with that of the possessions we call wealth, and with free persons more than with slaves. First, with regard to slaves, someone might be at a loss to know whether there is any virtue in a slave that goes beyond the excellent of instruments or menials and is superior to them, such as self-mastery, courage, justice and other such qualities, or whether the slave possesses no virtues beyond serving with his body. There is a difficulty either way you take it. For if there really is something more, what distinguishes slaves from free men? And if there is not, that is astonishing, since they are human beings and participate in reason. This question is almost the same as the one about a woman or a child. Do they have virtues? Should a woman be self-controlled, brave and just, and can a child be licentious and temperate, or not? And this needs to be asked generally about ruler and subject, whether their virtues are the same or different. Yet if both ought to have a share in nobility of character, then why should one always rule and the other always be ruled? For ruling and being ruled are by no means to be distinguished by greater or less but by a difference in kind. So it is strange that one ought to rule, the other not. If the ruler is not temperate and just how can he rule well? And if the subject is not, how can he obey properly? For if he is a useless wretch without control over himself he will fail to carry out any of his duties. So it is obvious that both must participate in virtue, but with the same difference that distinguishes those who are by nature subjects. This finds its immediate illustration in the soul, for the soul contains both natural ruler and natural subject, the former of which we refer to as virtue and the faculty of reason, the latter as irrational. Evidently the same thing applies to other relationships, so that most things in nature are either rulers or ruled. For the free man rules over the slave in a different way than the male over the female, or a man over a child. Yet the parts of the soul are present in each, though present in different degrees. The slave lacks the deliberative faculty entirely while the female has it to a limited extent, and the child also has it, but in an undeveloped state. The same conclusion must also be drawn about the moral virtues, that all must participate in them yet not in the same way, but each to the extent accordant with his function. Therefore the ruler should have moral virtue in its entirety, for his function in general is to direct and to reason about what he directs, while each of the others should possess as much virtue as pertains to him. Thus it is evident that all the persons mentioned have moral virtue, but that the self-mastery of a woman and that of a man are not the same, nor are their courage and sense of justice the same, as Socrates imagines, but that of the man is sovereign, that of the woman subsidiary. The same principle applies to the others. And this will be clear to those who examine the matter in more detail, for those who speak in general terms deceive themselves, saying that virtue is the proper disposition of the soul, or doing what is right, or something of that kind. Those who, like Gorgias, enumerate the virtues make better sense than these definitions. We ought to regard all these in the light of what the poet said about women: "Silence adorns a woman,"[3] but this does not apply to a man.

Since a child is incomplete, it is clear that his virtue does not relate to himself as such but to his final goal and his preceptor. The slave has a similar relation to his master. We have established that a slave is useful for the necessaries of life, therefore it is evident that he needs little virtue, but just enough so that he will not fail in his task through licentiousness or timidity. If what we have said is correct someone might be in doubt whether or not artisans ought to have virtue, for they often fail in their work through licentiousness. But is there not a great difference? For the slave is certainly a companion in life, the artisan far less so, and the former participates in virtue as much as he does in slavery. The low type of artisan has a separate kind of bondage, for the slave is a slave by nature, but not so the shoemaker or the rest of the artisans. Clearly the master is responsible for the virtues of the slave, but not because he has a special science of mastery to teach the slave his duties. Therefore those who maintain that slaves should not be talked to, saying they should only be given orders, are wrong. For slaves are even more in need of admonition than children.

Notes

1. *Iliad,* XVIII, 373 ff.
2. I.e., the famous *graphe paranomon.*
3. Sophocles, *Ajax,* 293.

10

The Revolt of Mytilene:
Can Punishment Deter?

THIS IS one of the best examples of Thucydides' use of speeches for presenting important historical issues. Cleon is well known to us elsewhere
(e.g., Aristophanes' play The Knights) as the leader of the war party after
Pericles' death, but this is our only evidence for Diodotus. The speeches
are shorter and more abstract than actual speeches would have been (for
a comparison, see selection 12), and they do not give the facts needed
by the Athenians to decide the issue. Rather, we have two discourses
on imperialism, nor is it at all clear that Diodotus' arguments are always
stronger. The reader is not pushed into a corner as he usually is when
Socrates takes the floor, at least the Socrates of Plato. The bitterness of
Thucydides' implied judgment on Athenian imperialism is found later in
the so-called Melian Dialogue (V. 86–111).

Thucydides, iii, 35-50

35] WHEN Paches arrived in Mytilene he forced Pyrrha and
Eresus to submit, and finding the Lacedaemonian Salaethus
hiding in the city he sent him off to Athens along with the Mytilenians he had detained in Tenedos and anyone else he regarded as
responsible for the revolt. He also sent back most of the army. With
those who remained he regulated matters in Mytilene and the rest
of Lesbos according to his liking.

36] When these men and Salaethus arrived the Athenians immediately executed Salaethus, although he promised, among other
things, to get the Peloponnesians to withdraw from Plataea, which
was still being besieged. They made up their minds about the men
and decided, in their anger, not only to kill those who were present
but to put to death all the grown men in Mytilene and sell the
women and children into slavery. They also blamed them for defect-
ing when they were not subjected to them like the others, but not

the smallest reason for their irritation was the fact that Peloponnesian ships had dared to take the risk of aiding them in Ionia. Nor did they appear to have revolted on sudden impulse. So a trireme was sent out posthaste to announce their decision to Paches, commanding him to kill the Mytilenians. But the very next day there was a change of heart and second thoughts about a sweeping and cruel decree, wiping out an entire city rather than merely those responsible. When the Mytilenian envoys who were present perceived this along with their friends among the Athenians, they persuaded the magistrates to bring the matter up again. They were easily convinced because they saw clearly that most of the citizens wanted to be allowed to reconsider the question. An assembly was called right away in which different speakers voiced their opinions. Then Cleon the son of Cleaenetus, who had successfully advocated death the previous day, a most violent man in every respect but one who at that time was much more trusted by the people than anyone else, came forward again and spoke as follows:

37] "I have often felt on previous occasions that a democratic state is incapable of governing others, but never so strongly as I do at your present change of mind about the Mytilenians. The fact that you have no fear of plots in your daily relations with one another causes you to feel the same way about your allies, and whenever you are led into error by their arguments or give way to pity you fail to realize that not only is this dangerous to yourselves, but that your allies cannot be cajoled into any sense of gratitude. You do not understand that your empire is a tyranny exercised over conspirators and unwilling subjects whom you cannot charm into obedience by harming yourselves, but whom you can keep in subjection only by our own strength not by their good will. But the worst possible thing we can do is to waver continually in our decisions, not realizing that a city with inferior laws which upholds them without flinching is preferable to one with good laws that are not observed, or that stupidity accompanied by self-discipline is better than brilliance without it, or that persons with mediocre talents usually govern cities better than their intellectual superiors. There are some who, fancying themselves to be wiser than the established laws, are forever trying to outtalk the speakers in the assembly as though there were no more appropriate place for them to air their views, yet this practice is very damaging to the city. Then there are others who, distrusting their own abilities, regard themselves as less wise than the laws, and while they are not so good at picking holes in a speech as a clever orator, they usually come to the right decision, acting like impartial referees rather than athletic competitors. And this is how we ought to behave rather than to come to your assembly with proposals in which we do not really believe, merely to show how clever and how witty we are.

38] Personally my views are unchanged and I am astonished at those who have proposed to waste time debating the Mytilenian question all over again, which can only help the criminals since the victim confronts his persecutor when his rage has cooled, though punishment closest in time to the offense comes nearest to requiting it. I am also astonished that anyone should try to demonstrate that the crimes of the Mytilenians are advantageous to us, or that our misfortunes are harmful to the allies. Such a man evidently intends to prove that you simply did not know what you were doing when you made your decision, or else he has been bribed to try to mislead you with a tricky speech. In such competitions others get the prizes but it is the city that takes the risks. And it is your fault for holding such contests, for you are in the habit of acting as though you were merely a sounding board for orators, arriving at a knowledge of events only through what you hear in a speech, and deciding what can be done in the future by what is eloquently expressed now. As to what has already happened you have less confidence in what you actually saw than in what the clever critics say. You are very easily beguiled by the novelty of an argument, but do not like to follow a beaten path, always carried away by a paradox you despise the conventional, each man wishing more than anything else to be a participant, but failing that you pit yourselves against the speakers in not seeming to lag behind them in their arguments and by applauding their wit even before the point has been made; being as eager to anticipate what is being said as you are slow to see what will come of it; demanding as it were a different world than the one we live in and not paying sufficient attention to present reality. In a word the pleasure of listening has got the better of you, and you sit there like a sophist's audience rather than men debating matters of public policy.

39] Now I will try to counteract this by showing you that Mytilene wronged you more than any one city. For I can feel some sympathy for those who rebel because they cannot bear your rule or because they have been forced to rebel by the enemy, but when men who have a fortified island, with no one to fear but our enemies on the sea, against whom they have triremes with which to defend themselves, who are self-governing and held by us in the highest regard, when such men act in this way what else are they doing but conspiring to attack us, rather than rebelling? For rebellion is only for those who have been subject to coercion, while they sought to destroy us by siding with our greatest enemies. And this is worse than if they had made war on us on their own account with their own forces. Neither the misfortunes of their neighbors, who had already attempted to revolt from us, served to instruct them, nor did their prosperity at the time make them hesitate to go into danger. Being confident of the future, with hopes beyond their resources but not beyond their greed, they went to war. Preferring might to right when the circumstances favored them, they attacked us without having been wronged. Cities to which very great prosperity comes unexpectedly and very rapidly, become oppressive, and for the most part it is safer for men to be fairly successful rather than immoderately so, and one might say they find it easier to counteract failure than to preserve prosperity. The Mytilenians ought long ago to have been treated by us in the same way as the rest and then they would never have behaved in such an insolent manner. For in other respects men are apt to feel contempt when indulgence is shown, and admiration when no concessions are made. Let them be punished now as their crime deserves and do not let the common people off by putting the blame on the Few, for all were together in attacking you, including those who could have come over to our side and now be citizens again in Mytilene. Instead, thinking it was safer to share the danger with the Few they joined them in rebellion. Then too, consider whether there are any allies who will not revolt on the slightest pretext, if you inflict the same punishment on those who are forced into rebellion by the enemy and those who revolt of their own free will, particularly when freedom is the reward for success while the punishment for failure is by no means unbearable. Meanwhile we shall be obliged to hazard our fortunes and our lives over each city. Even if we win we take over a ruined town, depriving you in the future of the revenue on which your strength depends. But if we lose we add enemies to those we already have, and the time we ought to use resisting our present enemies we will spend making war on our own allies.

40] No hope should be held out either based on fine words or bought with money, that they will be pardoned on the grounds of human fallibility. For they did not harm us without intending to do so, they knew they were engaged in a conspiracy, but pardon is for involuntary offenses. Therefore, now as before, I resist to the uttermost your changes of opinion lest you succumb to the worst corrosives of empire: pity, the pleasures of oratory and fairmindedness. For pity is rightly bestowed on our equals, not on those who can never feel pity in return since of necessity they will always remain our enemies; and politicians who delight in fine speeches should compete on less important occasions, not those where the city pays a heavy penalty for a brief pleasure while the orators are rewarded for their eloquence; and fairmindedness is reserved for friends who are expected to be and to remain friends, rather than for those whose enmity will not be lessened in any way. In a word, if you agree with me, I urge you to combine justice towards the Mytilenians with expediency; otherwise you will not so much win their gratitude as pass judgment against yourselves, for if they were right to revolt you have no right to rule. But if you mean to perpetuate your empire, no matter how, then you ought to punish them if it serves your interest even in violation of equity; otherwise put an end to your empire and play the honest man with no risks at all. You who have escaped ought not to be less resentful than the conspirators or fail to avenge yourselves with an equivalent punishment, bearing in mind what they would probably have done had they been victorious over you, especially considering the fact that they began the wrongdoing. For those who attack without provocation are bent on complete destruction, realizing their danger if the enemy should survive; for one who is not forced into hostile action by harsh treatment is more implacable, if he lives, than one who fights fairly as an enemy.

Do not be traitors to yourselves, but keep very closely in mind what you suffered and how above everything else you wanted to take vengeance on them. Now give them what they would have given you, without yielding to momentary softness, as you recall the danger that hung over you at the time. Chastise them as they deserve and you will give your other allies a clear demonstration that whoever rebels will be punished by death. Once they understand that, you will not have to neglect the enemy so often in order to fight against your own allies."

41] Those were Cleon's words, and after him Diodotus the son of

Eucrates, who had argued forcefully against him in the previous assembly not to kill the Mytilenians, came forward once more and spoke as follows:

42] "I do not blame those who reopened the discussion about the Mytilenians, nor do I commend those who are enraged that the most important matters should be discussed many times. I believe that the two greatest obstacles to sound judgment are haste and anger, the latter being usually accompanied by folly and the former by ignorance and lack of perspective. Whoever contends that words do not instruct us in deeds is either a fool or else has some private interest at stake. He is a fool if he believes it possible to provide for the obscure future by any other means; he is interested if, urging a course of action which is shameful and fearing he will be unable to make a good speech on a bad subject, he means to intimidate opposing speakers and those who listen to them, with effective slander. But hardest to deal with are those who make up their minds in advance that the speaker has been bribed. For if he were merely accused of ignorance the loser would take away with him a reputation for foolishness rather than criminality, but when the charge of corruption is added the victor is held under suspicion while the loser is held to be a rogue as well as a fool. Nor does the city profit by this, because its advisers are silenced by fear; yet the city would be greatly benefited if citizens of this stamp were poor speakers who were therefore less likely to induce the city to follow them in error. The good citizen ought not to intimidate his adversaries, but rather to present a better argument on equal terms. A rightminded city will neither bestow new honors on its best advisers, nor deprive them of those they had before; it will neither punish the adviser whose opinion is rejected nor hold him in less regard. In this way the successful speaker would be less likely to gratify his audience at the expense of his convictions in order to obtain high honors, and the unsuccessful speaker would have the same purpose, to persuade the people to accept what he himself believes in.

43] But we go even farther. If a speaker has given the very best advice, but is also suspected of bribery, we deprive the city of a definite advantage out of resentment for an alleged profit which it is not certain he will receive. The result is that good advice frankly offered is no less suspected than bad, and while the orator who presents a completely hare-brained proposal resorts to trickery to convince the people, his more judicious opponent must also tell lies in order to be trusted. Ours is the only city that cannot be served openly and without deceit, for the man who presents a proposal in a straight-forward manner, even if it is admirable, is suspected of profiting secretly in return. But even under these conditions we who offer our advice on the most important matters must look more carefully into the future than you who have only a short time to consider them, particularly since we are held responsible for the advice we give while you, our audience, are not. For if the speaker and the man who votes for his proposal were both subject to punishment you would be less reckless in your decisions. But now, whenever you happen to have made a mistake in judgment you angrily exact vengeance for the one faulty opinion which was adopted but not for your own numerous opinions which were also in error.

44] Now I have not come forward to speak in opposition, favoring the Mytilenians, nor yet to accuse them. If we are sensible men our dispute is not over their guilt but over what is the best policy for us. And even if I show that they are entirely to blame I shall not advocate putting them to death unless it is advantageous, nor if they are in any way excusable will I let them go unless that seems to be useful to our city. I think we are deliberating for the future rather than for the moment. Now Cleon's main contention that the imposition of the death penalty will be to our advantage in the future because there will be less revolts, represents my own view so far as the emphasis on future advantage is concerned, but I draw the opposite conclusion. And I do not think you ought to reject what is useful in my proposal for his fallacious argument. Probably in view of your present anger toward the Mytilenians his proposal seems more just. But we are not contending with them over a point of law, we are discussing how to make them useful to us.

45] Now states have prescribed the death penalty for many offenses, not only offenses such as this, but for many lesser ones. Nevertheless men are spurred on by hope to take this risk, and no one yet entered on a dangerous scheme unless he was convinced he would live through it. Will any city attempt to revolt with what, in their opinion, are insufficient resources, either in themselves or through outside help? It is in the nature of everyone to make mistakes both privately and in public affairs, nor is there any law that can prevent this, for men have already exhausted the whole list of penalties in the attempt to reduce the number of crimes. Probably in remote antiquity milder punishments were assigned to the most heinous offenses, but as time went on most of these were increased to the penalty of death, yet the crimes continue. Therefore some penalty still more terrifying than this must be found, for this stops no one. The pressure of poverty leads to boldness, and the arrogance and egotism of power to the desire of conquest. Other circumstances operate successively on the passions of man, each of which is governed by some fatal necessity to lead them into danger. And above all hope and greed, the one leading the other following, one suggesting the plan the other representing it as likely to work, do the greatest harm, their strength being greater than that of other dangers because it cannot be seen. Then, too, good fortune plays no minor role in stirring them up. Taking the individual by surprise good fortune leads him into hazardous enterprises with inadequate resources; and this applies no less to cities, for there the stakes are very high, freedom or empire, while men acting in groups absurdly exaggerate their own strength. In a word, whenever human nature is strongly moved to do something it is impossible, and only a fool would think it is possible to prevent, whether by force of law or any other deterrent.

46] Therefore we ought not to adopt an inferior policy from a reliance on the preventive effect of the death penalty, nor deprive rebels of all hope of repentance if they atone for their mistake in the shortest possible time. And consider what happens now, if a city in revolt finds that it cannot succeed, but is able to reach an agreement on the basis of repaying expenses now and tribute in the future. If this were otherwise do you not see that they would prepare more carefully in the future than they now do and hold out to the bitter end, if the results were the same whether they surrendered late or early? Meanwhile would we not have the burden of expenditures because of our unwillingness to offer terms, and if we prevailed would we not take possession of a ruined city whose future revenues would be lost to us? And yet they are our source of strength against our enemies. We ought not to be scrutinizing the crimes they have committed, like judges, but we ought to make provision for the future, so that we will have cities at our disposal well able to furnish us with money; we ought not to depend on the severity of our laws but on the consideration we give to our acts. We will do just the opposite of this if we now decide we ought to inflict severe punishments whenever we subdue a free people reluctantly subject to our empire, men who have obviously revolted in order to obtain their freedom. We ought not to punish free peoples vigorously when they rebel, but rather to take vigorous measures in advance to prevent the idea from occurring to them, and when they have been subdued to impute the blame to as small a number as possible. But now see what a serious blunder you will make if you listen to Cleon.

47] At present the common people in all the cities look on you with favor, and either they refuse to join the oligarchs in revolt or, if forced to do so, soon become hostile to the rebels so that you enter the war with the majority of the city on your side. But if you destroy the common people of Mytilene, who did not participate in the revolt but voluntarily surrendered the city as soon as they obtained weapons, then in the first place you wrong your benefactors by putting them to death, and secondly you are doing what the leading men desire most of all: that is they will have the common people on their side as soon as they revolt, because you will have prescribed the same penalties for those who are guilty as for those who are not. But even if they were guilty you ought to pretend that they were not, for fear that the only class which is on your side will be alienated. And I think it will be greatly to our advantage in preserving our empire to put up with injustice knowingly rather than to destroy men however justly, against our own interests. Therefore Cleon's contention that just punishment coincides with our own advantage is not substantiated in this instance.

48] But now knowing this is the best way, and uninfluenced by pity or generosity — for I do not allow either of them to be brought into it — but by virtue of the facts themselves, be persuaded by me to determine at your leisure the guilt of those Mytilenians Paches has sent to us as the wrongdoers, and let the rest stay in Mytilene. This will benefit us in the future and frighten the enemy at present. For good advice, when followed, is more effective against an enemy than unreasoning violence."

49] Such were the words of Diodotus. After these diametrically opposed views had been presented the Athenians struggled to reach a decision, and the voting was close; nevertheless the view of Diodotus prevailed. They despatched another trireme immediately and in great haste for fear that if the earlier ship got there first they would find the city destroyed; and it had started out a day and a night ahead. The Mytilenian envoys provided wine and barley for the vessel, promising a handsome reward if they arrived in time. The urgency was so great that they ate their barley gruel mixed with wine and oil as they rowed, and while some took their turn at sleep the others went on rowing. By good fortune they did not encounter a head wind; then too the previous vessel, on such a monstrous errand, proceeded with less enthusiasm. Pressing on in this way, they were just far enough behind to allow Paches to read the decree and to be on the point of carrying it out, when the second ship arrived in the wake of the first and prevented the massacre. So narrow was the margin by which Mytilene escaped.

50] On Cleon's motion the Athenians condemned the other men who had been sent by Paches as chiefly responsible for the revolt, to the number of a little more than one thousand, and they razed the walls of Mytilene and confiscated her fleet. They did not, however, exact tribute from Lesbos in the future; instead they divided up the land, exclusive of Methymna, into 3000 plots, 300 of which were set aside as sacred to the gods, while cleruchs of their own were chosen by sortition to take over the rest. The Lesbians were required to pay two minas a year for each lot if they worked the land themselves. The Athenians also received the towns Mytilene had controlled on the mainland and these towns remained subject to Athens. And that is what happened in Lesbos.

11

Corcyra: A Case Study in Revolution

THIS PASSAGE has never been surpassed as a clinical study in revolution. Corcyra, whose troubles with the mother city of Corinth led directly to the outbreak of the tragic Peloponnesian War (Thucydides, I, 24–55), suffers the consequences of her actions. With the democrats favoring Athens and the oligarchs relying on Sparta, the fortunes of both are dependent on the presence of naval contingents from either side in western Greek waters. The period (427 B.C.) is one when Athens' power approaches its zenith, reached two years later with her spectacular success at Pylos and Sphacteria (IV. 29–40). Thucydides chooses to describe the revolution in Corcyra as characteristic of the effects of the long war on the Greeks generally. Worth noting is the contrast between the statesmanlike behavior of the Athenian Nicostratus (ca. 75) and the callousness of the admiral Eurymedon, who let matters get out of hand (ca. 81). We would like to know more, but Thucydides is exasperatingly reticent.

Thucydides, iii, 69-85

69] THE FORTY Peloponnesian ships that had gone to help the Lesbians and then fled across the sea pursued by the Athenians, were blown to Crete by a storm, and from there they reached the Peloponnese dispersedly, finding thirteen Leucadian and Ambraciote triremes in Cyllene, together with Brasidas the son of Tellis who had come as an adviser to Alcidas. After missing out in Lesbos the Spartans wished to sail to Corcyra, which was in a state of revolution, with an enlarged fleet. There being only twelve Athenian ships at Naupactus, they wanted to get there before a larger fleet could come to the rescue from Athens, so Brasidas and Alcidas made their preparations accordingly.

70] The disturbances began in Corcyra with the arrival of the prisoners captured in the naval engagements near Epidamnus. The

Corinthians released them, supposedly because their proxeni had gone bail for them to the extent of 800 talents,[1] but actually because it was believed they would bring Corcyra over to the side of Corinth. The prisoners went around among the citizens individually, urging them to cause the city to break with Athens. When an Athenian ship and a Corinthian ship arrived, each with envoys, the matter was debated. The Corcyraeans voted to continue their alliance with Athens on the terms agreed to, but also to be friends with the Peloponnesians as they had been in the past. Also these same men haled Pithias into court, the leader of the popular party and a self-styled Athenian proxenus, on the charge of enslaving Corcyra to Athens. After he was acquitted he, in his turn, accused five of the richest of their number, claiming that they had been stealing vine props from the temple lands of Zeus and Alcinus. The penalty imposed for each vine prop was one stater, so when they were convicted the men took refuge in the temple as suppliants asking to pay their fine in installments because of the magnitude of the penalty. But Pithias, who happened to be a member of that body, persuaded the Council to enforce the law. Now being hard pressed by this law, and also because they learned that while he was still on the Council Pithias intended to persuade the people to have the same friends and the same enemies as the Athenians, they rose up and suddenly invaded the Council chamber with drawn daggers, killing Pithias and sixty others, both members of the Council and private citizens. However a few of those who shared Pithias' views managed to escape to the Athenian trireme which was still waiting.

71] After perpetrating this violent act they called the Corcyraeans together and urged that it would be advantageous, and also that they would be less apt to be enslaved by Athens if they resolved not to receive men from either side in the future unless they came peaceably in a single ship, but to treat any more than that as enemies. After speaking they forced the adoption of the resolution. Then they promptly sent envoys to Athens to explain their action; they were to demonstrate that it was for the best, and also to induce those Corcyraeans who had fled there not to do anything untoward for fear of retaliation.

72] On their arrival the Athenians arrested the envoys for fomenting revolution, and the others, whom they had corrupted, they removed to Aegina for safekeeping. Meanwhile, when a Corinthian trireme reached Corcyra with envoys from Sparta, the men now controlling the government attacked the democrats and defeated them in a battle. When night came on the democrats fled to the acropolis and the heights of the city, and established themselves there in force. They also held the Hyllaic harbor. Their opponents seized the market place, where most of them lived, and the harbor nearest it which faced the mainland.

73] The next day there was light skirmishing while each side sent around to the countryside to summon the slaves, promising them their freedom. Most of the slaves allied themselves with the democrats, but on the other side 800 mercenaries were brought over from the mainland to help.

74] After a day had passed there was another battle, and the democrats won, having the advantage of a strong position and greater numbers. Their wives boldly took a hand, hurling pottery from the houses and enduring the rage of battle despite their sex. The rout came late in the day, when the oligarchs now afraid the democrats might proceed unopposed to the arsenal and then destroy them, set fire to the dwellings and rooming houses around the market place to head off an attack. They did not spare their own property nor that of anyone else, so that quantities of merchandise were burned and the entire city might have been destroyed if a wind had sprung up to carry the flames on through. With this the fighting ended, and both sides spent the night peacefully but on the alert. Following the democratic victory the Corinthian vessel slipped out to sea, and most of the mercenaries succeeded in making their escape to the mainland.

75] Next day Nicostratus the son of Diitrephes, the Athenian general, arrived to help with twelve ships and five hundred Messenian hoplites from Naupactus. He brought about a settlement, persuading them to agree with one another to condemn ten men as being chiefly responsible, men who had not stayed to await the outcome, and to allow the rest to remain, making a treaty with them and with Athens, to have the same friends and the same enemies. After this was done he intended to sail away, but the democratic leaders urged him to leave five ships with them to lessen the possibility of a move by their opponents; they agreed to provide an equal number of their own ships to go along with him. He agreed, and they assigned their enemies to these ships. The latter, fearing they might be sent to Athens, took refuge in the Temple of the Dioscuri. Nicostratus raised them up and spoke words of encouragement to them. But they would not be persuaded, so the democrats armed themselves on the pretext that their refusal to sail showed their intentions were dishonest. Then they confiscated the weapons in their houses, and if Nicostratus had not intervened they would have killed some of their fellow partisans whom they encountered. The rest of the oligarchs, seeing what had happened, seated themselves as suppliants in the Temple of Hera, there being not less than four hundred of them. Then, fearing they might stir up a revolt, the democrats raised them up, persuading them to be transported over to the island across from the temple, where provisions were conveyed to them.

76] This was the status of the revolution until four or five days after the men had been taken to the island, when the Peloponnesian ships which had been based at Cyllene after their voyage back from Ionia, arrived, fifty-three all told. Alcidas was in command, as before, but Brasidas accompanied him as an adviser. Dropping anchor in the harbor of mainland Sybota, they sailed for Corcyra at dawn.

77] The Corcyraeans, greatly alarmed both over the state of affairs in the city and also over the naval attack, prepared sixty ships and sent them against the enemy piecemeal as fast as each was ready, despite the advice of the Athenians for them to be allowed to go first, leaving the others to follow later with their whole fleet united. Encountering the enemy in detachments, two Corcyraean vessels deserted at the outset, while on others fighting broke out among the crews. Nothing was done in an orderly way. When the Peloponnesians became aware of the confusion they drew up twenty of their ships opposite the Corcyraeans, and sent the rest against the twelve Athenian vessels — among which were the Salaminian and the Paralian galleys.

78] Now the Corcyraeans were roughly handled, engaging a few at a time and in an irregular fashion, while the Athenians, fearing encirclement by superior numbers, did not direct their attack at the whole fleet nor at the center of it, but moved against one of the wings and sank an enemy ship. Then they formed in a circle, sailing around the enemy to throw them into confusion. When the Peloponnesians engaged against the Corcyraeans saw this they came to the rescue, fearing a repetition of what had happened at Naupactus.[2] Forming all their ships into a single force they attacked the Athenians. The latter now began to retire, slowly backing water in the face of the oncoming enemy because they wanted to give the

Corcyraean ships as much time as possible to extricate themselves. The naval battle came to an end in this fashion at sundown.

79] Fearing their victorious enemies would follow them and attack the city, or pick up the men on the island or cause trouble in some other way, the Corcyraeans brought the men back from the island to the Temple of Hera, and kept guard over the city. But the Peloponnesians did not venture to follow up their victory at sea by attacking the city; instead they sailed away with thirteen of the Corcyraean ships to the point from which they had started on the mainland. Nor did they attack on the following day either, though the city was filled with terror and confusion. Brasidas, indeed, is said to have urged Alcidas to do so, but his vote could not outweigh that of the commander. They did make a landing at Cape Leucimme and laid waste the fields.

80] Fearing the ships would make an attack, the Corcyraean democrats discussed ways and means of preserving the city with the suppliants and others. In fact they persuaded some of them to serve in the fleet and managed to equip thirty ships. Meanwhile, after ravaging the countryside until midday, the Peloponnesians sailed off, and at night signal fires announced the approach of sixty Athenian ships from Leucas, a force the Athenians had sent under Eurymedon the son of Thucles as general, when they heard about the revolution and learned that Alcidas' fleet was sailing to Corcyra.

81] As soon as it was dark the Peloponnesians set out hurriedly for home, skirting the coast. Transporting their ships overland across the Leucadian peninsula to avoid being spotted while sailing around, they got away. But when the Corcyraeans knew that the Athenians were coming and the enemy ships had departed, they quietly brought the Messenians, who had previously been outside, into the city, and ordered the ships that had been made ready in the Hyllaic harbor to sail around. On their way around whenever they found an enemy they killed him. Finally, forcing the men who had been persuaded to serve with the fleet to come out they put them to death. Next, proceeding to the Temple of Hera they induced up to fifty of the suppliants there to undergo a trial, and condemned them all to death. But the majority of the suppliants, who had not submitted, when they found out what was happening slew one another right in the temple enclosure, some hanging themselves from trees, others employing whatever other method was available. And during the seven days that Eurymedon remained with his sixty ships the Corcyraeans went on killing those they regarded as their enemies, charging them with conspiracy against the government, though some died because of personal animosities and others because their captors owed them money. Every variety of death was shown, and as usually happens in such circumstances, there was nothing, even worse things than that, which did not happen. Father slew son, men were torn from the temples and slaughtered in front of them, while some were even walled up in the Temple of Dionysus and died there.

82] This was the course of the revolution, and it seemed all the more brutal because it was the very first to occur, whereas later one might say all of Greece was in turmoil, the Athenians being called in everywhere by the democratic leaders and the Spartans by the oligarchs. In peacetime there had been no excuse nor were they prepared to call on them, but during the war assistance was available to enable either party to damage their opponents or strengthen themselves, while outside intervention could easily be invoked by any faction desirous of revolution. Many painful things happen to cities during a revolution, and they always will happen so long as human nature remains the same, with greater intensity or less and in a variety of ways as the differences in the circumstances of each may determine. During peace and prosperity cities and individuals alike, through not meeting unbearable conditions, have more amiable sentiments; but war, depriving them of their everyday well-being, is a violent teacher, molding the tempers of the majority to resemble their present circumstances. And thereafter the cities were torn by revolution, those where it occurred late through a knowledge of earlier revolutions greatly surpassed them in new refinements, showing excessive ingenuity both in bringing them about and in making reprisals. They even took pleasure in altering the usual meaning of words to describe their actions. Hare-brained recklessness was denominated as loyal bravery, the hesitation of a reasonable man as veiled cowardice, moderation as camouflage for unmanliness, and great wisdom as inability to act. Mercurial adaptability was added to the qualities that make up a man, while prudent efforts to avoid disaster were held to be merely fine-sounding excuses for deserting one's party. The violent man was always believed while anyone who opposed him was subject to distrust. The man who succeeded in a plot was felt to be clever and the one who found it out in advance to be even more so. But anyone who suggested ways of avoiding the necessity of a conspiracy was said to be ruining his party and cringing in the face of the enemy. The man who successfully carried out some dastardly enterprise was praised, and so was he who incited someone else who had previously had no such intention. Also, blood ties came to be less binding than those of party, since men would dare anything for the party and without any excuse. These party associations were not formed for mutual aid in accordance with the established laws, but for gaining advantages in defiance of the law. Their trust in one another was not so much strengthened by divine law as it was by their breaking the laws together. Reasonable proposals from their opponents were accepted only as a precautionary measure, if they had obtained the advantage, not in a generous spirit. And when binding agreements were made under oath they were made only because of some dilemma on one side or the other, and therefore they held good only from moment to moment as long as neither was able to get help from outside. When the opportunity came the first party to catch its opponents off guard was greatly encouraged. It was more satisfying to take revenge on account of the oath, not only because it was safer than acting in the open, but also because winning through treachery was admired as an act of superior intelligence. For rogues have more often been called clever than stupid men have been called honest, for stupidity is also felt to be disgraceful while cleverness is admired. The cause of all these things was the pursuit of power, for personal profit or out of vanity, which caused furious rivalries. Leaders of both parties in the cities resorted to high-sounding phrases, advocating the equality of all citizens before the law, or the moderation of a government of the rich. While they paid lip service to the city they treated it as a prize. In frenzied competition they dared form outrageous plots to defeat one another and devised even more outrageous punishments, not with a view to the requirements of either equity or the public interest, but solely to what was agreeable to one side or the other. Grasping for power, either by a rigged vote or by violence, they were prepared to sate their desires with immediate victory. So it came about that neither side paid any attention to strict truth, but those who accompanied their invidious acts with plausible phrases were better regarded. Citizens who followed a moderate course were victimized by both parties, either for not helping them or merely out of spite that they were there.

83] In this way every form of viciousness arose out of the revolutionary disturbances in Greece, and that simplicity in which honor plays so large a part was laughed out of existence, while the division into opposing ideological camps brought about general distrust. There was no word strong enough, no oath terrible enough to reconcile them, for when they found themselves on top there was no one who did not take precautions against injury in the future, since their conviction that it was useless to depend upon oaths made it impossible to trust anyone. For the most part it was the inferior sort who succeeded in imposing their opinions. Being well aware of their own deficiencies and of the sagacity of their opponents and therefore fearing to get the worst of it in debate, they also dreaded that if they resorted to intrigue the versatility of their opponents would anticipate them; therefore they turned boldly to direct action. The others looked down on them, and even when they got wind of a plot in advance they saw no reason to do anything while discussion was still possible. As a consequence they were usually caught without defenses and destroyed.

[84] Now in Corcyra many villainies were attempted for the first time, such as men commit when given the opportunity to take their revenge, governed as they usually are by violent emotion rather than self-control. Some acted to rid themselves of congenital poverty, but in particular those who felt an irresistible urge to get possession of the property of their neighbors judged them unfairly; even when not aiming at personal aggrandisement and especially when attacking men of their own class they were carried away by partisan frenzy into perpetrating cruel and implacable deeds. Life in the city was thrown into confusion during this period and human nature, ever prone to injustice and law violation, obtained the mastery over law and did as it pleased, impotent to control its rage but prevailing over justice, and hostile to any kind of superiority. For revenge would not come ahead of piety, or profit ahead of justice were it not for the fact that power leads to envy, even when blamelessly exercised. Men think it right to have laws in common dealing with matters of this kind, laws by means of which everyone hopes that if he meets with some mishap he will find himself protected, but in revenging themselves on others they destroy the laws, so that later on when some one finds himself in danger and needs them, they are no longer in existence.

85] So it happened that the Corcyraeans were the first to display this vindictiveness in their relations with one another inside the city, and then Eurymedon and the Athenians sailed away. Later on the Corcyraean exiles, some five hundred of whom had escaped, seized the forts on the mainland and took over the Corcyraean holdings there. Using them as a base they made raids against the island, creating such destruction that a serious famine broke out in the city. They also sent envoys to Sparta and to Corinth about restoring them, but when nothing was done, the exiles procured boats and mercenary soldiers, then crossed over to the island with about six hundred men all told. They burned their boats, leaving themselves no alternative except to conquer, and then went up to Mt. Istonē, where they built a fort from which they harassed the city and dominated the open country.

[Chapter 84 is usually bracketed because scholars doubt whether it is genuine. If an insertion in the text, it was a very old one.]

Notes

1. Almost $1 million, an impossibly high figure even for plausible fiction.
2. See II, 84.

12

The Speech for the Prosecution: Lysias vs. the Thirty

LYSIAS was a metic whose father, Cephalus, came to Athens from Syracuse. In fact it was at Cephalus' house in the Piraeus that Socrates carries on the conversation immortalized by Plato in the Republic. The fall of Athens in 404 B.C. was followed by the setting up of a provisional government under the watchful eye of Lysander and his Spartan troops, a government which tried to perpetuate its control. The overthrow of this government of the Thirty Tyrants, as they came to be called, was brought about by the Athenian democrats in exile led by Thrasybulus, and made possible by the division at Sparta between Lysander and King Pausanias. Accordingly the democracy was restored and an amnesty granted every citizen regardless of how he had behaved under the Thirty—an amnesty that accounts for some unusual features in the trial of Socrates later on. However no such immunity was granted any of the surviving Thirty, but one of them, Eratosthenes, decided to stay in Athens and take his chances with the courts. It is he who is the defendant in the present trial, and the speech explains Lysias' own motives clearly enough. Lysias remained a metic, though on one occasion he was voted Athenian citizenship, only to have the action invalidated on technical grounds. We do not know whether Eratosthenes was acquitted or found guilty. The entire speech is given.

Lysias, Against Eratosthenes (Speech No. xii)

1] GENTLEMEN of the jury, it is not beginning that seems difficult to me, but bringing my speech to an end. So numerous and so serious are the crimes these men have committed that it is neither possible to invent charges against them more terrible than the facts, nor to relate everything even if one wishes only to speak the truth, for of necessity the accuser will fail either through exhaustion or because the time has run out.

2] And we seem to me to be relying on exactly the opposite procedure from that which has been used in the past. Previously it was incumbent on the prosecutor to show the reasons for his hostility towards the defendant but now the defendant must be asked to explain why his enmity towards the city was so strong that he dared to commit such crimes against it. Now I do not make this observation because of a lack of personal grounds for enmity, but because there is abundance of matter for everyone to be outraged both on private grounds and on behalf of the state.

3] Moreover, gentlemen of the jury, I have never before been involved in a lawsuit on my own account or for anyone else, and now that I find myself compelled by what has happened to accuse this man I have often been reduced to despair, for fear I might conduct the prosecution for my brother and myself in an unworthy and incompetent manner because of my lack of experience. Be that as it may, I shall try to explain the matter from the beginning as briefly as I can.

4] My father Cephalus was persuaded to migrate to this country by Pericles, and he lived here for thirty years, during which time neither he nor we sued anyone or were sued by anyone, but resided under the democracy in such a way as not to do any injury to others or to be injured by anyone else.

5] But when the Thirty came into power, rascals and cheats that they were, they said it was necessary to rid the city of evil citizens and to turn the rest into the paths of virtue and justice; though this is what they said, this is not what they ventured to do as I will now demonstrate, first speaking about myself and then reminding you of your own experiences.

6] Theognis and Pison kept talking among the Thirty about the metics and how hostile some of them were to the government: that this gave them a chance to acquire money on the plausible excuse of exacting punishment; that the city was completely bankrupt and the government needed funds.

7] They had no trouble persuading their hearers, who thought nothing of killing a man and everything of seizing money. So they decided to arrest ten men, two of them poor men to serve as proof that their actions against the rest had not been taken for their money, but in the interest of the state like everything else.

8] Dividing up the houses among themselves they started out. They found me entertaining guests, whom they drove away. They turned me over to Pison, while the rest of them went into the workshop to make a list of the slaves. I asked Pison whether he would save me for a sum of money.

9] He said he would, if it were a large sum. I replied that I was prepared to give him a talent of silver. He accepted the terms. Now while I knew he paid heed neither to gods nor men, still I thought it was very necessary under the circumstances to obtain some pledge from him.

10] And after he swore to save me in return for a talent, invoking destruction on himself and his children if he did not, I went into my bedroom and opened the strong box. Perceiving this, Pison followed me into the room and when he saw what was inside he called two of his underlings to seize the contents of the box.

11] Now, gentlemen of the jury, it contained not just the sum I had agreed on, but three talents of silver, four hundred Cyzicenes, one hundred darics and four silver bowls, so I begged him to leave me something for travel.

12] But he told me to think myself happy if my life was saved. As Pison and I were leaving we were met by Melobius and Mnestheides returning from the workshop. They overtook us at the threshold and inquired where we were going. Pison replied that we were going to my brother's to examine what he had in his house. They told him to proceed, but ordered me to follow them to Damnippus' house.

13] Pison came up to me and told me to say nothing, and not to worry, for he would join me there. At Damnippus' house we found Theognis guarding some other prisoners, and they turned me over to him and went away. In this situation I decided to take a chance since I expected to die anyway.

14] Calling Damnippus I addressed him as follows: "You happen to be my friend and I have come to your house. But I have done no wrong, it is my money that has ruined me. But do you use your good offices for me, afflicted as I am, and save me." He promised to do so, and decided it would be best for him to talk to Theognis, because he thought he would do anything if someone only gave him money.

15] While he was engaged with Theognis, since I was familiar with the house and knew there was another way out, I made up my mind to save myself that way, reasoning that if I got out unnoticed I would be safe, while even if I were caught and Theognis agreed to accept money from Damnippus I thought I would still be saved, and if he refused I would die anyway.

16] After mulling this over in my mind I took flight while they were keeping watch over the entrance to the court. Now there were three doors through which I had to pass, but by good luck all three were open. When I reached the house of Archeneus the ship chandler I sent him into the city to find out about my brother.[1] When he returned he told me Eratosthenes had arrested him in the street and taken him off to prison.

17] When I learned this I boarded a ship for Megara on the following night. The Thirty gave their usual order to Polemarchus to drink the hemlock, without first telling him why he was to die, let alone bringing him to trial or allowing him to defend himself.

18] And when his corpse was removed from the prison they rented a shed in which to lay out his body, not allowing him to be buried from any of our three houses. And although we had an abundant supply of garments they would not release any of them for burial when asked to do so, with the result that friends made donations for his interment, one giving a cloak, one a pillow, each what he happened to have.

19] They also robbed us of seven hundred shields and more silver and gold, bronze, jewelery, furniture and women's clothing than they ever thought to get their hands on, and also one hundred and twenty slaves; keeping the choice things for themselves they turned the rest over to the treasury. The extent of their greed and shameful avarice, as well as their bad manners, are shown by the following: Polemarchus' wife happened to be wearing some earrings she had owned when she first entered his home, and Melobius snatched them from her ears.

20] Nor did they leave us the smallest fraction of our property out of compassion. But they wronged us as greatly for our money as others are driven to do out of resentment for great injuries. But this is not what we deserved from the city, we who have held every choregic office, paid heavy property taxes, conducted ourselves in a respectable manner, done whatever was asked of us, made no enemies and have ransomed many Athenians from the enemy. Yet they treated us in this fashion, but we, metics though we are, have not behaved like them, though they are citizens.

21] For they have driven many citizens into exile in enemy lands, and they have killed many others without cause, even depriving them of burial; they have also robbed many honest men of their rights as citizens, and prevented many citizens who were planning to give their daughters away in marriage from doing so.

22] They have now grown so bold that they are here to defend themselves, claiming never to have done anything evil or shameful! And I wish they were telling the truth, for I would not be the one least benefited if they were.

23] But as it is now, this is not true, either in their relations with me or with the city. As I said before, Eratosthenes killed my brother, not because he had personally been injured by him nor yet because he had observed him doing anything against the government, but simply to find an outlet for his cruelty.

24] I want him called to the stand, gentlemen of the jury, and this is what I have in mind: I think it would indeed be an act of sacrilege to speak to this man to his own advantage even by means of a third party, but when it is to damage him, I regard it as religiously acceptable to address even a man such as this one.[2] Come up here now and answer my questions.

25] Did you or did you not arrest Polemarchus? — I was carrying out the orders of the government because I was afraid. — Were you in the Council chamber when were were under discussion? — Yes. — Did you support those who urged killing us or did you oppose them? — I opposed them. — So we would not die? — So you would not die. — Thinking we would suffer justly or unjustly? — Unjustly.

26] Well then, most wretched of mankind, you spoke in opposition in order to save us, and then you arrested us in order to kill us? And when our salvation depended on the majority you say you opposed those who wished to destroy us, but when it rested with you alone to save Polemarchus or not save him, then you carried him off to prison? You think, then, that for making a useless protest, according to you that is, you ought to be regarded as an honest man, while for arresting and killing my brother you owe no accounting to me and all those who are present?

27] But it is not even reasonable to believe he is telling the truth when he says he spoke in opposition to what he was later ordered to execute. For then they would surely not have tested his loyalty in the metics affair. For is anyone more unlikely to have been given such an assignment than the one who had opposed it and had made his opinion known? Who was less likely to have served in this capacity than the very man who was against what they wanted to do?

28] Now I think it is an acceptable excuse when other Athenians blame what happened on the Thirty, but how can you be expected to receive it when the Thirty put the blame on themselves?

29] Now if there had been any more powerful authority in the city which ordered him to put men to death unjustly you would probably make allowances for him, but if it is permissible for the Thirty to excuse their actions because they were ordered by the Thirty, then can you punish anyone at all?

30] Also, it was not in his house but in the public street, where he could have respected my brother's safety as well as the vote of the Thirty, but he arrested him and carried him off. You still feel resentment towards those who entered your houses to carry out such a search for you or one of yours.

31] Yet if it is necessary to be lenient towards those who destroyed others in order to save themselves, then you ought rather to be lenient towards them, since it was dangerous not to go where they were sent, and not to surrender those they found. But Eratosthenes could have said he had not met my brother, and then that he had not recognized him. For this did not allow of proof or contradiction, so that his enemies could not possibly have refuted him had they attempted to do so.

32] If you really were an honest man, Eratosthenes, you should have warned those who were to die unjustly instead of arresting men who were being destroyed unlawfully. But now your handiwork is revealed, not as that of a reluctant participant but one who rejoiced in what was happening.

33] Therefore the jury ought to base its vote on deeds rather than words, taking your actions, which they know, as an indication of your words, for which witnesses cannot be produced. Not only were we not allowed to be present at their meetings, we were not even permitted to remain at home. So it is that after wronging the city in every possible way they can perfectly well give a completely good report of themselves.

34] But I do not deny this, and if you prefer I will admit you spoke out against your colleagues. But I do wonder how you would have behaved had you agreed with them, when after you say you opposed them you killed Polemarchus.

But suppose you happened to be the brothers or the sons of that man. Would you vote for acquittal? Gentlemen of the jury, Eratosthenes must prove one of two things: either that he did not make the arrest, or that he was justified in doing so. But he has admitted he arrested him without justification, making it easy for you to vote on the matter.

35] Then, too, many residents and foreigners are here to find out how you feel about these men. Of these, your fellow citizens will depart with the knowledge either that they will be punished for their crimes, or else that those whose plots are successful will become the tyrants of the city, while those who fail will still be your equals. And the foreigners who are visiting us will find out whether or not they were right in proclaiming the exclusion of the Thirty from their own cities. But if you acquit the men who abused you now that you have arrested them, the foreigners will certainly think they have been oversolicitous in protecting you.

36] Would it not be strange if, when you condemned to death the generals who won a naval battle but said they had been unable to rescue their comrades from the sea because of a storm,[3] because you felt they owed an accounting to the valiant dead, and then, when these men who as private citizens did all that was in their power to cause defeat at sea, and who when they came into office agreed of their own free will to put many citizens to death without trial, you did not think it necessary to apply the ultimate penalty to them and to their children?

37] I might feel at this point, gentlemen of the jury, that the charges already made are sufficient, for I think the prosecution should continue until the defendant is shown to have done enough to deserve the death penalty, for that is the most that we can ask of them. Therefore I do not see that it is necessary to accuse these men of a multitude of crimes, when even though they died twice they would be unable to make an adequate atonement for even one of them.

38] Nor can they resort to a device which is customary in this city, when instead of answering any of the charges defendants sometimes deceive you by relating other things about themselves: demonstrating to you that they were brave soldiers; that they captured many enemy ships while acting as trierarchs; or that they induced enemy cities to become your friends.

39] But ask this man to show that they slew as many of the

enemy as they did of their fellow citizens; that they captured as
many ships as they betrayed; or that they won over any city to
compare with your city, which they enslaved.

40] Did they despoil the enemy of as many weapons as those
they took away from you? Did they capture other walls comparable
to the walls of their own fatherland which they tore down? But it
was they who destroyed the forts in Attica and made it clear to you
that they had not removed the walls of the Piraeus because the
Spartans ordered, but because they meant to strengthen their own
control.

41] I have often wondered at the boldness of this man's defenders,
except when I reflected that it is those who commit all the felonies
who are praising criminals of this kind.

42] However this is not the first time Eratosthenes worked
against the people. During the period of the Four Hundred,[4] after
establishing the oligarchy in camp he fled from the Peloponnese as
a trierarch leaving his ship behind, along with Iatrocles and others
whose names I need not mention. When he arrived here he opposed
those who wanted the democracy. And I will call witnesses in support of these facts.

Witnesses

43] I will leave out his activities in between, but when the naval
battle took place[5] and misfortune overtook the city which was still a
democracy, then the revolutionary movement began with the establishment of five Ephors by the so-called "club-members," men
opposed to your democratic majority who called meetings of the
citizens and acted as leaders in the conspiracy. Critias and Eratosthenes were among their number.

44] These men appointed phylarchs over the tribes. They also
controlled voting in the assembly, decided who should be elected to
office and had full authority to do anything else they wished. So it
was that you not only had the enemy to deal with, but at the same
time these fellow citizens of yours kept you from passing any useful
measures and reduced you to a state of privation.

45] They knew very well that under other circumstances they
could not possibly succeed, but only when things were going badly.
And they believed that in your anxiety over the evils of the moment
you would not trouble yourselves about those that lay ahead.

46] I will call witnesses to show you that he was one of these Ephors — not from among his fellow conspirators, for I would not be able to do that — but men who heard about it from Eratosthenes himself.

47] And yet, if his partisans were sensible men, they would not have felt bound by their oaths to the detriment of their fellow citizens, but might easily have broken them for the good of the city. But I have said enough about them. Call the witnesses. Now, come up on the platform.

Witnesses

48] You have heard the witnesses. Had he been a good citizen then he ought not to have governed illegally in the first place; next, he should have told the Council that all the charges were false: that Batrachus and Aeschylides were not making bona fide accusations but introducing false charges trumped up by the Thirty, and invented to the detriment of the citizens.

49] Then, too, gentlemen of the jury, those who were disaffected to your democracy lost nothing by remaining silent. There were others to speak and act for them, men unsurpassed in doing harm to the city. If they were as well-disposed as they say they were, why did they not show this at the time by proposing the best measures and deterring the evildoers?

50] He will probably say that he was afraid, and this will seem sufficient to some of you. But he is not shown to have raised an opposing voice in the Thirty, and if he did not do so then he evidently liked what they were doing, because he was in a position to speak out and not to suffer anything from them in return. He ought to have shown the same concern for your safety that he wrongly displayed for that of Theramenes, who wronged you in many ways.

51] But he looked on the city as his enemy, and on your enemies as his friends. I shall offer abundant evidence to prove both of these statements. Also, their internal differences were not concerned with you, but disputes among themselves to determine which ones would control the government and rule the city.

52] If they were quarreling over those who had been wronged, then what better opportunity was there for a man in the government to show his goodwill than at the time when Thrasybulus had taken Phylē? But instead of making some kind of announcement or doing something to help the men in Phylē, the defendant went to Salamis and to Eleusis with his colleagues, carried off three hundred citizens to prison and then condemned them all to die by a single vote.

53] Then when we arrived at the Piraeus, and tumults arose and talk of reconciliation, there were great hopes of reaching an agreement satisfactory to both sides. The men of the Piraeus, though the stronger, allowed the others to withdraw.

54] The latter, returning to the city, expelled the Thirty, except for Pheidon and Eratosthenes, and chose as their leaders those most hostile to them, rightly believing that men hated by the Thirty would be liked in the Piraeus.

55] Now Pheidon was one of these, and Hippocles and Epichares of Lamptrae, and others regarded as very much against Charicles, Critias and their faction. But after they were appointed to office they greatly increased the dissension and conflict between the Men of the Piraeus and the Men of the City.

56] By this they clearly demonstrated that they had not risen in behalf of the Men in the Piraeus, or those who had been unjustly put to death; they felt no remorse for the dead or those about to die, but only regretted that some men were stronger or growing rich more rapidly than themselves.

57] When they gained control of the city magistracies they warred against both sides: against the Thirty who had committed every crime, and against you who had suffered every indignity. This at least was evident to everyone: if the Thirty had been banished justly, then your banishment was unjust, while if you had been justly exiled then their exile was unjust; for they had not been expelled from the city for any other act, but for this alone.

58] Therefore you should be very angry with Pheidon, who was chosen to reach an agreement and bring about your restoration but who behaved like Eratosthenes and shared his views; being ready to injure those stronger than himself with your support, he was not willing to restore you, who had unjustly been exiled, to the city. Instead he went to Lacedaemon and urged them to march, pretending that the city would fall into Boeotian hands and saying anything else he thought would have the greatest effect on them.

59] When this failed, either because some festival interfered or because they themselves were reluctant, he borrowed one hundred talents to hire mercenaries, and asked for Lysander as their general, a man who was very favorable to the oligarchy and most unfriendly to the city, especially to the Men of the Piraeus.

60] After hiring men all of whom were bent on the destruction of the city, and inviting other cities, and finally the Lacedaemonians and any of their allies who could be persuaded to come, they were preparing, not to bring about a settlement but to destroy the city, had it not been for the intervention of some honest citizens — to whom you will show your gratitude by bringing their enemies to justice.

61] These things you know yourselves and I am not sure that witnesses are needed. Still, I need a rest, and some of you may like to hear the same report from as many witnesses as possible.

Witnesses

62] Well now, I will try to enlighten you as briefly as possible on the subject of Theramenes. I beg you to listen both for my sake and for the city; and let no one say that I am accusing Theramenes while it is Eratosthenes who is on trial. For I have learned that he will defend himself from these charges on the ground that he was his friend and shared his actions.

63] But I am sure that if he had served in the government with Themistocles he would lay claim to building the walls just as he does to tearing them down with Theramenes, though these two men are scarcely of equal worth. The former built them in the teeth of Spartan opposition, while the latter removed them by deceiving the citizens.

64] But matters have turned out just the opposite of what might have been looked for in the city. It would have been proper for Theramenes' friends to have perished with him, unless there happened to be one who was against him in some way. Yet now I see men defending themselves by referring to him, and trying to bring his friends into good repute as though he had brought great good instead of many evils to the city.

65] Yet he was chiefly to blame for the earlier oligarchy by persuading you to choose the government of the Four Hundred, and his father, who was a member of the special committee,[6] followed a similar policy. Theramenes himself was so acceptable to their government that they made him a general.

66] As long as he remained in favor he was loyal, but when he saw Peisander, Callaeschrus and others becoming more important than himself, and also that the majority of you were no longer willing to obey them, then because he was jealous of them and afraid of you, he joined forces with Aristocrates.

67] Wishing to win your confidence he brought charges against Antiphon and Archeptolemus, his closest friends, and brought about their death. He carried his villainy so far that he enslaved you to win the trust of the oligarchs, then he sacrificed his friends to gain your support.

68] Honored and held in the highest regard he took it upon himself to save the city, yet it was he who ruined it, claiming to have discovered something great and valuable. For he promised to procure peace without giving up a hostage, destroying the walls or surrendering the fleet. However, he was unwilling to divulge his plan to anyone, but asked that they trust him.

69] But, O Athenians, although the Council of the Areopagus was laboring to provide for your deliverance, and although many spoke out against Theramenes' proposal, aware of the fact that others were secretly working for the enemy; and though he was unwilling to tell his fellow citizens what he meant to say to the enemy, nevertheless you entrusted your country, your wives and children and yourselves to that man.

70] And he accomplished none of the things he had promised. So determined was he to make the city small and weak, that he induced you to do what even the enemy had never suggested and what no citizen expected — not because he was forced into it by the Lacedaemonians but because he agreed with them voluntarily — to demolish the walls of the Piraeus and to abolish the existing constitution. For he knew very well that unless every possible hope were removed you would soon take out your vengeance on him.

71] And finally, gentlemen of the jury, he did not allow the assembly to meet until he had purposely waited for what he called a suitable time, when Lysander's ships had been summoned from Samos and the enemy army was at hand.

72] Then when these things had been done an assembly was held to decide about the constitution in the presence of Lysander, Philochares and Miltiades, so no speaker would dare oppose them or make threats against them, and so that instead of deciding what was in the city's interest you would vote whatever your enemies wished.

73] Then Theramenes rose and bade you turn the city over to thirty men and adopt the motion about the constitution introduced by Dracontides. Despite the situation in which you found yourselves you made an uproar as though you meant to refuse to ratify these proposals because you knew that on that day the assembly was choosing between slavery and freedom.

74] Thereupon, gentlemen of the jury, and here I appeal to you as witnesses, Theramenes declared that your protests meant nothing to him, because he knew there were Athenians who supported him, and also that what he had in mind met with the approval of Lysander and the Lacedaemonians. After him Lysander got up. He said many things including the statement that he considered you guilty of violating the peace, and that if you failed to do what Theramenes asked it would be your own freedom rather than the form of government that was at stake.

75] Of the loyal citizens in the assembly some, recognizing the intrigue and the necessity they were under, remained quietly in their seats, while others left the assembly, telling themselves that at least they were not voting for anything that would harm the city; but a few rogues and ill-advised persons voted what was required.

76] They were enjoined to elect ten men designated by Theramenes, ten whom the newly established Ephors selected and ten from those who were present. They saw your weakness and understood their own strength so well that they knew in advance what the assembly would do.

77] For these matters you need not depend on me but on Theramenes, because he enumerated everything I have said when he was defending himself in the Council. He reproached the former exiles because it was he who had brought them back while the Lacedaemonians cared nothing about them; he also upbraided his colleagues in the government for the way he was being treated despite the fact that he was responsible for everything that had been done — by the methods I have already described — and despite the many proofs of loyalty he had given them by his deeds, and despite the oaths he had received from them.

78] And they dare to claim friendship with a man who was guilty of such crimes as well as acts of shame and infamy both old and recent. Nor did Theramenes die on your account but for his own villainy. He was rightly condemned during the oligarchy, for he was already undermining it; and he would rightly have been condemned during the democracy, for twice he enslaved you; despising whatever was near at hand and eager for whatever was at a distance, he inspired the most outrageous crimes under the fairest of names.

79] But I have said enough in accusation of Theramenes, and now the time has come when you ought not to think of pity or forgiveness, but to exact punishment from Eratosthenes and his colleagues in office. And do not, now that your enemies have been defeated in battle, let them prevail by your vote.

80] Do not show more gratitude for what they say they meant to do, than anger for what they actually did. And do not after planning the ruin of the Thirty in their absence, let them off now that they are here. When good fortune has delivered them into your hands do not help them and hurt yourselves.

81] I have brought accusations against Eratosthenes and against the friends he will invoke in his defense and who shared in his deeds. The contest between Eratosthenes and the city is not an equal one. He was both prosecutor and judge of those who were condemned, while we now permit both prosecution and defense.

82] Those men put others to death who had done no wrong without a trial, while you think it best to judge according to the law those who destroyed the city, men whom even if you wished to condemn them illegally, would still be unable to pay back for the wrongs they have committed against the city. What punishment could be inflicted on them commensurate with their deeds?

83] If you put them to death, and their children, would we be sufficiently revenged for our fathers, our sons and our brothers whom they slew without trial? Or if you confiscated their real property, would this compensate the city from which they took so much, or the private citizens whose houses they looted?

84] Since nothing you do can punish them as they deserve, is it not disgraceful to refuse to grant whatever retribution is asked of them?

I think the man is capable of anything now that he has appeared to make his defense before judges who are none other than the victims of his wrong-dealing, and who have themselves witnessed his criminal behavior. Either he has a sovereign contempt for you or else he is relying on others.

85] Both possibilities should alarm you. Consider that they would have been unable to do what they did do without the others who supported them, and that they would not dare to appear now unless they expected the same persons to save them. And these persons do not come just to help them, but they come forward because they imagine they will be free of all responsibility for their own actions and can do as they please in the future if, when you get hold of those responsible for the very greatest crimes, you let them off.

86] But these helpers of theirs also deserve our admiration. Will they ask like true gentlemen, demonstrating that their own virtues outweigh the wrong done by these others? I only wish they had been as eager to save the city as the others were to destroy it. Or will they speak with such eloquence in defending these men as to show that their deeds were meritorious? Yet not one of them ever tried to support the justice of your cause in a speech.

87] And it will be worth while to look at the witnesses who, in testifying for these men really accuse themselves, for they must think you are forgetful and simple-minded if they imagine a majority of you will let the Thirty go scot free, when under Eratosthenes and his fellow rulers it was even dangerous to be present when corpses were carried out for burial.

88] But men like these could ruin the city again if they were saved, while those they destroyed have lost their lives and so have no way to revenge themselves on their enemies. And would it not be a terrible thing if when the friends of those who were unjustly killed perished with them, that these men who destroyed the city should have many mourners at their funeral — since there are so many prepared to defend them?

89] Further, I think it was much easier to speak up on your behalf when you were their victims, than it is now to defend themselves for what they did. Still, they say Eratosthenes was the one of the Thirty who did the least harm and that on that account he ought to be spared. But when he committed more crimes against you than all the rest of the Greeks do you not think he ought to die?

90] You, however, show your own opinions on these events. For in condemning this man you will show your anger over what happened, but if you acquit him you will be felt to approve of their deeds, and you will not have the excuse that your action was forced on you by the Thirty.

91] But now no one can compel you to vote against your convictions, so I urge you not to condemn yourselves by acquitting them. And do not imagine that your vote will be kept secret when what you have decided becomes known in the city.

92] Before stepping down I wish to remind both of your groups, the Men of the City and the Men of the Piraeus, of one or two matters, so that when you vote you will be guided by what each of you suffered under these men. First, you who are of the City remember how harshly you were ruled by these men, who made you wage war against your brothers, against your sons and against your fellow citizens, a war in which if you were defeated you would be treated by your conquerors as equals, while if you were victorious you would have enslaved them to these men.

93] Also these men greatly increased their private fortunes by means of the government while yours was diminished by civil war. For they did not think you deserved any of the benefits, though they did force you to share in the blame. So contemptuous were they, that instead of courting your support by distributing favors they counted on your supporting them as their partners in shame.

94] And now that your confidence has been restored you in your turn should take whatever vengeance you can for yourselves and also for the Men of the Piraeus. Consider that then you were ruled by these detestable persons, and consider also that now you govern the city, make war on your enemies and deliberate on state policy along with the best citizens; and remember the mercenaries they stationed in the acropolis to watch over their rule and your slavery.

95] And let this suffice for you, though I could add a great deal more.

Now those of you who are of the Piraeus remember first your weapons, and how after you fought many battles on foreign soil your weapons were taken away from you, not by the enemy but by these men in time of peace; and then remember how you were banished from the city your fathers left you, and how they demanded your extradition from the cities where you were fugitives.

96] Recall the anger you felt at the time you were banished and the other evils you suffered from them: how they dragged some forcibly from the market place, others from the temples and killed them; how they snatched some from the arms of their children, their parents or their wives, forcing them to take their own lives; and how they refused them the customary burial, thinking their power to be stronger than the vengeance of the gods.

97] Those of you who escaped death met endless dangers, wandering from one city to another, continually being driven out, lacking the bare necessities, some of you leaving your children behind in the hostile city of your birth, others in a foreign land, yet despite every obstacle you reached the Piraeus. Then, like brave men, after facing many and serious dangers you freed some and restored others to their ancestral city.

98] But if you had been unlucky and had failed in your undertaking you would have returned to exile for fear of suffering the same indignities you had suffered before. For neither temples nor altars, which protect even the guilty, would have been any use to you, who were innocent, against men like these. As for those of your children who stayed here, they would have been mistreated, while those who remained abroad would have been enslaved for trifling debts, with no one to rescue them.

99] And now I do not wish to speak of what is going to happen in the future when I cannot even relate what they did. For this is not a task for one accuser or for two, but for many. Nevertheless I have not flagged in my determination, for the sake of the sacred objects they have sold or polluted by their presence, for the city which they made small, for the sake of the dockyards which they destroyed, and for the dead. You were unable to save them when they were alive, come to their aid now that they have died.

100] I fancy the dead have been listening to us, and that they are waiting for you to cast your vote, thinking that those who vote for acquittal will be condemning them to death again, while those who punish these men will also be taking vengeance on their behalf.

I will now end my accusation. You have heard, you have understood, you have suffered. You have the guilty man. Pronounce your verdict.

Notes

1. I.e., Polemarchus.
2. The difficulty is that the relative of a dead man was not supposed to speak to his murderer.
3. I.e., in the Battle of Arginusae, 406 B.C.
4. 411 B.C.
5. I.e., at Aegospotamoi, 405 B.C.
6. See Thucydides, VIII, 1.

13

The Governments of Sparta and Crete

SPARTA and her legendary lawgiver Lycurgus were greatly admired in antiquity, particularly by those who were shocked by the license of the Athenian democracy. Plato's Republic clearly shows this and in the Crito Socrates is made to refer to the excellent laws of Lacedaemon and Crete. The full extent of this idealization may be grasped by reading Plutarch's Lycurgus or the Lacedaemonian Constitution of Xenophon. So persuasive was this favorable image of Sparta created by non-Spartan, chiefly Athenian writers, that in the third century a serious attempt was made by Agis and Cleomenes to bring back the glory of ancient Sparta by restoring the old Lycurgan constitution—with tragic results for Sparta and Greece. When Aristotle wrote (the date is uncertain but probably in the last decade of his life; i.e., 333–322 B.C.) Sparta had long lost her hegemony over Greece, though she was still a powerful state. He rightly regards the resemblances with Crete as having a historical basis, though his historical knowledge is faulty.

Aristotle, Politics, *1269a29-1272b23*

THERE ARE two ways of examining the Spartan and Cretan constitutions, or any other constitution, the first of which is to determine whether any of its provisions are well designed or poorly designed when compared with the best form of government; and the second, whether any of them is in contradiction with the plan and spirit of the form of government proposed. It is admitted that if a city is to be well governed it must be relieved of concern about the necessities of life, but how this is to be managed is less easily understood. The serf class in Thessaly[1] frequently used to attack the Thessalians, and likewise the helots used to attack the Laconians, lying in ambush as it were for their misfortunes. But nothing like this ever happened to the Cretans, probably because neighboring cities never offered aid to rebels even when they were at war with one another, because it was not in their interest to do so when they had *perioeci*[2] of their own. But all the peoples bordering on Laconia — Argives, Messenians and Arcadians — were hostile. And the serfs first rose in Thessaly because of war with their Achaean, Perrhaebian and Magnesian neighbors. Probably, even if there were no other reason, it would have come about through the difficulties in managing them and the problem of how they ought to be treated. For if they were left to themselves they became arrogant, demanding equal rights with their masters; while if they lived under oppression they would become embittered and conspire. It is obvious from the troubles they have had with the helots that they did not discover the most satisfactory method. In addition to this, their laxity so far as the women are concerned is harmful to the principles of their constitution and the prosperity of the state. Just as man and wife are part of the household, so it is evident that a city should be regarded as divided into two virtually equal parts, the male and female inhabitants. Consequently, whenever the constitution fails to regulate the women, one half of the city must be regarded as uncontrolled by law; and that is what happened in this instance. For while the lawgiver wished to make the whole city well disciplined, as he clearly demonstrates with reference to the men, he was negligent in dealing with the women, who live in luxury and with absolutely no restrictions.

In such a state wealth necessarily comes to be held in high regard, particularly when the women are in control, as usually happens among military and warlike people — except for the Celts or any others who openly approve of male loves. The story teller who first linked Ares and Aphrodite was certainly no fool, for all such men are inclined to be given over to passion, either for men or women. And that is just what happened to the Laconians, for they have often been managed by women in their rule. For what difference does it make whether the women rule, or whether the rulers are dominated by their wives? The results are the same. Now excessive courage is of no possible use in daily life but perhaps only in war, and it was here that the Laconian women were most harmful. In fact they demonstrated this during the Theban invasion, when instead of helping out as they do in other cities, they created more confusion than the enemy. It seems likely that this indulgence of the Laconian women began early, and for good reason. The men lived away from home for a long time on campaigns abroad, making war on the Argives and then again on the Arcadians and the Messenians. Then when peace finally came they gave themselves over to the lawgiver, already prepared by their life as soldiers — for such a life has many elements of virtue. They say that Lycurgus tried to subject the women to his laws, but that when they resisted he gave way. Now it is evident that the causes of what happened go back to this mistake. But we are not examining the question of whether this was excusable or not, but whether it was right or wrong. And it appears that the regulation of women was not well handled. Not only, as was said before, was it the cause of a certain deformity in the constitution itself, but also it gave a distinct impetus to the love of money. But in addition to what has just been said, it is needful to criticize the inequitable distribution of property. For some have managed to acquire very large estates while others have exceedingly little land, with the result that the country has come into the control of a small number of persons. And this tendency has been increased by faulty legislation. Now the lawgiver attached a stigma to buying or selling the existing land, and he was right in doing so, but he allowed anyone who liked to give his land away or to dispose of it in his will, which necessarily led to the same result. Actually, nearly two-fifths of all the land belongs to women, as a result of giving them large dowries, and also because there are so many heiresses. But it would be better if they had no dowry at all, or at most a small or limited one. But now it is permissible for a man to marry off his heiress to anyone he likes, or if he should die intestate then whoever his heir may be is allowed to bestow her on anyone he chooses. For that very reason a country capable of maintaining 1,500 horsemen and 10,000 heavy infantry was cut down to a population of less than 1,000 men. Their own experience clearly shows that in this respect the government was faulty, for the city could not endure a single reverse but perished through lack of man power. They say that under the earlier kings they offered their citizenship to others, so that in those days there was no falling off in population despite long periods of fighting, but they assert that there were 10,000 Spartans. Whether this is true or not, it is better for a city to augment its population by equitable property regulations. But the law about child-bearing which was meant to correct this has had the opposite effect. With a view to producing as many Spartans as possible the lawgiver encouraged the citizens to have as many children as they could, for they have a law that the father of three sons is relieved of military duty and the father of four of all public burdens. But it is obvious that if there were more Spartans and the land were distributed as it is now, many of them necessarily would be impoverished. Then, too, the ephorate is badly managed. This magistracy, which handles affairs of the greatest importance, is chosen from all the people, with the result that all too frequently men of no means obtain this office, men whose poverty makes them venal. This was shown frequently in the past and recently in the matter of the Andrians, when some of the magistrates who had been corrupted by bribes did all that was in their power to ruin the city. Since this magistracy is very important and high-handed the kings are forced to pander to the ephors, as a result of which the constitution also suffers, and the aristocracy is changed into a democracy.

But this magistracy does hold the state together, because the people are mollified by having access to the most important office, and so whether this happened through the lawgiver or came about through chance, it is of advantage to the state. For in any government that is to survive it is necessary for every part of the city to favor it, and to wish it to continue unchanged. Now the kings have this feeling because of the position they hold; the better class citizens because of the Council of the Elders[3] — since this office is a reward of merit — ; and the common people on account of the ephorate, which is picked from everyone. But while this magistracy ought to be chosen from all of the people, it ought not to be constituted in the present fashion, which is extremely childish. Furthermore, though they are haphazardly selected yet they are responsible for deciding important cases, and it would be better if they gave judgment in accordance with the letter of the law, rather than relying on their own opinions. Then, too, the way the ephors live violates the spirit of the constitution, for they are much too free and easy while the others are subject to such a strict regimen that they cannot endure it, but evade the law in order to enjoy furtive bodily pleasures.

But besides this, the office of the Elders is not properly regulated. Very likely someone might argue that since they are men of ability sufficiently well schooled in upright conduct the institution ought to be advantageous to the state, but their sitting in judgment for life over important cases is questionable; for there is such a thing as old age in the mind as well as in the body. Moreover when their upbringing makes even the lawgiver distrust them, this is unsafe. And in fact members of the Council on frequent occasions are known to have betrayed the public interest for personal reasons, or for a bribe. Therefore they ought not to be free from liability as they are now. It might appear that the board of ephors has the authortiy to scrutinize all officials, but this gives excessive power to the ephorate; also, we maintain that the scrutiny should not be conducted in the present fashion. Then, too, the way the Elders are elected and validated is childish, and it is wrong for men deemed worthy of holding office to sue for it. The man worthy of office ought to hold it whether he wishes it or not. As it is now the legislator seems to have followed the same principle here as in the rest of his constitution: making the citizens ambitious, he has counted on this in the election of the Elders, for no one who was not ambitious would sue for the office. Yet the worst acts of deliberate injustice usually take place in mankind as the result of ambition and the love of money. Now whether it is disadvantageous or beneficial to have kingship in a city may be discussed elsewhere, but it would certainly be better to choose each of the kings on the basis of performance rather than in the way it is done at present. It is evident that the lawgiver himself did not conceive of the possibility of their being true gentlemen, for he distrusts them as not completely reliable. Therefore the Spartans were in the habit of sending their enemies along with them as fellow envoys, and felt that the salvation of the state depended on quarrels between the kings.

Neither were the common meals, known as the Phiditia, properly established by whoever it was that first introduced them. They ought to be paid for by the state as they are in Crete. In Laconia everyone is required to contribute, but some are so poor as to be unable to meet this expense; the result, therefore, is just the opposite of what the legislator intended. He wished to make the common meals very democratic yet, regulated in this way, they have turned into a most undemocratic institution. It is not easy for the poor to take part, yet this is their established method of defining citizenship, so that anyone who cannot meet this expense also loses his rights as a citizen.

Others have found fault with the law about admirals, and rightly so. For it creates conflict, since the office of admiral has been set up as virtually another monarchy added to that of the kings, who are perpetual generals. Then one might criticize the lawgiver's intentions, as Plato criticizes them in the *Laws*,[4] because the whole system of legislation is directed to one part of virtue, excellence in war, for this is useful in conquest. For that very reason they were preserved as long as they were fighting but ruined when they had won their empire, because they did not understand how to live in peacetime, having received no other training above and beyond their training for war. But there is another fault no less serious than this. They believe that things worth having are to be obtained by practicing virtue rather than vice, and that is admirable, but the fact that they value these things more than they do virtue is not admirable. Also the state finances are poorly managed in Sparta, for there is no money in the treasury when they are obliged to fight a major war and they are also remiss in paying taxes. Because most of the land belongs to the Spartiates they do not scrutinize one another's tax payments. The results have worked out contrary to the legislator's wishes, for he has rendered the city penniless and the private citizens lovers of money. Let what has been said on the Lacedaemonian constitution be sufficient, for these are the chief criticisms that can be made.

The Cretan constitution is similar to this, in a few respects not inferior but in most respects less advanced. It is said with some probability that the Laconian constitution is chiefly patterned after that of Crete, and in antiquity most things were less clearly worked out than in recent times. They say that when Lycurgus gave up the guardianship of King Charillus to go abroad, he spent most of his time in Crete because of their common origin. The Lyctians were Laconian colonists who when they went there to settle adopted the code of laws used by the previous inhabitants. Even now the dependent peoples in the area use them in the same form in which they were first promulgated in the laws of Minos. The island is admirably located, and seems to have been naturally intended to rule over Greece. For it lies right across the sea, and almost all the Greeks are established around that sea. It is not far from the Peloponnese on one side or Asia on the other, that is the part of Asia by Triopium and Rhodes. As a result Minos obtained the rule of the sea, conquering some of the islands and settling others, until finally he attacked Sicily and lost his life there near Camicus. There is a similarity between the Cretan and Laconian institutions. Helots do the farming for the Laconians and the *perioeci* for the Cretans; both have common meals. Originally the Laconians called them Andria like the Cretans, not Phiditia, which shows that the institution came from Crete. This is also true of their constitution.

The ephors have the same powers as the cosmoi, as they are called, in Crete, except that the ephors are five in number while there are ten cosmoi. The Elders resemble the Elders whom the Cretans call their Council. There used to be kingship also, but later on the Cretans abolished it, the cosmoi obtaining the command in war. Everyone is free to attend the assembly, but it has no authority except to ratify whatever the Elders and the cosmoi have decided. The common meals are better managed in Crete than in Laconia, for in Sparta each brings in a stipulated amount, and if he fails to do so the law bars him from the citizenship, as was explained previously; but in Crete there is more sharing. Out of all the produce and the cattle belonging to the state and out of the tribute paid in by the *perioeci* one part is set aside for the gods and for state services, and another for the common meals, so that everyone, men, women and children, are taken care of by the state.

The lawgiver has also devised many ways to encourage moderation in eating, as a beneficial practice, including divorcing one's wife to prevent their being too many children, and sanctioning homosexuality. Whether the latter is bad or not will be discussed at a later time. It is clear, then, that the common meals are better managed in Crete than in Sparta, but the board of cosmoi are an even worse institution than the ephors. They have the same defect as the board of ephors in that they are indiscriminately chosen, but they lack the compensating constitutional advantages they have in Sparta. For in Sparta, where they are selected from all the citizens, the common people wants the constitution to be maintained because they have a share in the highest office; but the cosmoi are chosen from a particular class, and the Elders from former cosmoi. The same objections can be made to them that have been made to the Elders in Sparta: namely, that the privilege of holding office for life without being held responsible for their acts, is greater than they ought to have; and also their being governed by their own opinions rather than by the laws is dangerous. The fact that the common people, who have no share in the magistracy, keep the peace is no proof of the excellence of this arrangement. Neither do the cosmoi derive any profit from their office as the ephors do, because they live on an island far removed from would-be corruptors. The remedy they employ to correct the flaws in this magistracy is bizarre, and it is not a constitutional act but the arbitrary procedure of a small faction. At frequent intervals some of their fellow magistrates or a group of private citizens join together to drive out the cosmoi. Before this happens the cosmoi are given a chance to abdicate their office. These measures would be better if they were based on law rather than the caprice of individuals, for this is a dangerous practice. But worse than anything else is having no cosmoi at all, which is frequently brought about by powerful men who do not wish to be brought to judgment. This clearly shows that while their government bears some resemblance to a constitutional state it is really not a polity, but rather a close oligarchy. When the people are divided they are wont to assemble their friends and stir up confusion, rioting and fighting against one another. And how is this any different than for the state periodically to cease to exist, and for the political community to be dissolved? This would be a very dangerous situation for any city when someone is able and willing to attack it. But, as has been pointed out, they are saved by their location, for their remoteness has kept foreigners away. Consequently the Cretans have kept their *perioeci* while the helots have often risen in revolt. Nor do the Cretans have any foreign possessions, though recently war did come to the island from abroad and demonstrated the weakness of the Cretan institutions. Let what has been said about this government be sufficient.

Notes

1. I.e., the penestae, as they are called.
2. I.e., half-citizens who fought for Sparta and paid taxes but had no vote.
3. The Gerousia.
4. *Laws,* I, 625C, 630E.

14

Ctesias: Physician, Historian, Romancer

CTESIAS came from Cnidus, famous for its doctors. Like the earlier Democedes of Croton he became personal physician to the Persian royal family. In fact he was in attendance on Artaxerxes when the younger Cyrus wounded him just before his own death at Cunaxa (401 B.C.); this is the battle we know so well through the Anabasis of Xenophon, who fought with the Ten Thousand Greeks in Cyrus' army. Ctesias was a man of influence at court and a born intriguer. Like Democedes he found it hard to get away, but after seventeen years (?) he insinuated himself into the negotiations between the exiled Athenian admiral Conon and the Persian court and returned to Greece. The negotiations resulted in Conon's destroying Spartan naval supremacy at Cnidus (394 B.C.) with a Phoenician fleet. Ctesias, once safely away from Persia, published two historical works, one about the history of Persia and the earlier Asiatic empires (the Persica), the other a separate work on India. Ctesias wrote to entertain rather than to inform. His popularity threatened to eclipse that of Herodotus, whom he maligned, though justice ultimately prevailed. Even the fragments that we have are still an important source for Persian history, and we regret that no more is left of the work of one of the most entertaining liars who ever wrote.

Diodorus Siculus, ii, 4-5, 7-9, 16-20, 23-28

4] SINCE Ninus campaigned against Bactria after founding this city, and since it was there that he married Semiramis, the most famous of all the women we know of, it will be necessary to speak about her and of how she attained such great glory from a humble beginning.

(2) In Syria there is a city, Ascalon, with a lake not far away, a large deep lake well stocked with fish. Beside the lake is a precinct sacred to an illustrious goddess whom the Syrians call Derceto. She has a woman's face, but the rest of her body is that of a fish, and for

these reasons: (3) The most informed natives say that Aphrodite took offense at the aforementioned goddess and inspired her with love for a youth, one of the mortals who offered sacrifice. Derceto, mingling with the Syrian, gave birth to a daughter. Shamed by her mistake she caused the young man to disappear and exposed the child in a rocky deserted region. (4) There great numbers of doves are in the habit of nesting, and strangely enough the child was saved and nourished. She herself plunged into the lake, overwhelmed with shame and anguish, and her body was transformed into that of a fish. As a result the Syrians refrain from this creature and to the present day they regard fish as divine.

Near the place where the child was exposed flocks of doves made their nests, and in wonderful fashion the child was cared for by them. For some wrapped their plumage all around the girl's body to warm it, while others kept an eye on the cattle pens nearby. When the cowherds and the other herdsmen were away they carried off milk in their beaks, dropping it between the child's lips. (5) When the child was a year old and in need of more solid food, the doves would snip off bits of cheese and provide sufficient nourishment. When the herdsmen went back and saw the cheese nibbled away they marvelled at the phenomenon. Then, keeping watch, and finding out the reason they discovered a child of surpassing beauty. (6) They promptly brought it to their shelter and presented it to Simmas, supervisor of the royal herds. He was childless, so he brought up the infant as his own daughter, treating her with every consideration and naming her Semiramis — which is derived from the word for doves in Syrian. And from that time on all Syrians have honored them as goddesses.

5] Now that is how the myth goes about the birth of Semiramis. When she was already of marriageable age and far surpassed other maidens in beauty, an official was sent out by the king to inspect the royal herds. This man was called Onnes, and he was chief of the royal council and designated as hyparch of all Syria. When he lodged with Simmas and beheld Semiramis he was enchanted with her loveliness. He begged Simmas to give him the maiden for his lawful wife, and then took her away to Nineveh where he married her and begat two children, Hypates and Hydaspes. (2) Semiramis, who excelled all women in every other way just as much as she excelled them in beauty, gained a complete ascendancy over her husband, who never did anything without consulting her, and who prospered in all his undertakings.

*　　*　　*

7] Now Ninus appropriated the Bactrian treasures which included quantities of gold and silver, and after arranging matters in Bactria he dismissed his army. Afterwards, when he had a son Ninyas, by Semiramis, he died, leaving his widow as Queen. Semiramis buried Ninus in the capital and built an enormous mound for him, nine stades high and ten stades across, according to CTESIAS. (2) Since the city lay in a plain beside the Euphrates the mound was visible for many stades, like an acropolis. It has remained down to my day, though Nineveh was destroyed by the Medes when they overthrew the Assyrian empire.

Since her nature inclined her to great undertakings Semiramis was eager to surpass the previous ruler, so she built a city in Babylonia, bringing in builders and craftsmen from every direction. After gathering together every necessary thing, she assembled 2,000,000 men from all over her empire to complete the work. (3) Leaving the Euphrates River in the middle she constructed a wall around the city of 360 stades, studded with many great towers; so mighty was this fortification that the wall was wide enough for six chariots to be driven abreast, while the height is incredible to those who hear about it as CTESIAS the Cnidian says. According to Clitarchus and some of those who later crossed over with Alexander, it was 365 stades. They add that she sought to make the number of stades equal to the number of days in the year. (4) Binding together baked bricks with asphalt she constructed the upper part of the wall to a height of 50 fathoms as CTESIAS says, but according to some later writers, 50 cubits. The wall was broader than needed for two horse chariots. There were 250 towers 60 fathoms high, or 60 cubits as the later writers say. (5) There is no need to be surprised that she built so few towers considering the length of the circuit, because most of the city area lay beside marshy ground where it was decided not to erect towers when the difficult terrain offered sufficient protection in itself. A road 200 feet wide ran along the whole distance between the houses and the wall.

8] To encourage speedy construction she assigned one stade to each of her friends, providing sufficient money and ordering each to complete his task in one year. (2) She rewarded those who carried out their assignments with particular zeal. She herself built a bridge 5 stades long over the narrowest part of the river, skillfully driving piles deep down and at 12-foot intervals. She clamped the stones together with iron tenons, and poured molten lead into the joints. In front of the piles on the sides facing the current she built cutwaters, rounded for the water to run off, and gradually contracted to the width of the piles, so that the sharp edges of the cutwaters would yield to its force and tame the violence of the stream. (3) The bridge was covered over with beams of cypress and cedar and even with the trunks of enormous palm trees to a width of 30 feet, so that Semiramis' work was second to none in the skill with which it was constructed. On each side of the river she built up a splendid embankment extending for 160 stades and with a width corresponding to that of the falls. She also built duplicate palaces by the river at either side of the bridge, which were intended for purposes of observation and control, the keys as it were to the most important parts of the city. (4) Since the Euphrates runs through the middle of Babylon and flows towards the south, one of the palaces faced east, the other west, but both were characterized by their magnificence. The part that lay towards the west was built with an outer perimeter of 60 stades and with lofty and imposing walls strengthened with baked bricks. But she built another circular wall inside this one, where all sorts of animals were depicted, their real life colors skillfully reproduced on unbaked brick. (5) This circuit was 40 stades long and 300 bricks thick; according to CTESIAS the height was 50 fathoms, while the towers rose to a height of 70 fathoms. (6) She then made still a third wall inside this one, which surrounded the citadel and which had a perimeter of 20 stades with the height and width of the masonry surpassing that of the middle wall. There were great numbers of animals depicted on the towers and on the walls, in color and with lifelike imitation of the originals. The whole represented a hunting scene crowded with all sorts of game animals over 4 cubits long. Semiramis was shown on horseback piercing a leopard with her spear, while nearby her husband Ninus was smiting a lion with his spear at close range. (7) And she set up triple gates, two of which were bronze and opened mechanically. This palace far surpassed the one on the other side of the river, both in size and ornateness, for the other was enclosed by a baked brick wall of only 30 stades. Instead of animal figures it contained bronze statues of

Ninus, Semiramis and their lieutenants as well as a statue of Zeus, whom the Babylonians call Bel. Battle scenes and various kinds of hunts were also depicted, furnishing a diversity of enjoyment to viewers.

9] Next she picked out the lowest part of Babylonia and there dug a square, 300 stades on each side. She made it of baked bricks and asphalt to a depth of 35 feet. (2) Diverting the river into this square, she built a tunnel from one palace to the other. She made the vaults on both sides of baked bricks bound together with asphalt smeared on to form a coating 4 cubits thick. The walls of the tunnel were twenty bricks thick, and the height, not counting the vault, was 12 feet, the width 15. (3) After seven days, in which this work was completed, she turned back the river into its former course, so that though the stream flowed above the tunnel, Semiramis could cross over from one palace to the palace on the other side without crossing the river. She also constructed bronze gates at either end of the tunnel, gates which lasted down to the Persian empire. (4) Next, in the heart of the city she built a temple for Zeus, whom we mentioned is called Bel by the Babylonians. Writers disagree about this temple, but it is impossible to find out the truth since the building has been destroyed by time. Admittedly, however, it was very tall. In it the Chaldaeans recorded their observations of the stars, accurately noting their risings and settings, thanks to the height of the building. (5) The entire building was elaborately constructed of asphalt and baked brick. At the top of the stairway she set up three images wrought in gold, of Zeus, Hera and Rhea. Of these Zeus was standing and striding forward, 40 feet high, and weighing 1,000 Babylonian talents. Rhea was seated on a golden pillow, and her statue was of the same weight as the preceding one. At her knees stood two lions and nearby were two enormous serpents wrought in silver, each weighing 30 talents. (6) Hera's was a standing figure weighing 700 talents, holding a snake by the head in her right hand and a gem-encrusted scepter in her left. (7) For all these in common there was a table wrought in gold, 40 feet by 15 and weighing 500 talents. On the table were two drinking cups weighing 30 talents. (8) And there were the same number of censers, each weighing 300 talents. There were also three golden bowls, of which Zeus' weighed 1,200 Babylonian talents and each of the others 600 talents. (9) But these things were later plundered by the Persian kings. Of the palaces and other buildings some were looted and others entirely destroyed by time. And today only a small part of Babylon is inhabited, most of the area inside the walls being farm land.

* * *

16] When Semiramis had regulated affairs in Ethiopia she returned to Asiatic Bactra with her army. Since her army was large and since she had remained at peace for a long time she was desirous of accomplishing something notable in war. (2) When she learned that the Indians were the most populous nation in the world, and that they occupied the largest and finest territory she decided to march into India, which was ruled then by Stabrobates with innumerable soldiers. He also possessed a very large number of elephants superlatively well trained for the terrors of war. (3) India is an extraordinarily beautiful land traversed by many rivers, and well watered throughout. It yields two crops every year, and supplies such an abundance of provisions that the inhabitants always enjoy inexhaustible supplies of food. It is said the climate is so propitious that there has never been a crop failure let alone a famine. (4) It produces an unheard of number of elephants which are far superior to the Libyan variety in courage and bodily strength. Likewise there are gold, silver, iron and copper. In addition there are quantities of all sorts of precious stones in India, and just about anything else contributing to luxury and wealth. Although Semiramis had heard only a part of this, still she was persuaded to make war on the Indians, who had not previously committed any offense. (5) Perceiving that she would need overwhelming forces she sent out messengers to all the satrapies ordering the *eparchs* to enlist the pick of the young men in numbers proportionate to the size of the district. She also ordered them to provide new armor and to appear with all the rest in military array at Bactra after the third year. (6) She also sent for ship builders from Phoenicia, Syria, Cyprus and other countries on the sea, ordering them to bring down an unlimited supply of timber, and to manufacture river boats capable of being broken up into sections. (7) Since the Indus River, which marked the boundary of the empire, was the largest in the region, many boats were required for transport and also to guard against the Indians. As there was no timber near the river the vessels had to be transported overland from Bactria. (8) Further, seeing that the lack of elephants was a great handicap she devised a most unusual scheme concerning these beasts, hoping by this means to startle the Indians, who were under the impression that no elephants existed anywhere except for the ones in India. (9) She collected 300,000 head of black cattle, then distributed their carcasses among the craftsmen and others who knew how to make things. She had them stitch hides together and stuff them with fodder, moulding them into exact replicas of elephants. Inside each dummy elephant was a man, to manipulate it, and a camel. When carried by a camel the dummy looked just like a real elephant to anyone who saw it from a distance. (10) The workmen who made these contrivances for her were kept under constant guard inside a walled enclosure with gates, to prevent any of the workmen from getting outside or anyone from the outside from getting in where the workmen were. She did this to stop anyone else from finding out what she was doing, lest a report about it might reach the Indians.

17] The ships and the beasts were finished within two years, so in the third year she summoned her forces to Bactria from all directions. According to the writings of CTESIAS the Cnidian the assembled armies amounted to 3,000,000 infantry, 200,000 cavalry and 100,000 chariots. (2) In addition the number of men riding camels equalled the number of chariots, and they carried swords 4 cubits long. She constructed 2,000 river boats in sections, the hulls being transported overland by camel. Likewise, as has been pointed out, camels bore the counterfeit elephants. The soldiers led their horses alongside to overcome their fear of these terrifying beasts. (3) Perseus the king of Macedon did something like this many years later when he was about to engage the Romans with their Libyan elephants. But all his ingenuity in contriving them failed to turn the war in his favor, just as it failed with Semiramis. (4) When the Indian king, Stabrobates, heard of the size of the aforementioned forces and of their excellent military preparations he was eager to surpass Semiramis in everything. (5) First he constructed 4,000 river boats out of reeds. India produces vast numbers of reeds along the river and in marshy places, reeds so thick a man can hardly grasp them. It is also said that reed vessels are remarkably durable because their wood will not rot. (6) Devoting great attention to the manufacture of arms and traversing the whole of India, he gathered together an army many times as large as the army of Semiramis. (7) In an elephant hunt he captured wild elephants in numbers many times the elephants he had before, and then equipped them magnificently with trappings calculated to terrify in warfare. (8) The result was that the towers they carried and their great numbers gave them the appearance of being beyond the powers of human beings to resist.

18] When his warlike preparations were complete he sent messengers to Semiramis, who was already on the move, upbraiding her for starting war without any provocation. He also reviled her in unmentionable language as a whore, calling on the gods as his witnesses that after victory he would nail her to a cross. (2) But Semiramis laughed when she read his letter, saying the Indian would find out about her courage by her deeds. When she reached the Indus with her forces she found the enemy fleet prepared for battle. (3) Thereupon she immediately put together her own ships, embarked the picked crews and began a naval action on the Indus, while the land forces, drawn up on the bank, lent them encouragement. (4) In the end Semiramis was victorious but only after a prolonged battle in which each side made a strong fight of it. She destroyed about 1,000 ships and took no small number of prisoners. (5) Puffed up with success she made slaves of the inhabitants of the river island cities and took more than 100,000 prisoners. The Indian king, meanwhile, withdrew his army from the river, pretending to fly in panic, but actually hoping to induce the enemy to cross the river. (6) And in point of fact, when Semiramis saw things going according to plan she constructed a long and elaborate pontoon bridge across the river. Leaving a guard of 60,000 men behind, she moved the rest of the army across the bridge and led them on against the Indians. In front were the dummy elephants, so that enemy scouts would tell the king she had a multitude of elephants. (7) And in this she was not deceived, for the Indian scouts reported the great numbers of elephants, and everyone was puzzled to explain where this vast assemblage of beasts had come from. (8) But the ruse did not remain undetected for long. Some of Semiramis' soldiers who had been remiss in night guard duty at camp, were so afraid of their impending punishment that they deserted to the enemy, and told them about the elephant hoax. Heartened by this news the Indian monarch told his soldiers about the dummy elephants, then turned back and drew his army up in line of battle against the Assyrians.

19] Semiramis followed suit, and when the armies approached one another Stabrobates, the King of the Indians, sent his cavalry and chariotry out ahead of the phalanx. (2) As the queen was bravely awaiting the cavalry attack with her dummy elephants posted at equal intervals in front of the phalanx, the Indian horses turned in panic. (3) From the distance the dummies resembled real elephants, so the Indian horses which were used to elephants came on with a will. But when they got close, the unaccustomed smell and other differences completely terrified the horses. As a consequence some of the Indians were thrown to the ground, while others were carried over intact inside the enemy lines when the horses refused to be guided by the reins. (4) Meanwhile, leading a picked body of soldiers, Semiramis took full advantage of this success and drove the Indians back. But when they reached the phalanx in their flight, King Stabrobates was undismayed. He brought up regiments of infantry preceded by elephants. Riding the largest elephant into battle on the right wing he advanced menacingly against the queen, who happened to be posted opposite him. (5) The rest of the elephants followed, and for a short time Semiramis' army resisted the onslaught of these beasts. But the elephants were very powerful. Confident in their own strength they easily overpowered anyone who tried to resist them. (6) Therefore, the slaughter was great and varied, some being trampled underfoot, others ripped up by the elephants' tusks, still others tossed on their trunks. The growing heap of the slain and the impending danger struck terror into those who beheld it. No one dared maintain his place in the ranks. (7) As the entire host turned in flight the Indian monarch pressed on after Semiramis. First drawing his bow, he hit her in the arm; then he hurled his javelin, striking the queen on the back with a glancing blow. But Semiramis was not seriously hurt and she soon got away on horseback, the pursuing elephant being much slower. (8) When the mass of fugitives reached the float there was such a crowding of people in a narrow space, that the queen's men caused one another's death, being trampled underfoot. The footsoldiers and the cavalry were unnaturally crowded together, while the Indians kept pressing them. There was a mighty rush for the bridge, inspired by terror, which resulted in many men being pushed off both sides into the river. (9) As soon as Semiramis had crossed the river safely with the majority of the survivors of the battle, she cut the cables. Thereupon the floating bridge was broken up into many separate sections, and the crowd of pursuing Indians on the bridge were caught, just as they were, by the swift current, and many of them destroyed. This was Semiramis' salvation, for it prevented the enemy from crossing over to attack her. (10) After this there were divine omens which the soothsayers interpreted as a sign not to cross the river, so the

Indian ruler called a halt. After exchanging prisoners Semiramis returned to Bactra, having lost two-thirds of her army.

20] Some time later, when she was informed by a eunuch that her son Ninyas was conspiring against her she remembered the oracle of Ammon. Instead of harming the conspirator in any way she turned the kingdom over to him and ordered her governors to accept his orders. She herself soon disappeared, as though translated to the gods in fulfillment of the oracle. (2) Some mythologers maintain she was turned into a dove, and that when a flock of birds flew down into her house, she flew away with them. For this reason the Assyrians honor the dove as sacred, and pay divine honors to Semiramis. Thus after ruling over all of Asia except India she died in the manner indicated above after living for sixty-two years and ruling for forty-two. This is the account of Semiramis given by CTESIAS of Cnidus.

*　　*　　*

23] Sardanapallus, the thirtieth king after Ninus established the Assyrian rule, was also the last. He outdid all his predecessors in luxury and frivolity, for not only were no outsiders allowed to see him, but he even lived like a woman. He spent his time with his concubines, spinning the finest purple-dyed wool while clad in a woman's robes. He painted his face, his entire body in fact, with white lead and other preparations courtesans employ, to make his skin softer than that of the most delicate women. He also affected a woman's voice. (2) At banquets not only did he partake of food and drink specially designed to prolong the pleasure, but he surrendered himself to the delights of both male and female love. He used both forms of intercourse without restraint, not troubling himself in the least over the shamefulness of his actions. (3) He reached such a pitch of luxury and shameless unbridled pleasure that he composed an elegy for himself which he ordered his successor to inscribe on his tomb after he died. While he wrote this in barbarian speech, some Greek later on translated it thus:

> Know well thou art mortal, gratify thy desires,
> Rejoice in merry-making. There is no profit after thou art dead.
> For I am but dust, though king of mighty Nineveh.
> All I keep are food, insolence and love,
> From which I received pleasure. The multitude of other possessions are meaningless.

(4) Such behavior not only brought about his own shameful death, but also finally ended the Assyrian rule, which had endured longer than any other recorded empire.

24] There was a certain Arbaces, a Mede, renowned for his valor and greatness of soul, who was the general commanding the annual contingent sent to Nineveh from Media. During his tour of duty he made friends with the Babylonian general, who exhorted him to overthrow the Assyrian dominion. (2) The general's name was Belesys, and he was the most distinguished of the priests called "Chaldaeans" by the Babylonians. His great skill in astrology and divination enabled him to make infallible predictions to people about what was going to happen. With this reputation, he informed his friend the Median general that he would rule the whole empire then held by Sardanapallus. (3) Arbaces praised the man, and promised to appoint him satrap of Babylonia when this prediction came true. He himself, as though elevated by divine ordinance, set out to win support from the leaders of the other nations. He cultivated all of them assiduously at banquets and meetings, establishing friendship with each. (4) But he wanted to see the king with his own eyes and, in general, to spy out the kind of life he led. Accordingly, after bribing one of the eunuchs with a gold cup he was introduced to Sardanapallus. When he had learned the truth about his effeminate pursuits he came to feel contempt for such an unworthy king, and was even more determined to embrace the prospects held out to him by the Chaldaean. (5) Finally he and Belesys made a sworn agreement, according to which he was to incite the Medes and Persians to revolt, while Belesys was to persuade the Babylonians to join in the undertaking as well as to induce his friend the Arab leader to take part in the attack. (6) When the period of one year's military service came to an end and another army was on the way, the previous forces were sent to their respective homes as usual. Then it was that Arbaces persuaded the Medes to attack the empire, and also induced the Persians to join in leading the fight for liberty. Likewise Belesys persuaded the Babylonians to strike for freedom, and by means of messengers sent to Arabia he also induced the leader of that people, who was his guest friend, to take part in the attack. (7) As the year ended all of these gathered together a multitude of soldiers whom they led en masse to Nineveh, ostensibly to furnish next year's contingent as was customary, but actually with the object of destroying the Assyrian dominion. (8) When the troops of the four nations mentioned above were assembled in one place their numbers reached a total of 400,000 men. Forming a single camp they consulted together for their common advantage.

25] As soon as Sardanapallus learned of the revolt he led the troops from the other nations out against them. In the first battle, which took place on the plain, the rebels got the worst of it, being driven back into the mountains some 70 stades from Nineveh with severe losses. (2) But afterwards, when they marched down once more to offer battle in the plain, Sardanapallus, drawing up his own army opposite them, sent heralds to the enemy camp with the following proclamation: "Sardanapallus will give 200 talents of gold to anyone who slays Arbaces the Mede, but to anyone who brings him in alive he will pay twice that sum and also make him governor of Media." (3) Similar rewards were offered anyone who would kill or capture Belesys the Babylonian. When the proclamation was ignored battle was joined. Again there was a slaughter of the rebels whom Sardanapallus chased back to their camp in the mountains. (4) Discouraged by these defeats Arbaces called a council of his allies and asked their advice on what should be done. (5) Most of them advised returning to their native lands, occupying the strong places there, and taking other necessary measures to prepare for invasion. But Belesys the Babylonian said the gods had given signs that after hardship and suffering they would attain their goal in the end. He also encouraged them in every other way he could and persuaded all of them to wait and take their chances. (6) In still a third battle the king was victorious again, capturing the camp of the rebels and pursuing the vanquished all the way to the Babylonian border. It happened, also, that Arbaces himself was wounded by the Assyrians after fighting bravely and slaying many men. (7) After such a series of defeats the rebel leaders lost all hope of victory and prepared to disperse to their respective countries. (8) Belesys, however, after spending a sleepless night in the fields watching the stars, told those who despaired of their cause that if they would only wait five days help would come to them automatically, and there would be a complete shift in their fortunes to the opposite direction. He said he knew the gods intended these things by his knowledge of the stars, and he begged them to stay that many days to make trial of his skill and of the benevolence of the gods.

26] When everyone had agreed and waited the prescribed time there came a man announcing that an army sent to the king from

Bactria was near at hand and marching rapidly. (2) Now Arbaces decided to intercept them as soon as possible with their generals, taking along the best, especially the swiftest, soldiers to explore the possibility of persuading the Bactrians to share their dangers by a show of force, even though they could not succeed by reasoning with them. (3) At first only the leaders favored the cause of freedom, but finally the whole army agreed, so they all camped together in one place. (4) Now it chanced that the Assyrian king, elated by his earlier victories and ignorant of the Bactrian defection, turned to relaxation. Animals for sacrifice, and great quantities of wine and other comestibles were distributed among the soldiers for a feast. So the entire army held a celebration. But when Arbaces heard about the drinking and laxity in the enemy camp through deserters, he made a surprise attack during the night. (5) Prepared as they were they threw themselves in battle formation against disorganized troops, who were not expecting them. They captured the camp, after slaughtering many, and pursued the remainder all the way to the city. (6) After that the king turned over the army to his wife's brother, Salaemenes, while he gave his own attention to the city. The rebels drew up their forces in the plain in front of the city, and defeated the Assyrians in two battles. Salaemenes was slain, and of the others some were killed in the pursuit, while the rest, cut off from the road back to the city, threw themselves into the Euphrates, where all but a few were drowned. (7) The dead were carried away in such numbers that for a considerable distance the river was dyed the color of blood. After that, when the king was besieged many peoples revolted, each deserting to obtain liberty. (8) Now when Sardanapallus saw his whole kingdom in the greatest peril he sent away his three sons and two daughters with ample funds to Cotta (?) the Paphlagonian governor and his most loyal subject. Meanwhile he himself sent messengers to all his subjects for reinforcements, and prepared to stand a siege. (9) An oracle had been handed down to him by his ancestors to the effect that no one would take Nineveh by force unless first the river became hostile to the city. Since he thought this could never happen he remained hopeful, planning to undergo a siege while waiting for the armies sent out by his subjects.

27] Elated by their victories the rebels turned their attention to the siege, but they were unable to damage the city in any way because the walls were so strong. In those days catapults, protective screens for besiegers and rams for overthrowing fortifications had not yet been developed. The men in the city had abundant supplies of everything they needed, thanks to the advance preparations made by the king to meet this contingency. As a result the siege was prolonged, and for two years they pressed the attack, assailing the battlements and depriving the inhabitants of access to the country outside. But in the third year there was a succession of very heavy rains which caused the Euphrates to rise high and flood part of the city, destroying 20 stades of the wall. (2) Then, thinking the oracle had been fulfilled with the river an avowed enemy of the city, the king gave up hopes of survival. To avoid falling into the hands of the enemy, he built a huge pyre inside the palace, heaping all his gold and silver and all the royal robes on top. Then he constructed a chamber in the middle of the pyre in which he confined his concubines and eunuchs, burning himself along with them and with the palace. (3) When the rebels learned of the destruction of Sardanapallus they occupied the city, forcing their way in over the ruined part of the wall. Investing Arbaces with royal robes they proclaimed him king, putting him in control of everything.

28] Then when the king was distributing rewards to his comrades in order of merit and appointing satraps over the nations, Belesys the Babylonian, the man who had prophesied he would be King of Asia, approached him. He reminded him of his services and asked for the rule of Babylon as he had been promised earlier. (2) He also revealed that during the fighting he himself had made a vow to Bel that when Sardanapallus had been conquered and the palace burned down, he would transport the ashes to Babylon near the temple of the god. There he would erect a mound to serve as an everlasting monument of the overthrow of the Assyrian dominion. (3) He made this request because he had learned about the silver and gold from one of the eunuchs who had taken refuge with him after running away, and whom he had kept in hiding. (4) But Arbaces, who knew nothing about this because the palace and everything in it had been burned along with the king, permitted him to transport the ashes and to hold Babylon without tribute. Thereupon Belesys brought up boats and immediately dispatched most of the gold and silver to Babylon along with the ashes. But he was caught in the act and the king appointed his fellow generals to act as his judges. (5) Since he had been caught and admitted his wrongdoing the tribunal condemned him to die. But the king was generous, and also he wished the beginning of his reign to be an auspicious one. So he released

Belesys from his peril, even letting him keep the gold and silver he had removed. Nor did he deprive him of the powers he originally promised him in Babylon, for he said the services he had performed earlier outweighed his later injuries. (6) When his magnanimous behavior was known he won the good will and admiration of the nations, for they all felt that a man who rose superior to his injuries was indeed worthy of empire. (7) Treating the men in the city with moderation Arbaces settled them in villages, allowing each to keep his own property, but he levelled the city with the ground. And then he carried off the gold and silver left outside the pyre, amounting to many talents, to Median Ecbatana.

(8) Thus it was that the Assyrian empire, which had lasted for thirty generations after Ninus and for more than 1,300 years, was destroyed in this manner by the Medes.

15

A Sentimental Appraisal of Alexander the Great

THE DISAPPEARANCE of all the contemporary histories of Alexander, except as they survive in phrases cited more or less inexactly by later writers, has permitted a variety of judgments on the Macedonian conqueror. His character has been molded to suit the changed ideals of each successive age. One of these judgments is given here in the De Alexandri Magni Fortuna aut Virtute of Plutarch of Chaeronea, a gentle soul who lived during the late first and early second centuries of our era. This youthful estimate is quite different from that in the well-known "Life" Plutarch composed in later years. It is a rhetorical exercise designed to answer the question: "Did Alexander owe his success to Luck?" in the negative. It is included here because it has been used by the late Sir William Tarn to support an interpretation of Alexander more widely known than any other to the English-speaking community.

Plutarch, De Alex. Magni Fortuna aut Virtute, Oratio i

1] NOW FORTUNE argues that Alexander belongs to her and to her alone. However, this ought to be denied in the name of philosophy and even more so because of the wrath and indignation of Alexander at the notion that he received as a gift of Fortune that empire which he purchased with a copious expenditure of his blood and repeated wounds,

> "And many sleepless nights he spent
> And bloody days consumed while making war,"[1]

contending with invincible forces, nations without number, impassable rivers, and rocks above the range of bow and arrow, helped only by good judgment, perseverance, courage and self-control.

2] And I imagine he might address Fortune when she claimed these deeds for herself in these words: "Do not depreciate my honor, or strip me of my fame. Darius was your work, the slave and royal courier whom you made ruler of the Persians; or Sardanapalus the carder of purple wool on whom you placed the diadem of empire. But I entered Susa as a victor after Arbela, and Cilicia opened the road to Egypt for me as Granicus, which I crossed using the bodies of Mithridates and Spithridates as a bridge, did to Cilicia. Plume yourself with pride at kings untouched by blood or wounds, for they were fortunate, at Ochus and at Artaxerxes whom you placed on the throne of Cyrus as soon as they were born. But my body bears many indications that Fortune was my adversary, not my ally. First I was struck in the head by a stone and clubbed on the neck in the Illyrian land. Later, at the Granicus, my head was broken by the lone knife of a barbarian, and at Issus my thigh was gashed with a sword. Before Gaza my ankle was pierced by an arrow, when I fell heavily, dislocating my shoulder. At Maracanda my shin was broken by an arrow. Then came blows and the ravages of famine in the Indian lands. Among the Aspasians I was shot in the shoulder by an arrow; in the land of the Gandridae in the leg; among the Malli a missile from a bow reached me, burying its iron point in my breast, and when I had also been struck by a club along the neck, the ladders that had been raised against the walls gave way, and Fortune, taking delight in such a deed, penned me up there alone, not to contend with famous adversaries but with unknown barbarians. And if Ptolemy had not covered me with his shield and if Limnaeus had not died in front of me after intercepting countless missiles, and if the Macedonians had not torn down the walls in their rage, then that nameless barbarian village would have been Alexander's tomb."

3] And in this same expedition gales, droughts, deep rivers, rocks higher than a bird can fly, monstrous beasts, savage customs, a succession of petty rulers and constant betrayals were also encountered. But even before the expedition itself, Greece fought back after the ways of Philip. The Thebans shook the dust of Chaeronea from their weapons, rising up after disaster while Athens extended a helping hand. All Macedon was ripe for rebellion, looking secretly to Amyntas and the sons of Aeropus. The Illyrians erupted and the state of affairs in Scythia threatened her troubled neighbors. Persian gold, diffused in every direction by popular orators, stirred up the Peloponnese. Philip's treasury was empty and there was even a deficit of two hundred talents, as Onesicritus relates. With such an appalling lack of money and with the government still in confusion a young man just barely beyond boyhood had the audacity to entertain thoughts of Babylon and Susa, and even of an empire embracing all mankind — and this, mind you, with 30,000 foot and 4,000 horse. Those at least are the figures given by Aristobulus; according to King Ptolemy there were 30,000 foot and 5,000 horse, while Anaximenes gives 43,500 foot and 5,500 horse. The great and magnificent sum which Fortune had provided for his travelling chest was 70 talents, as Aristobulus tells it, but Duris says he had only supplies for thirty days.

4] Then Alexander must have been an unthinking hothead to challenge such a formidable power with his meagre resources? Not at all. Did anyone ever start out for war with greater or better preparation for succeeding than nobility of character, intelligence, self-mastery and courage — with which philosophy had equipped him for his journey? He crossed over against the Persians with greater resources furnished by his teacher Aristotle than by his father Philip. In fact there are writers who allege that Alexander once said that he had brought the *Iliad* and the *Odyssey* along as provision for the army; and we believe them, honoring Homer. And if anyone maintains that he only used Homer for relaxation after toil and as a pleasant way of diverting his leisure moments, but that his real provision for the journey lay in the philosophic doctrines, in discourses on fearlessness and valor, on self-mastery and on high-mindedness we look on this with scorn. For obviously Alexander wrote nothing about syllogisms or propositions, and he never held forth in the Lyceum or presented a thesis for debate in the Academy, while such a view would restrict philosophy to things of this sort as though it were made up of words rather than deeds. Yet there were famous philosophers like Pythagoras, or Socrates, or Arcesilaus or Carneades who wrote nothing. And these men were not occupied with such great wars, or civilizing barbarian princes, or establishing Greek cities among savage peoples, nor did they continue pressing on against lawless and ignorant tribes in order to instruct them in law and peace. Instead, though they did have the time, they abandoned writing to the sophists. Then why are they believed to have been philosophers? Because of what they said, how they lived and what they taught. Then let Alexander be judged on the same basis and he will be revealed as a philosopher by what he said, by what he did and by what he taught.

5] But first and, if you will, most surprising, look at Alexander's pupils and compare them with those of Socrates and Plato. Now they were teaching adaptable scholars who spoke the same language, for even if they knew nothing else they all understood Greek. Despite this, there were many of them whom they failed to convince: the Critiases, Alcibiadeses and Clitophons went astray, spitting out their doctrines as a horse gets rid of a bit. But then look at Alexander's instruction: he taught marriage to the Hyrcanians, he showed the Arachosians how to farm, he persuaded the Sogdianians to support their fathers instead of killing them, and induced the Persians to respect their mothers and not to marry them. What an admirable philosophy, which caused the Indians to bow down before the gods of Greece, the Scythians to bury their dead instead of devouring them! We are astonished at the ability of Carneades if he hellenizes Clitomachus, who was a Carthaginian by birth formerly named Hasdrubal, and we also admire Zeno for his skill if he induces Diogenes of Babylon to become a philosopher. But thanks to Alexander Homer was read in Asia, and the sons of Persia, Susiana, and Gedrosia sang the choruses of Euripides and Sophocles. Now Socrates was brought to judgment for introducing foreign gods by informers in Athens, but Alexander caused Bactra and the Caucasus to worship the gods of Greece. While Plato drew up a single form of government which was so strict he could induce no one to adopt it, Alexander, by founding more than seventy cities among the barbarian tribes, and seeding Asia with Greek outposts, suppressed their savage and uncivilized customs. Although a few of us read about the laws of Plato, countless numbers have adopted and continue to use the laws of Alexander. Those whom Alexander conquered were more fortunate than those who escaped, because there was no one to correct their foolish way of life, while the conqueror forced his subjects to live in prosperity. Therefore Themistocles' remark when he received munificent gifts from the king during his exile and obtained three tribute-paying cities — one to furnish him with grain, one with wine and the other with condiments: "O my children, had we not been ruined, we would have been ruined indeed!" — was a remark that might have been made even more appropriately by those whom Alexander conquered. For they would not have been civilized unless they had been conquered. And Egypt would not have had its Alexandria, or Mesopotamia its Seleuceia, or India its Bucephalia, nor would the Caucasus have had a Greek city founded there, yet it is by means of such cities that savagery is gradually extinguished and bad customs changed into good ones. Now if philosophers really set such great store by refining and altering rough and ignorant dispositions then Alexander, who is seen transforming countless races and natural savages, ought truly to be regarded as a very great philosopher.

6] Now the much-admired *Republic* of Zeno, the founder of the Stoic school, adds up to this one thing: that we ought not to live in cities or in demes, each distinguished by its own regulations, but we should look on all men as fellow citizens and demesmen, having one life and one world, feeding together like a single herd sharing a common pasture. Zeno, however, wrote this as a dream, a philosophic image of a well-governed state, while Alexander expressed his views by deeds. He did not follow Aristotle's advice to treat the Greeks as a leader, the barbarians as a master, cultivating the former as friends and kinsmen, and treating the latter as animals or plants. Had he done so his kingdom would have been filled with warfare, banishments and secret plots, but he regarded himself as divinely sent to mediate and govern the world. And those whom he failed to win over by persuasion he overpowered in arms, bringing them together from every land, combining, as it were in a loving cup, their lives, customs, marriages and manner of living; he bade them all look on the inhabited world as their native land, on his camp as their citadel and protection, on good men as their kinsmen and evil doers as aliens, and not to distinguish Greek from barbarian by the chlamys, or the shield, or the sword, or the sleeved tunic but to associate Hellenism with virtue and barbarism with evil doing; and to regard their clothing, food, marriages and manners as common to all, blended together by their blood and their children.

7] Now Demaratus of Corinth, the mercenary and a friend of Philip's, wept tears of joy when he saw Alexander in Susa, exclaiming that those Greeks who had died earlier had been robbed of great happiness since they had not seen Alexander sitting on Darius' throne. But I, by Zeus, do not envy those who saw a spectacle which is associated with Fortune and lesser kings, but I think I would have been more pleased at the fair and blessed sight of the marriage procession when, bringing together one hundred Persian brides and one hundred Greek and Macedonian grooms into a single tent bedecked with gold, with a single hearth and a single table, he was the first, crowned with flowers, to raise the hymeneal song, singing as it were a song of friendship, while he joined together the greatest and most powerful peoples into one community by wedlock: the bridegroom of one, but for everyone at once a bride-giver, a father and a sponsor. I would gladly have said: "O barbarous and foolish Xerxes, your great efforts in putting a bridge across the Hellespont were wasted, for intelligent rulers do not join Asia to Europe in this way with planks, or floats or lifeless and unfeeling fetters; but they unite the races by true laws, and chaste marriages and common offspring."

8] With a view to adornment Alexander did not adopt the Median but the Persian dress, which is much simpler than the Median. Rejecting the bizarre and dramatic aspects of barbarian dress — such as the tiara, the long-sleeved cloak and the trousers —, he wore a garment which combined Persian and Macedonian features, as Eratosthenes has recorded. Like a philosopher he regarded these things as neither good nor bad, but as their common leader and benevolent ruler he won the goodwill of his subjects by honoring their dress, so that they would become firmly attached to their Macedonian rulers instead of hating them as their enemies. On the other hand, only a fool or a madman would admire the chlamys of one and the same color yet despise the purple-bordered tunic, or again, to despise some things and be filled with admiration for others, or like a silly child cling to the garments in which ancestral custom has swaddled him like a nurse. Men who hunt wild animals clothe themselves in deerskin, and when fowling they wear tunics with flaps; they also take care not to be seen wearing red tunics by bulls or with white ones by elephants, because these animals are wont to be driven into a rage by these colors. But when a great king, propitiating and mollifying unruly and warlike races as one tames wild animals, has managed to appease and placate them by adopting a dress and manner resembling their own, calming their resentment and brightening their sullen looks, why is he censured? Why do they not admire him for the wisdom with which, by a slight change in dress, he made himself popular in Asia, winning over by his costume the souls of those whose bodies he had already conquered in arms? Yet Aristippus the Socratic is admired because he looked like a gentleman whether he was wearing a threadbare cloak or the finest Milesian robe. But still they find fault with Alexander because, while very fond of his ancestral dress, he did not disdain that of the conquered, in laying the foundation of a great empire. For he did not cross Asia like a robber, nor did he have it in mind to ravage and despoil it for the booty and loot presented by such an unheard of stroke of fortune — the way Hannibal treated Italy later on, or the way the Treres acted earlier in Ionia or the Scythians in Media. Instead he conducted himself as he did out of a desire to subject all the races in the world to one rule and one form of government, making all mankind a single people. Had not the divinity that sent Alexander recalled his soul so soon, there would have been a single law, as it were, watching over all mankind, and all men would have looked to one form of justice as their common source of light. But now, that portion of the world that never beheld Alexander has remained as if deprived of the sun.

9] Now at the outset, the very purpose of his expedition commends the man as a philosopher for aiming not at wealth and luxury for himself but at bringing peace, harmony and mutual fellowship to all men. Secondly, let us examine what he said, since other kings and rulers reveal their character by the spirit of their pronouncements. When a certain sophist presented him with a treatise on justice, the elder Antigonus remarked: "You are a fool to prate to me about justice when you see me molesting the cities of others." The tyrant Dionysius used to say that children should be cheated with dice, men with oaths. And the tomb of Sardanapalus contains the following inscription: "I possess only what I have eaten and the lusts I have satisfied." On the basis of these sayings, would anyone fail to attribute injustice and greed to the first, impiety to the second, or voluptuousness to the third? But Alexander's sayings, once you separate them from his crown, and Ammon and his high birth, strike you like those of Socrates, or Plato or Pythagoras. For we will not count the grandiloquent words carved on portraits and statues of him by poets, not to call attention to his moderation but to his power:

> The bronze figure, looking at Zeus, seems to say:
> "Zeus, I will take care of the world, you look after Olympus!"

And also Alexander's, "I am the son of Zeus." For, as I pointed out, the poets invented these things, paying court to his good fortune. But in relating the sayings of Alexander we might begin with the youthful ones. He was a swifter runner than any young man of his age, and when his companions urged him on to the Olympics, he asked them whether there were kings competing. When they replied that there were not, he said it would not be a fair contest in which, if he won, he won over private citizens, while if he lost, he would be defeated as a king. When his father Philip was pierced in the thigh by a spear in the Triballi country, he escaped the danger of death but was grieved over being made lame. "Be of good cheer, Father," he said, "and show yourself in public. Every step you take will testify to your valor!" Are not these the thoughts of a philosopher, combating the weaknesses of the flesh with an enthusiasm for brave deeds? How do you imagine he would have delighted in his own wounds, each reminding him of a particular people and a victory, of the taking of cities and the surrender of kings — not hiding his scars but wearing them like graven images of his virtue and his bravery?

10] Also, when Homeric verses were being compared by way of diversion or on some convivial occasion, when each in turn selects a line, then he would always choose this verse in preference to any other:

Both a good king and a mighty warrior.[2]

This praise which another had gained in an earlier age, he regarded as a pattern established for himself, so that he said Homer had embellished the virtues of Agamemnon and prophesied those of Alexander in the same verse. In fact when he had crossed the Hellespont he surveyed the site of Troy, seeing the heroic deeds in his mind's eye. And one of the natives promised that if he so desired he would give him the very lyre of Paris, but he replied: "I do not need his lyre for I have the one with which Achilles used to play when he paused to refresh himself, and sang of the deeds of heroes"; but Paris' lyre played only languid and effeminate love songs. Now it is the mark of a philosophic soul to love wisdom and to admire wise men above all else. This was a trait possessed by Alexander to a degree unmatched by any other king. His relations with Aristotle have already been mentioned, and it is also said that he included Aristarchus among his most valued friends. When he first met Pyrrho of Elis he gave him 10,000 gold pieces, and he sent Xenocrates, Plato's friend, a gift of 50 talents. Many writers have related that he appointed Onesicritus, the pupil of Diogenes the Cynic, as his Chief Pilot. When he talked to Diogenes himself, in Corinth, he was so captivated and overwhelmed by the man's way of life and reputation that he would often refer to him later, saying: "If I were not Alexander, I would like to be Diogenes!" By this he meant: "I would have devoted myself to philosophic discussion, if I had not been a philosopher of deeds." But he did not say: "If I were not a king, I would like to be Diogenes"; still less: "If I had not been rich and an Argead" — for he did not prefer fortune to wisdom, nor the purple and the diadem to the threadbare cloak and wallet. But this is what he said: "If I were not Alexander, I would like to be Diogenes," by which he meant: "If I did not intend to blend the customs of the Greeks and the barbarians; to cross every continent and tame it; to search out the farthest points of land and sea; to make Ocean the boundary of Macedon; and if I did not mean to transplant the peace and the justice of Greece to every people, even then I would not waste my energies in useless luxury, but I would emulate the frugality of Diogenes. But now, Diogenes, excuse me. I am imitating Heracles, rivalling Perseus and following in the footsteps of Dionysus, the ancestor of my line. I wish to bring the chorus of victorious Greeks to India once more, and to renew the memory of Bacchic revels among the wild mountainous peoples beyond the Caucasus. And there are said to be holy men in those parts who live under laws of their own, a rough and naked sect devoting their lives to the god. They are even more self-denying than Diogenes, in that they require no wallet, for they do not save any food since the land continually provides them with a fresh supply. Flowing rivers furnish them with drink, trees shed their foliage over them and herbs of the field serve them as a bed. Thanks to me they will come to know of Diogenes, and Diogenes of them. I, too, must coin money, and stamp the form of a Greek constitution on a barbarian mould."

11] Well, then, do his deeds appear to be primarily the result of chance? Power in war? Government by force? Do they not rather suggest the great courage and justice, the great self-control and mildness of one who does everything in an orderly and intelligent manner and in accordance with a sober and sagacious plan? It is not my task, by the gods, to distinguish between them, assigning one of his actions to courage, one to humanity, another to his self-control, for each act was probably compounded of all his virtues, lending force to the Stoic doctrine that the sage exercises every virtue in everything he does. In each separate action a particular virtue probably takes the lead, summoning the rest and urging them on to the goal. Certainly in Alexander his warlike virtue is also seen to be humanitarian; his gentleness to be bravery, his liberality to be good management; his anger to be easily placated; his love to be accompanied by self-control; his relaxation not to be sloth; and his toil not to be without solace. Who else combined festivities with warfare? Revels with a campaign? Bacchic dances, marriages and wedding songs with sieges and battles? Who was more a foe to the unjust or kinder to the unfortunate? Harder on opponents in battle, or more generous to those who asked for mercy? And in this connection I might mention the words of Porus. When he was brought before Alexander as a captive and was asked how he wished to be treated, he replied: "Like a king, Alexander!" When he was asked whether there was not something else, he said: "Nothing, for everything is contained in that phrase 'like a king.'" And I think one might always describe Alexander's deeds as being performed like a philosopher, for that one phrase also includes everything. When he fell in love with Roxana, the daughter of Oxyathres, as she was dancing among the female prisoners, he did not abuse her but took her in marriage, "like a philosopher." On one occasion when he was reading a confidential letter from his mother, and Hephaestion, who happened to be sitting beside him, was quite openly reading the letter with him, Alexander did not stop him, but touching Hephaestion's lips with his ring he sealed him to silence by trusting him as a friend — "like a philosopher." If those are not the actions of a philosopher, then what actions are?

12] Let us compare his actions with those of admitted philosophers. Socrates allowed Alcibiades to share his couch. But when Philoxenus, the Prefect of the Coast, wrote Alexander that there was a boy in Ionia surpassing all others in charm and beauty, and asked Alexander in his letter whether he should send him the boy, he replied tartly: "Vilest of men, what evil have you ever seen in me to make you try to tempt me with such pleasures?" Why do we admire Xenocrates for refusing the 50 talents Alexander sent him as a gift, and yet fail to admire the giver? Or do we not see that the man who offers money shows as much contempt for it as the man who refuses it? Because of his philosophy Xenocrates had no need for money, but Alexander did need it because of his own philosophy, in order to bestow it on men of that kind. How many times Alexander used to make this remark when forcing his way through a hail of javelins! To be sure we believe the knowledge of what is right is implanted in all men, for nature herself leads them to what is good. But philosophers differ from the rest in that their judgment is strengthened and made firm by adversity, and they do not rely on sayings such as: "The one best omen,"[3] and "Death is the end for all men." But in time of peril the reasoning breaks down, and the sight of danger when near at hand destroys the judgment. Not only does terror steal away the memory, as Thucydides says, but all resolution, incitement and effort, unless philosophy binds them with her ropes.

Notes

1. Cf. *Iliad*, IX, 325–326.
2. Cf. *Iliad*, III, 179.
3. I.e., "The one best omen is to fight for one's country"— *Iliad*, XII, 243.

16

A Greek Account of India

UNLIKE Ctesias [14], who wrote the first separate work on India in Greek, Megasthenes had been to India, where he visited the court of Sandracottus (Chandragupta) on the Ganges during the reign of Seleucus I (312–281 B.C.), perhaps as his envoy. He did not rely entirely on his own observation but also made use of the works of his immediate predecessors, men like Onesicritus and Nearchus who had gone to India with Alexander. Like them he probably filled in gaps with gossip picked up on the spot and details borrowed from Ctesias' ever popular storehouse of misinformation. Nevertheless, no better account of India was written after Megasthenes by any classical writer because political developments severed India from direct relations with the Successor Kingdoms. Megasthenes thus remains the high-water mark of Greek knowledge about India, however low that may have been. Nor does India herself have a literature to replace his fragments for this period. The excerpts given here contain our earliest picture of Indian society.

a Strabo, xv, 1, 39-41, 45-49 (Megasthenes)

39] HE SAYS the whole Indian population is divided into seven classes, the philosophers being first in point of honor, though least in numbers. They are made use of individually by anyone who makes a private sacrifice or an offering to the dead, while publicly they are consulted by the kings in the Great Assembly, as it is called, the one at the beginning of the new year, when all the philosophers gather at the royal gates, and each presents in public whatever useful thing he has found or observed useful to crops, or animals or to the government. But whoever is caught three times in a false statement is required by law to remain silent for life, while whoever speaks truly is relieved of all taxes.

40] Second, is the class of the farmers, who are the most numerous and upright, and who are freed from military service, carrying on their work without any fear, never coming into the city for their needs or in time of public disturbance. It happens frequently that in the same time and place men are drawn up to fight against the enemy, while the farmers plough or hoe without risk, having the former as their protectors. All the land belongs to the king, and they work it for one-fourth of the produce.

41] The third class is that of shepherds and hunters, who alone are permitted to hunt and keep cattle, to sell yoke animals or to hire them out. In return for ridding the country of wild beasts and seed-devouring birds, food is given them by the king. They lead a wandering life in their tents. No private person is allowed to maintain an elephant or a horse, both being regarded as royal possessions, and these persons are their keepers.

*   *   *

45] . . . Let this be sufficient about these beasts. Turning back to Megasthenes we will resume where we left off.

46] After the hunters and shepherds, he says, the fourth class consists of those who follow a craft, the tradesmen and those who support themselves by physical labor. Of these some pay tribute and perform fixed services, but the armorers and the shipwrights receive pay and maintenance from the king, since they work for the king alone. The army custodian (stratophylax) supplies the soldiers with weapons, and the admiral hires out ships to shipmen and merchants.

47] Fifth is the class of the warriors, who spend their leisure time in amusement and drinking, being maintained at the expense of the king. To insure their rapid departure when the need arises, they take nothing with them but their persons.

48] Sixth are the ephors, who are assigned the task of observing everything that happens and reporting it secretly to the king, using prostitutes to help them — the ephors in town using the town prostitutes, those in camp the prostitutes there. The best and most trustworthy men are selected for this function.

49] Seventh are the counsellors and advisers of the king, by whom the magistracies, the courts and the whole government are administered. It is not permissible to marry into another class, or to change from one profession or employment to another; nor yet is any man allowed to follow more than one occupation, unless he happens to be one of the philosophers. Then he is allowed to do so because of his excellence.

b   Arrian, Indica, *13-14* (*Megasthenes*)

13] THE INDIANS hunt other wild animals just the way the Greeks do, but their method of hunting the elephant is unlike anything else, even as these beasts are unlike others. Choosing a warm flat place large enough for a sizeable army to camp, they surround it with a trench, which they dig thirty feet broad and twenty-four feet deep. On either side of the trench they heap up the earth obtained by digging, and make it serve as a wall. They dig shelters for themselves below the mound — the one along the outer rim of the trench — and they leave openings through which the light penetrates and through which they can watch the beasts approach and enter the enclosure. Then, placing three or four female elephants of a very amenable disposition within the enclosure, they leave only one entrance by way of a bridge over the trench. Here they pile earth and quantities of green stuff, so that the elephants will not be aware of the bridge and suspect trickery. They then take themselves out of the way, and go down into their tents below the trench. Wild elephants will not approach an inhabited area in the daytime, but at night they wander widely and graze together, following the strongest and most spirited animal, as cattle follow bulls. When they draw near, and hear the voices of the females and smell the female odor, they break into a run for the enclosure. They circle around the outside of the trench until they chance upon the bridge, and press across it into the enclosure. When they perceive that the elephants have gone inside some of the men quickly remove the bridge, while the rest run off to the nearby villages to announce that the elephants have been penned up in the enclosure. When the villagers hear this, they mount the liveliest tame elephants and ride off to the enclosure. But they do not join battle immediately on arrival. Instead, they wait for the wild elephants to be weakened by hunger and overcome by thirst. When they seem to be in a bad way, the Indians replace the bridge and ride across. At first there is a violent struggle between the tame elephants and the captives, but in the end the wild elephants, probably weakened by hunger and despair, are subdued. But the riders, climbing down from their mounts, bind together the ends of the feet of the already weary wild elephants, and then order the tame animals to rain blows on the wild ones until they drop to the ground exhausted. Standing beside them the riders fasten cords around their necks, and then mount them as they are lying there. To prevent the riders from being thrown and to forestall any other mischief, they cut their necks all the way round with a sharp knife, then fasten a rope in the wound so that the beast will not move his neck or head because of the wound. Should he unwisely twist his neck around the rope would rub against the sore. Thus they are made placable, and with a spirit already cowed they are led off in fetters by the tame elephants.

14] But young elephants, or those not worth keeping because of some defect, are allowed to return to their herds. The others they take to the village, and first offer them green stalks and grasses to eat. But they are too dejected to feel any desire for food, and so the Indians stand around them in a circle, and soothe them by beating drums and cymbals, and singing songs. For if any beast is naturally clever it is the elephant. Some of them, when their drivers have died in battle, have even snatched them up and carried them off for burial. There are others who have protected prostrate drivers, and others who have borne the brunt of battle for their fallen riders. And there was one elephant which slew his driver in a rage, and then died afterwards of remorse and despair. I myself have seen an elephant play the cymbals while other elephants were dancing. The one playing the cymbals had two of them fastened to his fore-legs and another to his so-called "proboscis." And he beat the cymbal on his trunk alternately and rhythmically against the cymbals on each of his legs. Meanwhile, the other elephants danced round in a circle, raising and bending their front legs in turn, and in rhythm; wherever the cymbal-playing elephant led, they followed.

Now the elephant is impregnated in the spring just like a cow or a mare, when the spiracles on the temples of the females are open and pour forth exhalations. The period of gestation is at least sixteen months, and eighteen at the most. Like the horse the elephant has only one offspring, which it nurses with milk until the eighth year. The longest-lived elephants live up to 200 years, and while many die of sickness, it is possible for elephants to reach this age. For eye ailments cow's milk is infused, while for other sicknesses they are forced to drink black wine. Roasted swine's flesh is applied to their wounds. Such are the remedies used for them by the Indians.

c   Strabo, xv, 1, 42-43, 50-52, 53-55, 58-60, 68 (Megasthenes)

42] THIS IS how they hunt elephants. Encircling some bare spot of four or five stades with a ditch, they build a very narrow bridge for an entrance, and then introduce three or four very tractable female elephants, while they themselves lie under cover in ambush. Now while the wild elephants do not approach during the daytime, at night they enter, one by one. Then the entrance is shut secretly, and the hunters bring in the strongest of the tame elephants to fight with them; at the same time they wear them down with hunger. When they have become weakened the boldest drivers climb down unobserved, and each darts under the belly of his own elephant, and from there he darts under a wild elephant and puts fetters on his feet. When this has been done, they order the tame elephants to strike the wild ones until they fall to the ground. When they fall, the hunters fasten their necks to the necks of the tame elephants with rawhide thongs. Lest the wild elephants shake off those who are trying to mount them, they make a circular gash around the animal's throat, and run a rawhide rope along the cut, to make them submit to their fetters because of their pain, and to remain quiet. Removing the captured animals that are either too young or too old to be used, they bring the rest to the stables, binding their feet together and fastening their necks to well-driven posts, and tame them by hunger. Then they restore them with cane shoots and grass. Afterwards they teach them to obey, some by words — others they charm by song and drum. Rarely are they hard to tame. They are naturally gentle and amenable, and very close to being a reasoning animal.

They have been known to pick up their drivers, fallen from loss of blood and to rescue them from the battle; others have fought for and saved men who darted in between their front feet. And if an elephant happens to kill one of his keepers or trainers in a rage, so much does he long for him, that in his grief he refuses to eat and sometimes persists until he dies of hunger.

43] They couple and bear offspring in the manner of horses, usually in the spring. The proper time for the male is when he is stung to fury and becomes enraged, for then a kind of fatty substance pours through an opening beside the temples; and for the female, when this same orifice happens to be open. The period of conception is eighteen months at most, and at least sixteen. The mother gives suck for six years. Most elephants live as long as very old men, but some have been known to live for 200 years. They are subject to many diseases and are hard to cure. For ophthalmia the only remedy is to be washed with cow's milk, but for most ailments they are made to drink black wine. Melted butter is applied to wounds; it draws out the particles of iron. Ulcers, they foment with the flesh of pigs.

*   *   *

50] Of the officials, some are market supervisors (agoranomi), others police magistrates (astynomi) and still others are in charge of military affairs. The first group control the rivers and measure the land, as in Egypt, and they regulate the closed canals from which the water is distributed to the ditches so everyone shares equally in the use of the water. The same men also supervise the hunters, and assign rewards and punishments to those who deserve them. They collect taxes and inspect the crafts connected with the land — woodcutters, carpenters, smiths and miners. They also build roads and set up posts every ten stades, indicating the turn-off points and the distances.

51] The police magistrates are divided into six groups of five men each. One supervises the handicrafts, another looks after strangers — they assign them lodgings, give them companions suitable to their way of life, send them on their way, or if they die send their money back, and look after them when they are ill and bury them when they die. Third are those who keep a record of births and deaths, when and under what circumstances these occur, both with a view to taxation, and to determine whether the number of births is greater or less than the number of deaths. The fourth group have to do with retail trade and barter; they regulate the measures and see to it that seasonal fruits are sold according to stamp. The same person may not sell different products unless he pays a double tax. Fifth are those who control the sale of handicrafts, having them sold according to stamp; for brand new goods and used goods must be sold separately; and whoever mixes them is punished. Sixth and last are those who collect the tenth on what is sold. The tax evader pays the death penalty.[1] These are their separate duties. Collectively they manage private and public business, are responsible for and repair public buildings — for prices (?), the market, harbors and temples.

52] After the police magistrates, the third board is that in charge of military matters, and it too is divided into six groups of five men each. One of these is associated with the admiral, another with the supervisor of ox carts — for they are used to transport the implements of war as well as food for man and beast, and the other things an army requires. They also supply the servants: drummers, bell-ringers, grooms, engineers and their underlings. They also send out foragers at the sound of a bell, encouraging speed and safety by rewards and punishments. Those who control the infantry are third; fourth the cavalry; fifth the chariots; and sixth those who manage the elephants. There are royal stables for these beasts and for the horses, and there is also a royal armory. The soldier turns in his equipment at the armory, and puts his horse in the stable — likewise the elephants. They use no bridles. Oxen draw the chariots on the march, while the horses are led by a halter to prevent their legs being chafed; thus the energy with which they draw the chariots will not be wasted. There are two warriors in each chariot in addition to the charioteer; each elephant carries a driver and three bowmen. . . .

53] The Indians are all simple in their living habits, but particularly on military expeditions. They do not care for unnecessary numbers, and accordingly they maintain strict discipline. Moreover, there is a truce on stealing. Megasthenes says that when he was in Sandrocottus' camp, consisting of 40,000 men, he never heard of any theft beyond the value of 200 drachmas — and this despite their having no written laws. For they do not know how to write, but manage everything by memory. They prosper because of their simple frugal living, for they never drink wine except at sacrifices, but drink a beverage brewed of rice instead of barley, and their usual diet is rice gruel. The simplicity of their laws and contracts is also demonstrated by their not being litigious. They have no actions on pledges or deposits, nor do they need witnesses or seals; for deposits they depend on good faith. Property at home is usually unguarded. Now these regulations are all admirable, but they have others of which one can scarcely approve: the fact that each man always eats by himself, and that there is no special time for everyone to breakfast or dine, for everyone eats when he feels like it. But the opposite arrangement is better, both for social life and for the state.

54] They specially sanction rubbing as a means of conditioning the body, and among other methods they massage themselves with smooth ebony rods. Their tombs are small plain mounds. Their dress, however, is in contrast with their plainness in other matters. They array themselves in gold, wear jewelled ornaments, dress in flowered linen, and have parasols carried behind them. Devotees of beauty, they will use anything to enhance their appearance. Truth they regard as synonymous with virtue. Therefore they grant no privileges to the old men because they are old, but only if they excel in wisdom. They marry many women, purchased from their parents for a yoke of oxen: some they marry to be obeyed, others for pleasure and child-bearing. Women are not required to be chaste, but are permitted to prostitute themselves. No one sacrifices, or offers incense, or pours a libation with a wreath on his head. Nor do they butcher the sacrificial animal; instead they strangle it, so it may be offered whole and unmutilated to the god. Anyone convicted of bearing false witness has his hands and feet cut off; if anyone deprives a workman of a hand or an eye, he is put to death. He[2] says no Indian owns a slave. Onesicritus cites this as peculiar to the Land of Musicanus and he mentions it as an improvement, just as he attributes many other innovations to this country as though it had the best laws.

55] The care of the king's body is entrusted to women purchased from their fathers. Outside the gates are the bodyguards and the rest of the soldiery. A woman who kills a drunken king is rewarded by marrying his successor. The sons succeed. The king may not sleep in the daytime, and even at night he is obliged to change his couch at intervals, for fear of plots.

One of the occasions on which he goes out, aside from war, is to give judgment; and he continues the hearing even when it is time for his bodily exercise, which consists of a rub-down with rods. Four rubbers station themselves beside him, and he is massaged while giving audience. Another occasion is when he goes out for a sacrifice; and a third is a Bacchic-style hunt, where he stays on the inside surrounded by women while the spearbearers are outside. Access is blocked off by ropes, and anyone who passes them and reaches the women, is put to death. Drummers and bell-ringers go on ahead. When he hunts in an enclosure, he shoots with his bow from a platform — two or three women stand by his side — but when he hunts in the open, he shoots from an elephant. Some of the women ride in chariots, some on horseback, and some on elephants, just as they do on campaign; for they are trained to use every kind of weapon.

*   *   *

58] Speaking of the philosophers, the ones in the mountains, he says they are votaries of Dionysus. As evidence they point to the wild grape which grows among them, to the ivy, the laurel, the myrtle, the boxwood and to other evergreens, none of which is found beyond the Euphrates except for a few kept in parks — and there only by special pains. Bacchic also is their wearing linen and chaplets, anointing themselves and using bright colors, and also the fact that when their kings go out, they are escorted with bells and drums. But the philosophers of the plains honor Heracles. Now this is pure fiction, refuted in many details, especially the part about grape-vines and wine. For a large part of Armenia and all of Mesopotamia are beyond the Euphrates, and Media — all the way to Persia and Carmania; yet each of these regions is said, for the most part, to abound in grapes and good wine.

59] But he divides the philosophers in another way, saying that there are two kinds, whom he calls the Brachmanes and the Garmanes. The Brachmanes are more highly regarded, for they agree better in their doctrines. Now from the very time of their conception in the womb men of repute are put in charge of them, ostensibly to cast spells to bring about a happy nativity for mother and child, but actually for the purpose of giving sage admonition and advice. It is believed that those women who hear them most willingly, will be fortunate in their children. When they are born, one group after another takes over the supervision, their instructors being more and more distinguished persons as the child grows older. The philosophers stay before the city in a wooded enclosure of moderate size, living simply, lying on straw and hides and abstaining from animal food and from all sexual intercourse, while listening to discourses on elevated subjects — which they impart to those who request them to do so. The pupil is not allowed to clear his throat or to spit, on the penalty of being expelled from the society that day as a licentious person. After living this way for thirty-seven years, each returns to his possessions and leads a more relaxed life free from care, wearing linen, and using gold ornaments in moderation — in their ears and on their heads — and enjoying the flesh of such animals as do not share in their work, but abstaining from pungent herbs and seasonings. They marry as many wives as possible, in order to have many children. The more there are, the more good ones there will be, and since they have no slaves the services of their children are the nearest equivalent; therefore they need to beget more of them. The Brachmanes do not discuss philosophy with their wedded wives lest, if they are of low character, they tell what it is a sacrilege to divulge to the profane; and if they are virtuous, lest they abandon them. For no one who despises pleasure and pain, as well as life and death, would willingly be subject to another. Yet this characterizes the virtuous man and the virtuous woman. Most of their talk is about death, for they regard life here as the end of the prenatal period, and death as the beginning of a true and happy life for those who have practised philosophy. Therefore their training is chiefly concerned with preparation for death. The things that happen to people are neither good nor bad. Otherwise, some would not be grieved and others pleased by the same things, their views resembling dream fantasies; nor would the same persons feel annoyance at one time, delight at another, for the same occurrences. He[2] says their views about nature show a certain simple-mindedness, for they are better at deeds than words, trusting largely to myth. But they have many points of resemblance to the Greeks. They, too, believe the world came into existence and is destructible; that it is spherical in shape; and that the god who rules and creates it permeates the whole. They have different views on the origins of the universe, but it is water that shapes the world. In addition to the four elements there is a fifth substance, from which proceed the heavens and the stars. Earth is established in the center of the universe. About seed (sperma) and soul they have like views, and many others as well. They weave myths as Plato does about the immortality of the soul, the judgments of Hades and the like. That is what he has to say about the Brachmanes.

60] He says the most honored of the Garmanes are called Hylobioi, and that they live in the woods on leaves and wild fruits, clad in the bark of trees and avoiding both sexual intercourse and wine. They are in touch with the kings, who question them by messenger about the causes of things, and who use them in serving and supplicating the godhead. Next in honor after the Hylobioi are the physicians, philosophers of man as it were, who live simply but not in the country, subsisting on rice and barley; for these things as well as hospitality are bestowed on them by anyone who is asked.

They are able to promote fecundity by their skill in medicine, and to cause either male or female children to be born. They usually heal by the use of a diet rather than by medicines. But of medicines they favor salves and poultices, on the theory that other remedies have very bad after effects. Like the others, these men practice endurance, both of hardships and in maintaining postures: they will continue all day long in the same position without moving. The others are: fortune-tellers, conjurors, men skilled in the lore and practices concerning the dead, and those who beg in the cities and villages. There are still others, more accomplished and refined than these, who none the less repeat the nonsense which is told about Hades, whenever it seems to promote piety and holiness. Women, too, avoid sexual intercourse.

*   *   *

68] The account of Calanus will serve to demonstrate the inconsistency of these historians. They agree that he joined Alexander and died a voluntary death by fire in his presence, but they differ on the manner of his death and on his motives. Megasthenes says the philosophers have no doctrine in favor of suicide. Those who commit suicide are held to be foolhardy. Men of violent natures dispatch themselves with a blow, or by flinging themselves over a cliff, while the slothful ones plunge into the water and the long-suffering ones hang themselves; those who are of a fiery disposition thrust themselves into the fire. Such a man was Calanus, an intemperate person captivated by the dainties of Alexander's table. Consequently he is blamed, but Mandanis is praised; for when messengers from Alexander summoned him to the Son of Zeus, promising gifts if he obeyed and punishment if he refused, he replied that that man was no Son of Zeus who ruled such a minute portion of the world; furthermore he needed no gifts from a man who had no son; neither did he fear his threats. So long as he lived India would give him all the food he wanted, and when he died he would be released from a body wasted away by old age and enter upon a better purer life. Thereupon they say Alexander praised him and accepted his excuses.

Notes

1. Literally "tax stealer."
2. I.e., Megasthenes.

17

Heraclea, A Greek City on the Black Sea

MEMNON, a citizen of Heraclea in the imperial days of Rome, wrote the History of Heraclea from which the following passage has been taken. He is less interesting on his own account than for the lost historian whom he follows here, Nymphis of Heraclea, a truly respectable historian who lived in the third century B.C. Nymphis was one of those who returned to Heraclea with other exiles whose families had been banished for something over eighty years. Perhaps there is no better illustration of the tenacity with which a Greek clung to his city-state nationality. The glimpses given us of Heraclea under the Successors, and the account of the earlier fourth-century tyrants, are very welcome, though they also remind us of the historical literature that has disappeared. Even Memnon, who preserves Nymphis, reaches us in an abbreviated form, as the two hundred and twenty-fourth work read aloud by Photius and his friends in the ninth century. Photius was a famous scholar and also the Patriarch of Constantinople. Since his brother missed the readings, Photius summarized them for him in the work we still possess, his Bibliotheca.

Photius, Bibliotheca, No. 224 (Memnon)

BOOKS IX-X

i

1] HE WRITES that Clearchus was the first to obtain tyranny in the city.[1] He also says that he was not without training in philosophy, having been one of Plato's students, and that he also studied under Isocrates the rhetorician for a period of four years; but that he was cruel and murderous towards his subjects if anyone ever was, and that he reached such heights of arrogance as to call himself the Son of Zeus. He could not bear to have his face preserve its natural coloring, but had it tinted artificially to look fresh and rosy. He also kept changing his outer garments to present now a terrifying, now a dazzling appearance.

2] But these were not his only faults, for he was also very ungrateful to his benefactors, and he was violent in everything he did and shrank from no act of infamy. He was naturally inclined to cause the murder of anyone with whom he came into opposition, not just his own people but even outsiders, if he thought any of them stood in his way. However, he built up a library superior to those of other tyrants.

3] Now this man escaped many plots, for plots were frequently made against him because he was so bloodthirsty, so violent and such an enemy of mankind; but at last Chion son of Matris, a highminded man related to him by blood, and Leon and Euxenon and a number of others planned the fatal blow, so that he died a bitter death of his wound.

4] The tyrant was conducting a public sacrifice when Chion and his men, finding this a suitable opportunity for the deed, plunged the sword Chion had in his hand through the side of their common enemy. But the tyrant, suffering prolonged agony and terrified by apparitions (the apparitions were images of the men he had cruelly murdered), finally expired on the second day, having lived for 58 years during 12 of which he held the tyranny. At that time Artaxerxes held the Persian throne (359–338 B.C.). Clearchus, during his life, had frequently sent embassies to both.

5] Of the men who killed the tyrant, almost all were cut down by the bodyguards at the time of the attack, though they defended themselves bravely, but a few were arrested later and put to death after undergoing cruel punishments.

ii

1] Satyrus, the tyrant's brother who was left in charge of the boys Timotheus and Dionysius, took over the rule; not only did he surpass Clearchus in cruelty but all other tyrants as well. He took vengeance on the men who plotted against his brother, and not only that, but he also inflicted unbearable punishments on their children, who had played no part in what happened, and he also made charges against many who had done nothing wrong.

2] This man was utterly unconcerned with the study of philosophy, or with anything else worthy of a free man, but he had a mind which only took a lively interest in bloodthirsty deeds, with nothing kindly, nothing gentle about it, and with no desire and no ability to learn. While in time he became sated with the slaughter of kinsmen and relaxed his cruelty to some extent, his first concern remained devotion to his brother.

3] He made it so much a cardinal principle to preserve the rule intact for his brother's children, that he even avoided having children from his own wife, of whom he was enamoured, using every means to avoid having any offspring, so that there might be no one at all to plot against his brother's children.

4] Now while still alive but weighed down by age Satyrus turned the government over to Timotheus, the elder of his brother's children. Not long afterwards, after suffering from a severe and incurable ailment — he had a cancerous growth between groin and scrotum which spread inwards and became more and more painful, and there was a constant discharge from his flesh which caused an insufferable stench, and neither his retinue nor the physicians could stop this unbearably putrid flow — and unremitting sharp pains reached out over his entire body, causing sleeplessness and convulsions, until the disease finally reached the vital organs and deprived him of his life.

5] As in the case of Clearchus, he seemed to those who witnessed it to have rendered an account by his death for his cruel and illegal acts against the citizens. For they say that many times while he lay ill he prayed vainly for death to remove him. Thus, day after day, by his painful and grievous disease he paid back his debts after living 65 years, during 7 of which he held the tyranny. At that time Archidamus was ruling over the Lacedaemonians.[2]

iii

1] Timotheus, who took over the government,[3] made it milder and more democratic, to such an extent that for his deeds he came to be called Euergetes (Benefactor) and Soter (Savior) rather than tyrant. For he himself settled debts owing to money lenders, and took care of those who needed money in business or for their livelihood, without interest, and not only did he release all the men held in prison without cause, but the guilty ones as well. He was a fair judge and at the same time a kindly one. He was virtuous in every way and his acts were distrusted by no one. With such principles not only was he like a father to his brother Dionysius, but he immediately made him a partner in the rule and designated him as his successor.

2] Nor did he conduct himself any less excellently in warlike matters. For he was noble in spirit and also strong in body. In coming to an understanding after battle he showed himself to be reasonable and not harsh. He was well equipped to understand matters of state and also to implement whatever his reason suggested. He was a virtuous man, compassionate by nature yet bold and persistent in what he ventured. He was gentle, kind and moderate. Therefore, as long as he lived he was a terror to his enemies, who all feared to incur his wrath, and a joy and a delight to his subjects. When he died he left behind a great longing for him, and this longing was intensified by corresponding grief.

3] Now his brother Dionysius[4] had his body burned with lavish expenditure, and groans poured from his breast and tears from his eyes. He established an equestrian contest, and not only that but also theatrical, musical and gymnastic contests, some right away, more lavish ones later on.

This is a summary of the 9th and 10th books of Memnon's History.

BOOKS XI-XII

iv

1] Succeeding to the rule,[5] Dionysius added to it. For the battle of Granicus between Alexander and the Persians enabled those who wished to do so to increase their holdings, since the Persian strength, which had always stood in the way, was removed.[6] Afterwards he experienced varied changes of fortune, particularly because of the exiles from Heraclea who sent envoys to Alexander when he was clearly winning control of all Asia, and begged him to restore them, and also to restore the ancestral democratic constitution to their city. Because of this Dionysius came within an ace of losing his throne. And he would have lost it if he had not managed to elude the enemies who threatened him, with great ingenuity and shrewdness, aided both by his subjects' good will and the help of Cleopatra. He succeeded in part by giving way to their rage and then continuing to delay, and in part by taking counter measures.

2] But when Alexander died (of violence?) or disease in Babylon[7] Dionysius dedicated a statue to Joy (Euthymia) when he heard the news. He was so overcome with delight on first hearing the news that he acted like a man in pain — for he spun around and almost fell, and seemed to be out of his mind.

3] When Perdiccas took over the control the Heracleote exiles pressed him with the same requests. But Dionysius used the same arts as before, and with everything balanced on a razor's edge, he won through every danger that threatened him. But Perdiccas, becoming hated by his subjects was killed, and the hope of the exiles was extinguished, and all Dionysius' affairs took a turn for the better.

4] The greatest support for his fortunes was his second marriage. For he married Amastris. She was the daughter of Darius' brother, Oxathres, that same Darius whom Alexander overthrew, and whose daughter Statira he took to wife. These two women were cousins, and they had a special affection for one another which had been implanted by their growing up together. Now at the time when Alexander married Statira he married Amastris off to Craterus, his intimate friend. After Alexander departed from the world of men Craterus turned to Phila, daughter of Antipater, and Amastris, with his consent, joined herself to Dionysius.

5] After that his power was greatly increased, both because of the additional wealth that came from this marriage, and also because of his own policies. And it came into his head to purchase all the furnishings of Dionysius the Sicilian tyrant, whose rule had been overthrown.

6] But his power was not only strengthened in these ways, but because he was lucky and because he had the goodwill of his subjects. And he came to exercise dominion over many who had not been his subjects before. He also concluded a brilliant alliance with Antigonus, the ruler of Asia, when he was besieging Cyprus.[8] As a reward for his support he was able to obtain Ptolemaeus, Antigonus' nephew, who was the general in charge of the area near the Hellespont, as husband for his daughter. She was the child of an earlier marriage. In this way he built a great reputation. Disdaining the name of tyrant, he took the title of King instead.

7] Getting rid of fears and anxieties he gave himself over to unremitting luxury, as a result of which his body became fat and swollen far beyond its natural size. Consequently he grew careless about the government, and even had to have his body pierced by long needles as the only remedy for somnolence and lethargy. Even then he could barely be aroused from his stupor.

8] He had three children by Amastris — Clearchus, Oxathres and a daughter who was named for her mother. When he was about to die he turned everything over to his wife and he also made her, along with some other persons, a guardian of the children, who were still very young. His subjects he left in a state of great longing and sorrow, for he had lived 55 years, 30 of them as a ruler and had governed very mildly — as has been said — earning the soubriquet of Chrestus by his conduct.[9]

9] Nevertheless the city continued to prosper after his departure from mankind. Antigonus took more than a casual interest in the children of Dionysius and in the citizens. And when his attention was directed to other matter Lysimachus again gave his attention to Heracleote affairs and to the children. He made Amastris his wife, and at first he was very fond of her, but when matters of state became pressing he left her in Heraclea while he occupied himself with those matters. Not long afterwards, getting the better of his many difficulties, he sent for her and continued to cherish her. But later he transferred his affections to the sister of Ptolemy Philadelphus — her name was Arsinoe — and this caused Amastris to separate from him. She left him to take over Heraclea. Returning, she built and colonized the city of Amastris.

v

1] Clearchus, who had now reached man's estate, ruled the city,[10] and he took part in a number of wars, some as the ally of others, some against those who made war on him. On one occasion, when he was campaigning with Lysimachus against the Getae, they were both taken prisoner. Lysimachus was released from captivity, and by his assistance Clearchus later obtained his own release.

2] Now this Clearchus together with his brother succeeded to the rule, but they departed greatly from their father's mildness and kindness towards his subjects, and they ended up with a terrible and bloody deed. Their mother, who had done nothing much to offend them, they contrived by a most despicable and evil act to have strangled at sea, after she had gone on board a ship.

3] On this account Lysimachus, who is mentioned frequently — for he was the king of Macedonia — and who despite the fact that

Amastris had been ready to leave him because of his union with Arsinoe, still felt the glow of his old passion. He decided that this loathsome act of savagery was not to be borne. However, he concealed his real intentions, and made a show of his old friendship for Clearchus, and resorted to many schemes and plots to avoid being found out — and he is said to have been a very clever man at concealing his intentions. He arrived in Heraclea ostensibly to further the interests of those who welcomed him. Hiding his real intentions from Clearchus under the guise of affection for his father, he destroyed the matricides — first Clearchus, then Oxathres, demanding their punishment for the cruel death of their mother. Taking the city under his care, and appropriating as booty most of the money collected by the tyrants, he permitted the citizens to have a democratic government, which they desired, and he returned to his own kingdom.

4] When he regained his own kingdom he extolled Amastris, and he was impressed both by her actions and by her dominions, and how she had strengthened them in size, dignity and power. He singled out Heraclea particularly, but he also devoted part of his praises to Teum and to Amastris, which she had built and named after herself. By his remarks he aroused in Arsinoe the desire to control the places he praised. She begged him to grant her wish, but at first, out of respect for his gift,[11] he would not yield. But being entreated he finally gave in. For Arsinoe was clever in getting what she wanted. Then too, old age had already softened him.

5] When Arsinoe was granted control of Heraclea she sent out Heraclides of Cyme, a man devoted to her interests, but also clever and unscrupulous with a shrewd ability to achieve his ends. When he set foot in Heraclea he ran things with a very strong hand, and he ruined many citizens by bringing charges against them and an equal number by inflicting punishments. So it was that they lost the happiness they had so recently obtained.

6] Meanwhile Lysimachus, beguiled by Arsinoe, slew his finest child, his elder son Agathocles — he had been born of an earlier marriage — in a most shameful way. Agathocles had avoided the effects of poisoning on an earlier occasion by vomiting, and Lysimachus cast him into prison and ordered him torn to pieces on the false charge of plotting against him. Now Ptolemy, who perpetrated this outrage with his own hands, was Arsinoe's brother. He was called Ceraunus[12] for his roughness and his folly.

7] Now Lysimachus was justly hated by his subjects for murdering his son. When Seleucus learned about it, and heard that it would be easy to deprive him of his kingdom with the cities in revolt, he joined battle against him.[13] Lysimachus fell in battle, struck by a javelin. The man who threw it was a Heracleote named Malacon serving under Seleucus. When Lysimachus fell his kingdom was surrendered and added to that of Seleucus.

That is the point reached by the 12th book of Memnon's History.

BOOKS XIII-XIV

vi

1] In Book 13 he says that when the Heracleotes learned that Lysimachus was dead and that the man who killed him came from Heraclea their hopes rose and they bravely desired to reassert the independence of which they had been deprived for 85 years, first at the hands of domestic tyrants and afterwards by Lysimachus.

2] At first they approached Heraclides, urging him to evacuate the city, not only without reprisals but furnished with splendid gifts in return for their recovering their independence. But when, instead of allowing himself to be persuaded, they saw him fall into a passion and carry off some of their number to be punished, then the citizens concluded an agreement with the phrourarchs[14] giving them isopolity and the right to receive the wages of which they had been deprived. They arrested Heraclides and kept him under guard for the time being. Then, relieved of all fear, they tore down the walls of the citadel to their very foundations, and sent off an embassy to Seleucus. They installed Phocritus as the manager of the city (epimeletes).

3] Zipoetes the Eparch of Bithynia was hostile to the Heracleotes on Lysimachus' account first, and then on account of Seleucus, for he was at odds with both. He made a raid against them and committed acts of destruction, but his army did not do this without suffering injuries in return for the injuries they inflicted, for their sufferings were almost as great as those they caused.

vii

1] Meanwhile Seleucus sent Aphrodisius his administrator (dioecetes) out to the cities in Phrygia and to those along the Black

Sea. After carrying out his instructions he returned with only praise for the other cities, but he charged that the Heracleotes were not well disposed towards Seleucus' government. Thereupon Seleucus flew into a rage, and when the envoys arrived he treated them with contempt and terrified them with threats. But one man, Chamaeleon, did not quail before him. "Heracles is 'Carron,' Seleucus!" he said.[15] But Seleucus did not understand what he said, for he was in a rage and had turned away. The envoys decided it would not be to their advantage to return home, nor yet to remain.

2] When the Heracleotes did learn what had happened they took other measures and also they collected their allies. They sent envoys to Mithridates, King of Pontus, and to the Byzantines and the Chalcedonians.

3] The remaining exiles from Heraclea at that time included Nymphis among their number, and he advised them and showed them that it would be easy to bring about their return provided they made no aggravating claims for repayment of what their ancestors had lost, and he was able to persuade them easily. Their restoration was brought about just as he advised, and those who returned as well as the city which received them alike turned to pleasure and merriment, those inside welcoming them in friendly fashion and allowing them to want for nothing necessary to satisfy their needs.

4] In this way the Heracleotes recovered their ancient felicity and their constitution.

viii

1] But Seleucus, encouraged by his success against Lysimachus, set out for Macedonia. He felt a longing for his native land, from which he had marched out with Alexander, and he wished to spend the rest of his life there now that he was an old man. He planned also to turn Asia over to his son, Antiochus.

2] Ptolemy the Thunderbolt, when Lysimachus' empire came into Seleucus' hands, served under him also, and he was not looked down on as a prisoner of war, but was held in honor and consideration befitting the son of a king. He also prided himself on Seleucus' promise that if his father died he would restore him to Egypt and his father's kingdom.

3] But while he was treated with such consideration, these acts of generosity did not make a bad man good. He organized a plot against his benefactor, whom he attacked and slew. Then he jumped on his horse and fled to Lysimacheia where he had himself crowned, and then returned to the army with a strong escort. Under the pressure of necessity the men who had formerly acknowledged Seleucus now received Ptolemy and called him king.

4] Antigonus, son of Demetrius, when he heard the news, attempted to reach Macedonia with an army and a fleet before Ptolemy arrived. But Ptolemy intercepted him with Lysimachus' ships, and offered battle.

5] There were other ships and also some sent from Heraclea. These included hexeremes, quinqueremes and undecked ships, but there was one octoreme called the Leontophorus which was much admired for its size and beauty. In this ship 100 men rowed in each bank, so that there were 800 of them on each side and 1,600 on both sides. The numbers who fought on deck were 1,200 and there were two helmsmen.

6] When battle was joined Ptolemy prevailed, turning back the fleet of Antigonus. The Heracleote ships were handled more gallantly than the rest. Among the Heracleote ships themselves the Leontophorus octoreme stood out. Antigonus, coming to grief with his fleet, withdrew to Boeotia. Ptolemy went on over to Macedonia and took firm possession of the kingdom.

7] But he soon displayed his characteristic harshness. He married his sister Arsinoe — as this is customary among the Egyptians — but he murdered the children she had had by Lysimachus, and then banished her from the kingdom.

8] After he had committed many atrocities over a period of two years, it happened that a part of the Galatae were driven out of their land by famine. Invading Macedonia they met him in battle. And he lost his life in a manner appropriate to his savage nature, being torn to pieces by the Galatae; for he was taken alive after the elephant he was riding was wounded and pitched him off. Demetrius' son Antigonus, defeated in the naval battle, took possession of Macedonia after the death of Ptolemy.

ix

1] After Antiochus, son of Seleucus, had just barely managed to recover his father's empire — though not all of it — he sent Patrocles with an expeditionary force beyond the Taurus. And he chose as his deputy Hermogenes, an Aspendian by birth. This man began to make attacks on other cities and he also attacked Heraclea.

2] After the Heracleotes sent envoys to him he withdrew from their territory and made a friendship pact with them, and marched against Bithynia by way of Phrygia. However, he was waylaid by a Bithynian ambush and he and his army were destroyed after he performed prodigies of valor against the enemy.

3] On account of this Antiochus decided to make war on the Bithynians (279 B.C.). Their king, Nicomedes, sent envoys to Heraclea to ask for an alliance, promising that if he obtained their support he would pay them back in their own time of need.

4] Meanwhile the Heracleotes succeeded, at great expense, in recovering Cierus and Tium and the Thynian land, but their efforts to get back Amastris — for it had been lost along with the others — were not successful, despite repeated efforts, both military and monetary. Eumenes, who held it, was foolishly led by his spite into handing it over to Ariobarzanes the son of Mithridates, for nothing, rather than to take money for it from the Heracleotes.

5] At the same time war overtook the Heracleotes, war against Zipoetes the Bithynian who held sway over the Thynian region of Thrace, a war in which many Heracleotes were killed fighting bravely. And Zipoetes won a victory by his arms, but he disgraced his victory by fleeing when an allied army came up to help the Heracleotes. The vanquished recovered their own dead safely and burned them. Then, taking possession of everything for which the war had been fought and transporting the bones of those who had died to the city, they gave them a splendid burial in memory of their brave deeds.

x

1] About this time (279) war was threatening between Antiochus son of Seleucus and Antigonus son of Demetrius, and considerable time was spent collecting forces on both sides. Nicomedes, King of Numidia,[16] allied himself with the latter, while many others sided with Antiochus.

2] Therefore, clashing with Antigonus, Antiochus stirred up a war against Nicomedes. Now Nicomedes collected troops from various places, and he also sent envoys to conclude an alliance with the Heracleotes, from whom he obtained 13 triremes. Subsequently he drew up his fleet over against the fleet of Antiochus. Remaining opposite one another for some time, neither offered to fight so they separated without a battle.

xi

1] When the Galatae invaded Byzantine territory and plundered most of it, the Byzantines, damaged by the war, sent to their allies asking for help. And everyone did what they could. The Heracleotes sent 4,000 gold coins, for this was the sum requested by the embassy.

2] Not long afterwards Nicomedes agreed to transport the Galatae who were attacking Byzantium, into Asia, despite the fact that when they attempted to cross before on numerous occasions they had been prevented from carrying out their plan by the Byzantines. The agreement was as follows: The barbarians were always to maintain friendship with Nicomedes and his descendants; they were to make no alliances with those who sent envoys to them, except with Nicomedes' approval, but were to be friends with his friends and enemies with those who were not his friends; that they might, if necessary, ally with the Byzantines, and also with the Tianians, Heracleotes, Chalcedonians, Cieranians and with certain others who controlled certain specified peoples.

3] In accordance with this treaty Nicomedes transported the Galatian horde (plethos) to Asia. There were seventeen leaders, but the most important of these were Leonnorius and Luturius. Such was the crossing of the Galatae into Asia. At first it was thought this would be to the detriment of the inhabitants, but in the long run it was shown to have been beneficial.

4] For while the kings were anxious to destroy democratic government in the cities, the Galatae tended rather to strengthen it, arraying themselves against those who attacked it.

5] First, assisted by his allies from Heraclea, Nicomedes armed the barbarians against the Bithynians, and he took possession of the region and killed the inhabitants. The rest of the booty the Galatae divided among themselves.

6] After overrunning a large area the Galatae again withdrew, marking off for themselves what is now called Galatia, from the conquered territory. This they divided up into three parts, one for the so-called Trocmi, one for the Tolostobogii and one for the Tectosages.

7] They also built towns — the Trocmi, Ancyra; the Tolostobogii, Tavium; and the Tectosages, Pessinus.

xii

1] Nicomedes, becoming very prosperous, erected a city named after himself, opposite Astacus.

2] Colonists from Megara founded Astacus early in the 17th Olympiad.[17] They chose the name Astacus in accordance with an oracle after a man named Astacus, one of the so-called earth-born Sparti descendants of the ones in Thebes, and a noble and high-minded man.

3] After the city had endured many attacks from its neighbors and become exhausted by the succession of wars, it was colonized next, after the Megarians, by the Athenians.[18] Then the city outgrew its misfortunes and became strong and famous. At that time Diodalsus held sway over the Bithynians.

4] When he died Boteiras ruled, living for 76 years. His son Bas succeeded him, and Bas got the better of Alexander's general, Calas, despite his great experience in warfare, and forced the Macedonians to keep their hands off Bithynia. Now he lived 71 years, ruling for 50 of them.

5] His son and the successor to his rule was Zipoetes, a famous warrior who killed one of Lysimachus' generals and drove another far away from his dominions. In fact he even proved too strong for Lysimachus himself, and also for Seleucus' son Antiochus, who ruled respectively over Macedonia and over Asia. He founded a city below Mt. Luperus and named it after himself. He lived 76 years and ruled his dominions for 48 years, leaving four sons.

6] His eldest son, Nicomedes, succeeded him, and proved no brother but an executioner to his brothers. But he too strengthened the Bithynian realm, and he it was who was responsible for bringing the Galatae to Asia. Also, as has been mentioned, he established a city bearing his own name.

xiii

1] Not long afterwards war broke out, the Byzantines against the Calatians — who were colonists of Heraclea — and the Istrians, concerning the trading post of Tomi, adjacent to Calatis, when the Calatians decided to establish a trading monopoly there. Both sides sent envoys to Heraclea seeking an alliance. The Heracleotes gave military support to neither, but sent men to both to act as conciliators; but their efforts were not successful at that time. However, after suffering many losses from their enemies the Calatians later made a settlement, but they were scarcely able to recover their strength after this disaster.

xiv

1] Before a long period had elapsed Nicomedes, King of the Bithynians, found himself approaching his end. His son Zeilas, by a previous marriage, had fled to the King of Armenia, driven out by the schemes of his stepmother, Etazeta, whose sons by Nicomedes were still infants.[19] Accordingly, he declared the sons by his second marriage to be his heirs, and appointed as their guardians Ptolemy and Antigonus, as well as the people of Byzantium, Heraclea and Cius.

2] But Zeilas returned to his ancestral kingdom with an army furnished by the Galatian Tolostobogii. The Bithynians, anxious to keep the kingdom for the children, married off their mother to the brother of Nicomedes; then, getting an army from the before mentioned guardians, they waited for Zeilas. After each side had fought many battles with varying results, they finally came to an understanding. The Heracleotes gave a good account of themselves in the fighting and brought about a favorable treaty.

3] Consequently, the Galatae treated Heraclea as an enemy, overrunning their territory all the way to the Calles River. Obtaining great booty they returned home.

xv

When Antiochus made war on the Byzantines the Heracleotes assisted them with 40 triremes and caused the war to stop at threats.

xvi

1] Not long afterwards it happened that Ariobarzanes departed from among men, leaving behind him a son Mithridates, as well as a dispute with the Galatae. The latter, despising the boy, plundered his kingdom.

2] The result was a shortage of food, so the Heracleotes sent grain from Heraclea to Amisus, where the men of Mithridates could easily provision themselves and end the shortage. On this account the Galatae once more sent an army into Heracleote territory and laid it waste, until the Heracleotes sent envoys to them. The historian, Nymphis, was chief of the delegation. He obtained their withdrawal from the land by presenting the army as a whole with 5,000 gold coins, and giving 200 gold coins separately to each of the leaders.

xvii

Ptolemy, King of Egypt, reaching the height of prosperity, was moved to bestow magnificent gifts on the cities, and he sent 500 (?) artabas of wheat to the Heracleotes,[20] and he built a temple of Heracles for them on the acropolis, made of Proconnesian stone.[21]

xviii

1] When he reaches this point the historian digresses on the subject of Rome — on the origins of the race, how they came to settle in Italy, what happened and what deeds were done before the founding of Rome; and he briefly describes the early days and enumerates the peoples on whom they made war, what happened under the kings and how the monarchy later was changed in favor of consuls, how the Romans were defeated by the Galatae and how the city would have fallen had not Camillus come to the rescue and saved it.

2] And how when Alexander crossed over into Asia and wrote them to the effect that they must conquer if they were capable of empire and otherwise submit to their conquerors, the Romans sent him a gold crown of considerable value; and how they made war on the Tarentines, who had allied themselves with Pyrrhus of Epirus, in such a way that after both suffering defeats and inflicting them on the enemy, they subjugated the Tarentines and drove Pyrrhus out of Italy.

3] And of the deeds of the Romans against Hannibal and the Carthaginians; and of the achievements of Scipio and others against the Iberians, and how he refused to accept the title of King of the Iberians which was offered him; and how Hannibal fled in defeat.

4] And how the Romans crossed the Ionian sea; and how Perseus, son of Philip, inherited the Macedonian throne, and how, after youthful impetuosity led him to break the treaty made by his father with the Romans, he was defeated and Paulus set up a trophy for his defeat.

5] And how, defeating Antiochus, King of Syria, Commagene and Judaea, in two battles, they drove him out of Europe.

6] The historian digresses on the Roman empire to this point. Resuming the narrative, he tells us that the Heracleotes sent envoys to the Roman generals who had crossed over to Asia,[22] and that they were favorably received, and obtained a gracious letter sent by P. Aemilius[23] in which the Senate promised friendship to them along with other indications of interest and concern, and which also promised that if they asked for anything they would not be refused.

7] Later they sent an embassy to Cornelius Scipio, the man who had won Africa for the Romans, to confirm the friendship that had been agreed upon.

8] Afterwards they sent another embassy to him for the purpose of reconciling the Romans with King Antiochus, and they passed a decree which they sent Antiochus, urging him to put an end to his enmity with the Romans. And Corneilius Scipio replied to the Heracleotes, and this is what he said: "Scipio, general, proconsul of the Romans, to the senate and people of Heraclea, Greetings!" And in the letter he confirmed his regard for them, and said that the Romans would end the war with Antiochus. And Publius Cornelius Scipio, his brother and the commander of the fleet, replied to the Heracleote embassy to the same effect as Lucius.

9] Not long afterwards Antiochus again met the Romans and was defeated. They ended hostilities with a treaty which deprived him of all Asia[24] and also of his elephants and the ships in his fleet; but he retained the rule over Commagene and Judaea.

10] The city of Heraclea sent ambassadors in the same way to the successors of these Roman generals, and they were received with the same consideration and good will. Finally, a treaty was made between the Romans and the Heracleotes, not merely a treaty of friendship but one of alliance, specifying against whom and for what purposes it was to be invoked. Two bronze tablets contained the agreement in identical terms; the copy in Rome was nailed up in the Temple of Capitoline Zeus, the one in Heraclea was also in the Temple of Zeus.

Notes

1. 364/3 B.C.
2. 361/0–339/8.
3. 346/5.
4. 338/7.
5. 338/7.
6. 334.
7. June 323.
8. Droysen prefers Tyre here.
9. 306/5.
10. I.e., Heraclea.
11. I.e., of free government.
12. I.e., "Thunderbolt."
13. I.e., at Corypedion in 281.
14. I.e., garrison commanders.
15. "Carron" means "stronger" among the Dorians.
16. I.e., Bithynia (MS faulty).
17. 712/1.
18. 435/4.
19. 255/3?
20. 247/6?
21. A white marble.
22. 190.
23. The text is somewhat confused here.
24. I.e., Asia Minor, as is usual in Memnon.

18

Polybius and
the Writing of History

POLYBIUS came from a political family. His father Lycortas was one of the leading statesmen of the Achaean League, the supporter and friend of Philopoemen, and was himself elected General of the League in 185 B.C. and perhaps twice thereafter. As a man of about thirty-five Polybius was one of the Greek hostages brought to Rome after the Third Macedonian War in 167 B.C. More fortunate than others, he won the respect and friendship of Scipio the Younger whom he accompanied on his campaigns, notably to Africa in the Third Punic War. In addition to his History, Polybius wrote a tribute to Philopoemen, which is lost. His History, in forty books, described the events from 220 down to 145/4 B.C., with the first two books giving the background of Roman history from 264 B.C. on. Unhappily only the first five books have survived intact, the rest in fragments that vary from long usable excerpts to bare citations. Yet they remain the most impressive torso of what was once a vast historical literature in the Hellenistic period. His strength and weaknesses as a historian will both be evident to the attentive reader in the passages that follow.

Polybius i, 1-4; ii, 56-63

i

1] IF IT HAD happened that those who preceded us in recording events had neglected the praise of history itself, it would probably have been necessary to impress everyone with the value of studying such works, because nothing is more suited to straighten men out than the knowledge of past events. However, not only have some writers done this to a certain extent, but everyone has made this the "sum and substance", as the phrase goes, proclaiming that the study of history is the truest education and a veritable training school for political life; that the only really effective teacher for nobly enduring the vicissitudes of fortune is the remembrance of the changes experienced by others. Obviously, therefore, no one, least of all ourselves, ought to be called on to repeat what many have said already, and so eloquently. Moreover, the startling nature of the events we have chosen to describe is sufficient to invite, even impel, young or old to read this work. For what man is so indifferent or so lazy that he does not care to know how, and under what form of government, Rome brought virtually the whole oecumene[1] under her rule in barely fifty-three years, a result never achieved before? Or, again, could anyone be so much attracted by some other subject or study as to prefer it to an understanding of this?

2] But just how great and how extraordinary the subject of our investigation is can best be shown if we consider the most famous of the preceding empires, about which a great many histories have been written, and measure them against the worth of the Romans. Now these are the empires that deserve such comparison and measurement: For some time the Persians possessed great empire and dominion, but as often as they attempted to overstep the boundaries of Asia, not only their own empire but they themselves were endangered. Then the Lacedaemonians, who disputed for many years over the rule of Greece, after they were victorious held that rule unchallenged for barely twelve years. Subsequently the Macedonians held sway over Europe from the region of the Adriatic to the Ister[2] River, which seems a very small part of the continent, though later they added to this the rule of Asia when they destroyed the Persian Empire. Now while they are regarded as having controlled the largest number of regions and governments they still left a major part of the oecumene under the rule of others. For they did not even attempt to exercise dominion over Sicily, Sardinia and Libya, and to speak plainly they were not even acquainted with the very warlike races of western Europe. The Romans, however, have subjected not merely a part but virtually the whole of the oecumene[3] to their rule. They have made their rule irresistible for the present time, and one which cannot be surpassed in the generations to come. Now this work will make it possible to arrive at a better understanding of why they were universally successful. Furthermore a historical narrative is calculated to furnish the lovers of learning with details of its magnitude and extent.

3] Our history will begin at the time of the one hundred and fortieth Olympiad[4] and the events among the Greeks known as the War of the Allies waged by Philip, the son of Demetrius and the father of Perseus, in conjunction with the Achaeans against the Aetolians; and among the inhabitants of Asia with the war Antiochus and Ptolemy Philopator fought against one another over Coele-Syria; and in the regions of Italy and Libya with the war undertaken by the Romans and the Carthaginians which is usually called the Hannibalic War. Now these events occurred in the world separately, as it were, since each thing that happened was differentiated by what was being attempted, by what resulted from it and likewise by the region in which it occurred. But during this period history becomes, so to speak, an organic whole. What happens in Italy and in Libya is bound up with what happened in Asia and in Greece, all events culminating in a single result. That is why we have chosen this as the beginning of our history. Having conquered the Carthaginians in the war mentioned above, and thinking that they had already accomplished the hardest part of acquiring universal dominion, the Romans were then first emboldened to stretch out their hands to grasp what remained and cross over with their army to Greece and to the regions of Asia. Now if the governments that were about to contend for universal rule were familiar and well known to us, then we would probably not need to sketch in the preceding events or to show the calculations and resources which led them to make such great efforts. But in view of the fact that most Greeks lack available information on the resources and achievements both of Rome and of Carthage before this time we have felt it to be necessary to compose this book and the one that follows it as an introduction to our history. Then, when he has given his attention to the narrative of these events, no one will be puzzled or lack the information on what the Roman plans were or what military and financial resources they had at their disposal, when they began the undertaking by which they obtained dominion both over the land and also over the whole of our sea. But these books and the introductory material they contain will make it clear to those who read them that the Romans began their undertaking with a well thought out plan, by completing which they arrived at universal empire and dominion.

4] Now here is what is unique in our work and amazing about the times in which we have lived: Fortune has tilted all the affairs of the world in one direction, forcing everything towards the same mark, so that it also becomes necessary through this history to present readers with an overall view of the handiwork of Fortune in shaping world affairs. This has been the chief reason that has led us to undertake our history, but there is also the fact that no one in our time has concerned himself with writing a general history; otherwise I would have been much less zealous in the matter. But now, noticing that most historians deal with individual wars and some of the events connected with them, while no general systematic explanation of what happened, when it happened, what the causes were and what the final results, has been offered, so far as we are aware by anyone, I felt that it was absolutely essential not to neglect or to pass over unnoticed the most excellent and profitable example of the workings of Fortune. For although she has wrought many changes by her constant interference with the lives of men, never has she labored so mightily or accomplished so much as in our period. Now this is a fact which cannot be grasped from those who write particular histories, unless someone maintains that in visiting the most illustrious cities one by one, or even, God help us, that by examining the pictures of each separately he can at once see the whole world pattern, and how everything fits into its place! Generally speaking, I think those who believe that they can obtain an overall view by means of particular histories are afflicted in much the same way as anyone would be who thought that the examination of the scattered parts of what had once been a beautiful living animal would be all that was needed to enable him to apprehend the vitality and charm of the living creature. Yet if such a man were immediately shown a reconstruction of the entire animal depicted on a life-sized scale, with proper proportions and an animated appearance, I imagine he would admit at once that previously he had missed the truth by a wide margin, like a man in a dream. It is possible to get some inkling of the whole from the part, but it is not possible to understand it or even to form an accurate opinion of it. Consequently separate histories must be regarded as of very little use in arriving at a realistic conception of the total picture. For it is only by exposing side by side the threads that connect each event with the whole complex, and also by pointing out resemblances and differences, that it becomes possible to achieve this, and to be able to derive profit as well as enjoyment from the study of history.

*　　*　　*

ii

56] In view of the fact that while some have looked with favor on Phylarchus among the writers who lived at the same time as Aratus, I frequently find myself in disagreement with him, contradicting him in what I write, it might be helpful, in fact it is incumbent on us who have chosen to follow Aratus on the War of Cleomenes, not to leave this matter unexamined, lest we allow falsehood to carry equal weight with truth in the writing of history. Now this historian makes a practice of writing many things carelessly and in a random fashion throughout his work. Although it will probably be unnecessary to find fault with the other parts of it at present or to speak about them in any detail, whatever falls within the period we are describing, and that is the period of the War of Cleomenes, those passages we must examine thoroughly. Furthermore, this will be quite sufficient for understanding the tendencies and abilities he exhibits throughout his history.

Wishing to expose the cruelty of Antigonus and the Macedonians along with that of Aratus and the Achaeans, he says that when the Mantineians suffered great misfortunes at their hands all Greece was moved to tears over the fact that the most ancient and the most important city in Arcadia should have met with such great calamities. In his effort to evoke the pity of his readers and to win their sympathy for his account he introduces women clinging to the altars with disheveled hair and bared breasts, and he also adds the tears and groans of men and women as they are led off together with their children and aging parents. And this is the sort of thing he does throughout his history, always endeavoring to present each horror before our eyes. Disregarding what is ignoble and effeminate in this approach, let us consider its appropriateness as well as its utility in a history. Now the historian surely ought not to startle his readers by putting marvels into his history, nor ought he to look for the words that men might actually have used or yet to enumerate the hypothetical results of the events under consideration, in the manner of a tragic poet; but instead he ought to give an entirely truthful account of what was done and what was said, even though it happens to be very restricted. For the object of history is not the same as that of tragedy, but the opposite, for tragedy moves its audience at the present moment and charms them by the persuasiveness of its language, while history instructs and convinces the lovers of learning for all time by means of the actual deeds and words. For in a tragedy plausibility is the essential thing even if it is untrue, in order to beguile the spectators, while in history truth is the essential for those who are intent on learning.

But aside from these considerations he[5] usually gives an account of sudden reverses of fortune without also giving the origins and purposes that lie behind the events, yet without these it is impossible to feel reasonable pity or appropriate indignation over anything that takes place. Surely there is no one who does not feel that it is a terrible thing to see free persons beaten? Yet if a man suffers this because he was guilty of far worse acts of injustice then he is held to have been punished justly. And if this is done with a view to instruction and improvement then those who beat free persons are thought to deserve honor and thanks. Likewise, killing citizens is regarded as an impious act deserving the most severe penalties, yet the man who kills a thief or an adulterer is obviously innocent, while whoever slays a traitor or a tyrant receives honors and the respect of everyone. All such acts, then, are to be judged with reference to their purpose, not merely on the basis of the acts themselves, but in accordance with the differences they show in the motivation and intent of those who commit them.

57] Now the Mantineians voluntarily renounced their Achaean citizenship, first entrusting themselves and their country to the Aetolians and later to Cleomenes. After they had made this choice and had become partners with the Lacedaemonian government, in the fourth year before the arrival of Antigonus[6] they were seized by the Achaeans when Aratus took the city by surprise. And on that occasion they were very far from suffering any unpleasantnesses for their aforementioned guilt, but what did happen was much talked about because of the sudden change that took place in the policies of both sides. For as soon as he captured the city Aratus sent out instructions forthwith that none of his men was to take anything belonging to their adversaries. Then, calling the Mantineians together, he urged them to set aside their fears and remain in their own land, guaranteeing their safety if they accepted Achaean citizenship. Thereupon the Mantineians promptly changed their minds at a proposal as remarkable as it was unexpected. And the very men they had been fighting a short time before, at whose hands they had seen many of their kinsmen destroyed and many others severely wounded, these men they invited into their own houses, sharing the same hearth with them and the rest of their kinsmen; nor was any token of mutual friendship omitted. And this was natural, for I do not know that any men ever encountered a more generous foe, or that any men ever came through what seemed to be such a great disaster with less harm than the Mantineians did, thanks to the humanity shown them by Aratus and the Achaeans.

58] Later on, foreseeing internal disorders as well as plots by the Aetolians and the Lacedaemonians, they thought it best to send envoys to the Achaeans asking them for a garrison. They agreed and chose three hundred of their own men by lot. Those who were selected abandoned their ancestral lands and way of life to go out to live in Mantineia, protecting the freedom as well as the security of the Mantineians. But two hundred mercenaries were also sent along with them to help the Mantineians maintain the existing arrangements. Not long afterwards when an internal revolution broke out the Mantineians called in the Lacedaemonians and turned the city over to them, slaughtering the Achaeans who were living in their midst. It would not be easy to cite any greater breach of faith or any more atrocious act. When they decided to break off their ties of gratitude and friendship with that nation they should at least have spared the men referred to, and have allowed them all to leave under a truce. It is customary to grant this even to the enemy according to the common laws of mankind. But in order to give Cleomenes and the Lacedaemonians sufficient confidence to make an attack they deliberately committed the most impious of acts, violating the common justice of mankind. What reprisals do they deserve who took vengeance with their own hands on those who, when they had captured them by force earlier, let them off scot free, and then continued to protect their independence and security? What ought they to have suffered to give appropriate satisfaction to the claims of justice? Perhaps someone might say by being sold into slavery along with their wives and children after being defeated in war? But that is prescribed by the rules of war even for those who have committed no act of impiety. But surely they deserved some much more terrible punishment, and even if they suffered what Phylarchus says they did it is unlikely that the Greeks would have been sorry for them; instead they would have praised those who had punished their impiety. Nevertheless, nothing more happened to these Mantineians when their fortunes were reversed than confiscation of property and the selling of the free population into slavery. In striving for effect the historian not only falsified the whole incident but his falsehood is not even plausible, and his ignorance is so great that he is unable to see the obvious: how it was that when the same people took Tegea by force in the same period they did none of these things to the Tegeans. Yet if the cruelty of those who acted was responsible then surely the Tegeans would have suffered the same treatment experienced by others at the same time. But since the Mantineians alone were treated in this way it is obvious there must have been some special reason for the wrath displayed against them.

59] Then again he says of Aristomachus of Argos, a man of the most distinguished family who had formerly been tyrant of Argos and who was descended from tyrants, that his sufferings were the most unjust and the most terrible known to man. Carefully examining this episode in his own peculiar way the historian invents certain cries which he says were carried to nearby houses during the night he was being tortured. He says that some persons were shocked at the impiety, others refused to believe what they heard, while still others ran off towards the building in anger at what was going on. Let us ignore the great exaggerations in his account, for they are sufficiently evident. It is my contention that if Aristomachus had committed no other crime against the Achaeans he deserved the most severe punishment for being the kind of man he was and for the lawless way he had treated his own country. But wishing to enhance his own reputation and to cause the reader to share his indignation at the sufferings of that man, the historian refers to him as a former tyrant and also as a descendant of tyrants. Yet no one could make a more serious charge or a harsher one than that, since the word itself has the most sinister implications and embraces every unjust and illegal act known to man. And if Aristomachus had indeed received the most cruel punishment, as he says that he did, even then he could not have atoned for what he did the day Aratus and the Achaeans got into the city. After strenuous efforts and after risking great danger in order to liberate the Argives, Aratus was finally driven out because none of the men drawn up inside the city stirred to help him because of their fear of the tyrant. Thereupon Aristomachus, on the questionable grounds that the Achaeans had got into the city with the help of conspirators, slaughtered eighty of the leading citizens who had done nothing wrong, after torturing them in the presence of their relatives. I will omit the outrageous acts of this same man throughout his life and also those of his forebears, for that would take too long.

60] Now if he had met with treatment of the same kind it ought not to be regarded as shocking, since it would have been much more shocking had he died unpunished without suffering any of these things. Nor should Antigonus or Aratus be charged with lawlessness for putting to death under torture a tyrant whom they got their hands on in time of war. For honor and praise are bestowed on those who exact retribution of death on such a man even in peacetime by right-thinking people. When, in addition to what has already been mentioned, he broke a treaty with the Achaeans what did he deserve to suffer? Not long before this he had laid down his tyranny under the pressure of circumstances brought about by the death of Demetrius[7] and, surprisingly, his safety was guaranteed, thanks to the lenience and noble-mindedness of the Achaeans, who not only granted him immunity for the impious acts of his tyranny but admitted him into their confederacy, even giving him the very highest office as their general and leader. But he, promptly forgetting these benefactions when he entertained sanguine hopes for the future based on Cleomenes, renounced his own commitments and those of his city and deserted the Achaeans to join the enemy at a very critical time. When he was caught he ought not to have been tortured to death in Cenchreae at night as Phylarchus tells us he was, but instead he should have been carried all around the Peloponnese as a spectacle and tortured until he died. Nevertheless, despite the kind of man he was he suffered nothing worse than being drowned by a detachment of soldiers in Cenchreae.

61] In addition to these things he[8] has given a rhetorically exaggerated account of the misfortunes of the Mantineians, evidently regarding it as the responsibility of the historian to point out unlawful acts, yet he does not so much as allude to the generosity displayed by the Megalopolitans in the same period, as though the enumeration of instances of bad conduct is more a part of history than calling attention to noble and just actions, and as though the readers of historical commentaries are less improved by examples of illustrious deeds worthy of imitation, than by those of lawless ones as actions to be avoided. Now he has told us how Cleomenes captured the city,[9] and how, without damaging it he sent messengers to the Meglopolitans in Messene offering to let them return safely to their city and to take part in the government, for he wishes to show that Cleomenes was magnanimous and reasonable towards his enemies. Also he tells us how when the letter was being read aloud the Megalopolitans would not allow the reading to continue, but came very near stoning the envoys — he carries the narrative down to this point. But he leaves out what also belongs here and is a part of history: the praise and commemoration of noble principles. And yet this is clearly a case in point. And if we regard as good citizens men who merely submit themselves to war by law and decree to help their friends and allies, and if we bestow not merely praise but gratitude and the highest privileges on those who undergo siege and the destruction of their country, what should be our judgment of the Megalopolitans? Should it not be one of the highest respect? For first they gave up the territory awarded to Cleomenes; then again, after that, they lost their country entirely because of their friendship for the Achaeans; and finally, when they had the opportunity against all hope and reason of recovering their city unharmed they chose to give up lands, tombs, shrines, fatherland — everything in short most necessary to human life — rather than to betray the trust of their allies. What nobler deed was ever done, or ever could be done? Is there anything to which the historian ought to direct the attention of his readers more than to this? What action offers a greater inducement to keeping faith and sharing in the enterprises of a truly resolute commonwealth? Yet Phylarchus makes no mention of these things because, as it seems to me, he is blind to the most deserving deeds and those most worthy of the historian's attention.

62] However, he goes on to relate that six thousand talents came into the hands of the Lacedaemonians out of the booty from Megalopolis, two thousand of which were given to Cleomenes in accordance with their practice. Now with reference to this sum, is there anyone who is not immediately amazed at such naïveté and ignorance of what is common knowledge about the resources and expenditures of Greek states? And I am not speaking of the days when they were subject to the kings of Macedonia, still less of the times when the Peloponnese was utterly ruined by a succession of internal wars, but of our own day when everyone agrees that it has enjoyed the greatest prosperity. Yet, despite this fact, no such sum could have been collected from all the movable property in the Peloponnese, not counting the slaves. And this is no careless statement, but it will be clear from what follows that we are speaking reasonably. Who has not read how the Athenians when they entered the war against the Lacedaemonians on the Theban side, and sent out ten thousand soldiers and manned one hundred triremes, that they then decided to make an inventory of all the lands in Attica, including the houses and all the rest of their possessions in order to levy a property tax on the basis of valuation to meet the expenses of the war?[10] Yet the total estimate came two hundred and fifty talents short of reaching six thousand. From this my previous statement about the Peloponnese will not seem to be unreasonable. For at that time, even speaking with exaggeration, no one would venture to maintain that there were three hundred talents in Megalopolis itself, considering that they had fled to Messene with most of the slave population. And there is the strongest kind of support for what I have said, because the Mantineians who, as he himself says, were second to none in Arcadia either in power or wealth, were captured by treachery during a siege. Therefore it was not easy for anyone to flee or get away by stealth, yet the entire booty they yielded, slaves included, was three hundred talents in that same period.

63] And who would not be even more bewildered by what comes next? After describing these events he says that ten days at most before the battle[11] an envoy arrived from Ptolemy informing Cleomenes that Ptolemy refused to continue his subsidy and bidding him make terms with Antigonus. When he learned this, Phylarchus tells us, he decided to stake his all at the soonest possible moment before his troops found out what had happened, since there was no hope of paying them out of his own resources. But if he had been in possession of six thousand talents at that time he would have been in a position to surpass Ptolemy himself in wealth. And even though he only had control of three hundred talents he was more than able to meet the expenses of the war with Antigonus. When he states that all Cleomenes' hopes depended on Ptolemy because he lacked money to meet expenses, and when he also maintains that at the same time he was possessed of such an enormous sum, how can this fail to be regarded as an indication of complete confusion and carelessness? Many other instances of this kind could be mentioned, both in the period under consideration and throughout his history, but I think what has already been said is sufficient for the purposes with which I began.

244

Notes

1. I.e., the inhabited world.
2. I.e., the Danube.
3. The text here is defective.
4. 220–216 B.C.
5. I.e., Phylarchus.
6. Antigonus Doson, the Macedonian king, came to the Peloponnese in 224 B.C.
7. I.e., Demetrius II, the King of Macedonia 239–229 B.C.
8. I.e., Phylarchus.
9. I.e., Megalopolis.
10. The date is 378 B.C.
11. I.e., of Sellasia in 222 B.C. (?).

19

The Greek Traveler

Heracleides Creticus (or Criticus) is the author of the first excerpt, which is all that is left of his Notes on the Greek Cities. Almost nothing is known about him except that he probably lived early in the second century B.C. It is a pity we do not have the entire work but we are grateful for what remains, which at least is not an abridgement. We are enabled to visualize the Greek countryside when travel was chiefly by foot. The writer speaks from experience, however anxious he is to interlard his account with quotations from the comic poets. It is our earliest description of Greek cities from the point of view of the traveler. Since Heracleides rigorously excludes the Peloponnese as not part of Hellas proper, the passages from Pausanias on Olympia and the Games have been added. Pausanias was a guidebook writer of the second century A.D., and his description of lost statues and paintings are very important for the history of art. It seems not inappropriate to end with this account of the Olympic Games which retained their vitality to the end, though standards of athletic behavior seem not to have improved.

a Heracleides, Notes on the Greek Cities

— THIS IS where the Peloponnese begins —

1] From there to the city of the Athenians. The road is a pleasant one all the way, through cultivated land offering an attractive prospect to the eye. But the city is quite dry and poorly watered, while because it is so old the arrangement of the streets is bad. Most of the houses are shabby though there are a few respectable ones. A stranger seeing it for the first time might refuse to believe that this was the famous city of Athens, but after a little while he will believe it. For it contains the most beautiful buildings in the world: a memorable theater, spacious and handsome; a splendid temple of Athena worthy of the goddess, called the Parthenon, which rises above the theater and makes a striking impression on the viewer; the Olympeium which, though only half-finished, is very impressive because of the scale on which it is built — and it would have been the very finest had it been finished. Three gymnasiums: the Academy, the Lyceum and the Cynosarges, each provided with fine trees and lawns. A great variety of festivals; also diversions to cheer the soul of every kind of philosopher; many amusements; continual exhibitions.

2] The fruits of the soil are inimitable and have the very finest flavor, but there is a certain lack of quantity. But having strangers living there closely associated with them, and sharing in their tastes diverts their attention to pleasing them, and at the same time causes them to forget their hunger. With its amusements and exhibitions the city seems not to admit of hunger so far as the common people are concerned, for it almost makes them forget food; but for those with money there is nowhere else that offers so much in the way of enjoyment. But the city has many other delights, since the neighboring towns are all suburbs of the Athenians.

3] The people who live there have the power to give any artist a high reputation, bestowing their approval on every success. A wonderful school for men, creatures subject to illusion.

4] Now of the inhabitants some are Atticans, others Athenians. The Atticans are inquisitive chatterers, treacherous and always spying and ready to denounce foreign ways. But the Athenians are magnanimous with frank manners, tenacious and honorable friends. However, there are a few pettifoggers wandering about in the city who extort money from visitors and wealthy foreigners. When the democracy catches them, though, they are severely handled. But the genuine Athenians are a discriminating audience at artistic performances and tireless spectators.

5] In brief, just as other cities are superior to the countryside in the pleasures and the amenities of life, so does the city of the Athenians leave other cities behind. But one must be on guard against the prostitutes for fear of being sweetly ruined unawares. These are the lines of Lysippus:[1]

If you have not seen Athens you are a clod.
If you have seen her without being enchanted you are an ass.
If you are pleased yet leave her — a pack animal.
This Greek city is like a rose,
Containing both fragrance and unpleasantness.
For the Sun Festival stirs my wrath,
The solar year drives me mad.
And when anyone speaks euphemistically of the white poplar

As the "Sun's Diadem" I am so choked
By these expressions that I would prefer
Taking my own life rather than go on listening to such stuff.
Such a fog enwraps the stranger here.

6] From here to Oropus by way of Aphidnae and the temple of
Zeus Amphiaraus is about a day's walk for anyone without a pack,
and steep. However the great number of guest houses supplied with
all the necessities of life, and places to rest prevent the traveler from
becoming weary.

7] The city of the Oropians belongs to Thebes. Active retail trade,
insatiable greed on the part of the customs officials, fostered by un-
rivalled knavery over a long period of time. For they levy a toll on
goods even before they are brought into Oropus. Most of the people
are boorish to meet, having gotten rid of the intelligent ones. Belying
the Boeotians, they are the Athenians of Boeotia. Here are Xenon's[2]
verses:

> Tax collectors all, and all of them are greedy.
> May the Oropians come to a bad end!

8] From here to Tanagra 130 stades. The road winds through
dense woods and olive trees, and is entirely free of the fear of rob-
bers. The city stands on a stony height, the land looks white and the
soil is clayey; its beauty is enhanced by houses with impressive entrances, and by carvings ornamented by colors in wax. The land does
not provide the city with an unlimited supply of grain crops, but the
wine is the best in Boeotia.

9] The inhabitants are very well off but live frugally. They are
all farmers not laborers. They are excellent men for fair-dealing,
keeping their word, and hospitality. They freely offer a share of anything they have to needy citizens or foreign vagrants, and they
entirely avoid illegal sharp practices. This city is the safest place in
Boeotia for a stranger to live. There is a downright intolerant hatred
of vice, thanks to the self-sufficiency and industriousness of the inhabitants.

10] In fact, I noticed very little inclination to debauchery of any
kind in the city, which usually causes the greatest crimes among
mankind. And where there is sufficient means there is nothing to
stimulate the desire for gain. Among such people it is difficult for
vice to arise.

11] From here to Plataea the distance is 200 stades. The road is rather lonesome and stony, rising up near Cithaeron, but it is not particularly dangerous. This is what the comic poet Poseidippus[3] says about the city:

> There are two temples, a hall, and the name,
> And a bath, and Sarambus' fame —
> Most of the time a desert, but during the Eleutheria a city.

The citizens have nothing to say except that they are Athenian colonists and that the battle between the Greeks and the Persians took place there. They are Athenians among the Boeotians.

12] From there to Thebes 80 stades. The whole way is smooth and level. The city lies in the center of the Boeotian land and has a circuit of 70 stades. It is all flat and circular in shape, with black soil. Although an ancient city the streets are laid out in modern fashion because, as history tells us, it was levelled with the ground three different times, thanks to the oppressiveness and the arrogance of its inhabitants.

13] Also the city is fine for breeding horses, very well-watered, green and fertile, with more gardens than any city in Greece. The two rivers that flow through it water the whole plain below the city. But water is also brought down from the Cadmea in underground pipes which they say were laid out in ancient times by Cadmus.

14] Such is the city. The inhabitants are high-spirited and extraordinarily confident under all circumstances; they are bold, violent and oppressive. They quarrel with everyone, making no distinction between foreigner and native, and they have an utter contempt for justice.

15] In disputes over agreements they do not talk matters over but resort to the power of their fists, employing the strong-arm tactics of athletes in the games in their legal contests.

16] Consequently lawsuits are brought into court only after at least thirty years have gone by. For if anyone suggests anything of this kind in the assembly and fails to leave Boeotia at once he will soon be waylaid in the night and meet with a violent death at the hands of those who do not wish the lawsuit concluded. Murders are committed there on the slightest pretext.

17] This then is the kind of people they are. But there are a few worthy men going about among them, men of high principles who deserve the friendship of anyone. Of all the women in Greece their wives are the fairest and best proportioned in stature, bearing and grace of movement, as Sophocles[4] testifies:

You speak to me of Thebes with the seven-mouthed gates,
Where mortal women give birth to gods.

18] Their garments are draped around the head in such a way that the whole face seems to be veiled, for only the eyes are visible, all the other parts of the face being entirely hidden by their cloaks. These female garments are always white.

19] They are blond and they wear their hair bound up in a knot. This is called a "torch" by the natives. Their shoes are plain and not high, but low-soled and red; they are pierced through so the feet seem almost bare.

20] In behavior they are less like Boeotian women than the women of Sicyon. Their voices are charming while those of the men are heavy and disagreeable.

21] The city is at its best in summer, for it has an abundance of cold water and gardens. Also there are fresh breezes and the city has a green look and is rich in fruits and all sorts of summer produce. But there is no wood and it is the worst place to spend the winter on account of the rivers and the wind. Also it snows and there is a great deal of mud.

22] Here are the verses of Laon[5] (he writes to praise them and does not tell the truth; he was convicted of adultery but released after he bought off the man he wronged for a small sum):

Love the man of Boeotia. The woman of Boeotia also
Is not to be shunned. He is a fine fellow and she is charming.

23] From here to Anthedon is 160 stades. This is a side road,[6] but passable, wandering past cultivated fields. The city is not of great size; it lies on the Euboean sea; the market place is covered with trees, and has a hall with a double colonnade. The city is well supplied with wine and fish, but poor in grain because of the wretched soil.

24] Almost all the inhabitants are fishermen, some of whom gain a livelihood by angling, others go after purple fish and sponges. They grow old on the beaches, in the seaweed and in their huts. In appearance they are all slight and redheaded. The ends of their fingernails are worn down by their labors in the sea. Most of them are devoted to the sea and build ships. So far are they from cultivating their land that it is as though they did not have any. They themselves claim they are descended from the maritime Glaucus, who is admitted to have been a fisherman.[7]

25] This is what Boeotia is like. For Thespiae has only the pride of its men and statues that are not carved,[8] nothing else. The Boeotians give an account of their individual shortcomings, to the following effect: that covetousness is at home in Oropus, envy in Tanagra, contentiousness in Thespiae, violence in Thebes, greed in Anthedon, inquisitiveness in Coroneia, boasting in Plataea, malaria in Onchestus, obtuseness in Haliartus. Thus the blemishes of all Greece pour into the cities of Boeotia. Here is the verse of Pherecrates:[9]

If you are wise, give Boeotia a wide berth!

Such then is the Boeotian land.

26] From Anthedon to Chalcis is 70 stades. As far as Salganeus the road is even and smooth along the coast, touching the sea on one side, with a not very high mountain on the other — wooded and channeled by water from springs.

27] The city of the Chalcidians has a circuit of 70 stades, which is longer than the road that goes there from Anthedon. All the land is fertile and there is plenty of shade; the water is mostly brackish but there is some which, while slightly salty, is cold and conducive to health. This comes from the spring called Arethusa, and the water from this spring is sufficient to take care of all the inhabitants of the city.

28] The city is also excellently provided with public buildings: with gymnasiums, pillared halls, temples, theaters, paintings, statues and with a market place unsurpassed in meeting the needs of tradesmen.

29] The stream which comes from Salganeus in Boeotia and from the Euboean sea discharges itself in this direction into the Euripus, and flows alongside the walls of the harbor where the gate to the warehouse area is adjacent to the market place. The market place is broad and enclosed by three pillared halls. Now since the market is situated near the harbor and cargoes are quickly unloaded from the ships, they sail into this harbor in large numbers. Then, too, the Euripus, which can be reached from two directions, attracts merchants to the city.

30] Their whole country is planted with olive trees. The sea is also productive. The inhabitants are Greek, not only by descent but in speech. The sciences are cultivated here and the people are fond of travel and educated. They bear up nobly under misfortunes that befall the city. Living under foreign domination for a long period their behavior is still that of free men, and they have acquired the habit of putting up with whatever happens with equanimity. Here is a verse of Philiscus:[10]

A city of truly worthy Greeks is Chalcis.

ii

1] The mountain called Pelion is large and forested, with as much land given over to fruit trees as it has farm land. The longest and most heavily wooded spur of the mountain is 7 stades from the city[11] by sea and 20 by land.

2] The entire mountain is covered with soft loam and rich vegetation. Every kind of tree grows there, but it has a particularly large number of beech trees and silver fir and field maple, as well as cypress and juniper. There are also flowers, including the lily and the rose campion.

3] A plant is also found there, chiefly in the waste areas, the adder's wort, which cures snake bites and averts the danger from them. It drives snakes far away from the region where it grows, by its odor. If they do approach it makes them languid and if they touch it the smell kills them.

4] Such power does it have, but to men it seems to be sweet-smelling. The fragrance is similar to that of the thyme blossom. When taken in wine it will restore anyone to health no matter what snake may have bitten him.

5] Then there is a thorny plant growing on the mountain with berries like those of the white myrtle. If anyone grinds it up fine and then rubs it on his body he becomes insensitive even to very great cold, or at least he will feel it only slightly. Nor will he feel the summer's heat, because this drug thickens and stops the outside air from penetrating deep into the body.

6] These berries are scarce, growing in ravines and precipices, so they are hard to find; and even when they are found it is difficult to pick them for fear of falling down from the rocks and being dashed to pieces. Its potency lasts for a year, but as it grows older it loses its effectiveness.

7] Two rivers traverse the mountain, the Craysindon, as it is called, and the Brychon. The former waters the fields below the heights of Pelion, the other empties into the sea after flowing past the thicket of Pelaea.

8] On the very highest part of the mountain is a cave named for Chiron, and a shrine of Zeus Actaeus. When the Dog Star rises and it is intensely hot, the leading citizens and those who are in the prime of life who have been chosen in the presence of the priest, climb up there wearing new fleeces of triple wool. For on the mountain it happens that it is very cold.

9] Now on one side the mountain extends past Magnesia and Thessaly, towards the west and the setting sun. The other side, towards Athens and the so-called Macedonian gulf, lies entirely along the coast and is rockier than the part opposite Thessaly.

10] The mountain abounds in herbs with many different powers of healing, if you know what they look like and are able to make use of them. Among others there is one in particular. This is a tree which grows to a height of not more than a cubit wherever it shows above ground, and the color is black. The root extends for the same distance below the surface.

11] When this root is ground up and applied as a poultice, it removes the pain from those afflicted with gout and prevents the inflammation of the tendons. And the bark, when pounded smooth and drunk in wine cures complaints of the bowels. The leaves, when ground up and then smeared on a bandage are used for those suffering from ophthalmia or troubled with a discharge that threatens their sight. It gently checks the flow as though to prevent it from any longer reaching the eyes.

12] One family among the citizens understands this remedy, and they are believed to be descended from Chiron.[12] Each father explained the remedy to his son, and in this way secrecy was preserved, and no other citizens learned about it. Those who do understand these medicines are not allowed to help the sick for a fee, but only gratis.

So this is what Pelion and Demetrias are like.

iii

1] Taking Hellas as beginning after the Peloponnese, I define it as extending to the Gulf of Magnesia. There will probably be some who say we have included Thessaly as a part of Greece out of ignorance, but they are not aware of the truth of the matter.

2] For Hellas was once a city in ancient times, named for Hellen the son of Zeus who was also its founder, and it belonged to the land of Thessaly, being situated between Pharsalus and the city of the Melitaeans. The Hellenes, in fact, are those who are lineally descended from Hellen and who also inherit their Greek speech from him. The Athenians are those who live in Attica, whose race is Attic and who speak in the Attic dialect, just as the Dorians speak in the Dorian speech inherited from Dorus, the Aeolians speak the Aeolian tongue inherited from Aeolus and the Ionians speak Ionic as the descendants of Ion son of Xuthus. Therefore Hellas was in Thessaly, as things used to be, and not in Attica. For the poet says:[13]

They called themselves Myrmidons, Hellenes and Achaeans,

by which he means that the Myrmidons are the people living around Phthia in Thessaly, the Hellenes those whom I spoke of a little earlier, and the Achaeans those who still live in Meliteia, Larissa Cremastē and Achaean Thebes. The last-named was earlier called Phylacē, and was the place from which came the Protesilaus who campaigned against Troy. Thus Hellas is the city and country colonized by Hellen.

3] And Euripides[14] offers his testimony:

For Hellen, as they say, came from Zeus,
And Aeolus was his son; and from Aeolus came Sisyphus
And Athamas and Cretheus, and also he who into Alpheus'
    stream
Threw the thunderbolts, maddened by the god.

4] Hellas, then, as we said a little earlier, was what Hellen the son of Zeus founded, and from him also the expression "to speak Hellenic" was derived; and the Hellenes are the descendants of Hellen. And these are Aeolus and Sisyphus, also Athamas and Salmoneus and their natural descendants.

5] What is now called Hellas, though spoken of, does not exist. For I maintain that "to speak Greek" depends not merely on speaking Greek correctly, but also on having inherited this speech, and that means from Hellen. And Hellas is located in Thessaly, so we say that those people live in Hellas and speak true Greek.

6] Therefore, if Hellas belongs in a special sense to the people of Thessaly then it is right and proper that in the general meaning of the word "Hellenes," Thessaly be included as a part of Hellas.

7] The comic poet Poseidippus supports our contention that all those we have enumerated belong to Hellas. Being annoyed with the

Athenians for claiming that their speech and their city were part of Hellas he writes as follows:

> Hellas is one, though there are many cities.
> You talk Attic when you speak your native tongue,
> But we Hellenes speak Hellenic.
> Why do you lavish your time on syllables, letters even,
> Refining your wit to the point of nausea?

8] For those who do not regard Thessaly as part of Hellas, or the Thessalians, the descendants of Hellen, as speaking Hellenic let this be sufficient. And so we allow Hellas to extend as far as the Thessalian gulf and to Homolion in the land of the Magnesians. Having finished our description we bring this work to an end.

b   Pausanias, Book v

vii

1] THOSE WHO travel to Olympia will discover that there the Alpheius is already a large river and a most attractive sight, other rivers having emptied themselves into it, of which seven are specially noteworthy. Flowing through Megalopolis the Hellison pours into the Alpheius; the Brentheates emerges from the Megalopolitan land; and near Gortyna, where there is a shrine of Asclepius, flows the Gortynius; and from Melaenae between Megalopolis and Heraea, the Buphagus; from the Clitorian fields the Ladon; from Mount Erymanthus a stream named for that mountain. These rivers flow into the Alpheius from Arcadia, but the Cladeus joins its stream from Elis. The source of the Alpheius itself is not in Elis but in Arcadia.

2] The following tale is told about the river. There was said to have been a hunter named Alpheius who fell in love with Arethusa, herself a huntress. And they say that since she was unwilling to marry him Arethusa crossed over to the island off Syracuse, called Ortygia, where she was changed from a woman into a spring; because of his love Alpheius was turned into the river.

3] These things indeed are told about Alpheius and Ortygia.[15] And there is no reason I should not believe that the river travels there under the sea and unites itself with the spring, when I know the god in Delphi says the same thing. When he bade Archias of

Corinth found a colony in Syracuse he granted him the following oracle:

> There is a certain Ortygia which lies on the misty sea
> Above Trinacia,[16] where the mouth of the Alpheius gushes forth
> Mingling with the springs of fair Arethusa.

And I am convinced that the fact that the water of the Alpheius mingles with the springs of Arethusa gave rise to the fable of the river's infatuation.

4] Greeks and Egyptians who have gone up beyond Syene to the Ethiopian city of Meroë report that the Nile flows into a lake which it crosses just as though it were dry land and then continues its course through Lower Ethiopia into Egypt, entering the sea at Phares. And in the land of the Hebrews is a certain river Jordan, and I know myself that it crosses the lake named Tiberias and then enters another lake called the Dead Sea, after which it disappears under that lake.

5] The Dead Sea is different from any other body of water in that all living creatures float on top, even without swimming, while dead ones sink to the bottom. The result is that the lake has no fish, since they avoid the manifest danger by swimming back to more congenial waters. Now there is another stream in Ionia that is subject to the same effects as the Alpheius. Its source is in Mount Mycale, and after crossing the sea that lies in between, it rises again near Branchidae at the harbor called Panormus. These things then occur in the way mentioned.

6] In connection with the Olympic Games the Elean experts on very early times tell us that Cronus was the first to obtain the rule in heaven, and that the men of that day, who were known as the Golden Race, dedicated a temple to Cronus in Olympia. When Zeus was born Rhea is said to have entrusted the child to the so-called Dactyls of Ida — who are also identified with the Curetes — and they are said to have come from Mount Ida in Crete. They were: Heracles, Paeonaeus, Epimedes, Iasus and Idas.

7] For amusement Heracles, who was the oldest of them, arranged a racing contest among his brothers, crowning the winner with a branch of wild olive. The wild olive was so plentiful that they covered the ground under them with fresh olive leaves when they slept. They say the wild olive was brought to Greece from the land of the Hyperboreans by Heracles.

8] The Hyperboreans are men who live beyond the north wind.

First the Lycian Olen wrote in his *Hymn to Achaeia* that Achaeia came to Delos from these Hyperboreans; later Melanopus of Cymē in his *Ode to Opis and Hecaerges* says they both came to Delos from the Hyperboreans even ahead of Achaeia.

9] And Aristeas of Proconnesus, who also mentions the Hyperboreans, seems to have learned more about them from the Issedones whom he visited, as he tells us in his poems. So Heracles of Ida is reported to have first instituted the games at that time, and to have given them the name of Olympic. Also they were celebrated every fifth year[17] because he and his brothers were five in number.

10] There are also those who maintain that Zeus wrestled there with Cronus for the kingdom, while others say that Zeus held the games to celebrate his victory. Other gods are related to have won victories there; Apollo is said to have outstripped Hermes in a foot-race, and to have defeated Ares in boxing. They say that is why it is the tradition for flutes to play a Pythian melody during the pentathlon jumping — the flute being sacred to Apollo, and Apollo himself having won in the Olympics.

viii

1] Later on, they say about fifty years after Deucalion's flood in Greece, Clymenus the son of Cardys arrived from Crete, being descended from Heracles of Ida. He established games at Olympia and erected an altar to the other Curetes and to his ancestor Heracles, whom he denominated as Heracles Parastates. Then Endymion, Aëthlius' son, deprived Clymenes of his kingdom and then proposed to his sons that they race at Olympia for the kingdom as the prize.

2] Then about one generation after Endymion, Pelops raised the games for Olympian Zeus to greater fame than they had ever enjoyed before his time. But when Pelops' sons were scattered away from Elis all over the Peloponnese, Amythaon the son of Cretheus, and on his father's side the nephew of Endymion — for they say Aëthlius was really the son of Aeolus despite being called the son of Zeus — this Amythaon celebrated the Olympic Games; and after him Pelias and Neleus held them jointly.

3] In addition to these Augeas held them, and Heracles the son of Amphitryon after he took Elis. He crowned many victors, including Iolaüs for his victory with Heracles' horses — for in ancient times it was customary to compete with another man's horses. Indeed

Homer relates that Menelaus raced Agamemnon's mare, Aetha[18] along with another horse of his own. Then, too, Iolaüs was once the charioteer of Heracles.

4] So he won the chariot race, but Iasius an Arcadian, won the race on horseback, and the sons of Tyndareus were also victorious: one of them in the footrace and Polydeuces in boxing. Heracles is said to have been the winner in the same games both for wrestling and for the pancration.[19]

5] After Oxylus — for he too held the games — after his reign the Olympics were not held until Iphitus was king. Then, when as I have said Iphitus renewed the games, men had already forgotten the earlier ones; they gradually remembered them, and whatever they remembered was added to the games.

6] This much is clear, that at the time when the continuous series of the Olympic Games begins,[20] the first contest was the footrace won by Coroebus of Elis. There is no statue of Coroebus in Olympia, but his tomb is found on the borders of Elis. Later, in the fourteenth Olympics, a race of double the distance was added.[21] Hypenus of Pisa won the olive crown for this race, and in the next Olympics it was won by Acanthus.

7] With the eighteenth Olympics the pentathlon and wrestling contests were brought back, when Lampis won the former and Eurybatus was victor in the wrestling, both being Lacedaemonians. In the twenty-third Olympics the boxing contest was revived, and was won by Onomastus of Smyrna, Smyrna already counting as one of the Ionian cities at that time. In the twenty-fifth Olympics the race for full-grown horses was introduced, and was won by Pagondas of Thebes with his chariot.

8] In the eighth Olympics after this the pancration for men and the riding race were introduced. Crauxidas of Crannon was first in the horse race and Lygdamis of Syracuse defeated his rivals in the pancration. There is a monument to him near the quarries in Syracuse. Whether Lygdamis was really as large a man as the Theban Heracles I do not know, but the Syracusans say he was.

9] There is no earlier reference to the boys' competitions, but the Eleans say they established them on their own initiative. Racing and boxing for boys were held in the thirty-seventh Olympics, in which Hipposthenes the Lacedaemonian won the wrestling and Polyneices of Elis won the footrace. In the forty-first Olympics boxing for boys was added, and Philetas of Sybaris defeated his rivals.

10] The race for men in armor was admitted in the sixty-fifth Olympics, as I see it, because it was good training for war. In the race for those carrying shields the first winner was Demaretus of Heraea. The race with a pair of full-grown horses called the "synoris" was established in the ninety-third Olympics, being won by Evagoras the Elean. In the ninety-ninth Olympics colt-drawn chariots competed and Sybariades the Lacedaemonian won the crown with his chariot and colts.

11] Then they offered the chariot race with a pair of colts and the riding race for colts. They say the former was won by a woman from the Macedonian seacoast, Belistiche, while Tlepolemus the Lycian was proclaimed victor in the riding race for one colt, this contest occurring in the one hundred and thirty-first Olympics while Belistiche with her pair of colts raced in the third Olympics before that. In the one hundred and forty-fifth Olympics a pancration competition for boys was introduced, and won by Phaedimus the Aeolian from the city of Troas.

ix

1] Some contests were discontinued in Olympia when the Eleans changed their minds about them. The pentathlon for boys was held in the thirty-eighth Olympics, but after Eutelidas the Lacedaemonian won the olive crown the Eleans were no longer willing to hold the pentathlon for boys. Although they introduced the mule-cart race in the seventieth Olympics and the trotting race in the following Olympics, a proclamation was made in the eighty-fourth Olympics that neither the mule-cart race nor the trotting race would be held in the future. When they were first held the mules of Thersius the Thessalian were victorious, and the trotting horse of the Achaean, Pataecus of Dyme, won.

2] Mares were used in the trotting race, and in the stretch the riders sprang from their mounts and ran alongside the mares holding them by the bridle — just the way the Anabatae, as they are called, still do in my day. The only difference from the trotting race is that the Anabatae wear special insignia and ride male horses. The mule-cart race, however, was neither an ancient institution nor did it have any special merit. Also the Eleans were under an old curse which even forbade them to permit the animal to be bred in their country.

This race was like the synoris except that mules were used instead of horses.

3] The order of events in my day, when the sacrifices to the god for the pentathlon and the chariot races are offered later while those for the other sports come earlier, was established at the seventy-seventh Olympics. Before that the contests for men and for horses came on the same day. But on that occasion the pancratiasts continued until it was dark because they were not called up in time, the horse races and still more the pentathlon competition having prevented their being called during the daytime. And Callias the Athenian was the victor in the pancration. It was provided that in the future neither the pentathlon or the horse races would interfere with the pentathlon.

4] But in my day the games are not managed the same way they were in the beginning, for Iphitus managed them alone. And after him the descendants of Oxylus followed the same practice. But the management of the fiftieth Olympics was entrusted to two men chosen by lot from among all the Eleans, and for a long time thereafter the number of directors was kept at two.

5] For the ninety-fifth Olympics nine Hellanodicae were appointed as judges. Three of them were put in charge of the horse races, three others over the pentathlon and the rest handled the other events. In the second Olympics after this a tenth official was added. In the one hundred and third Olympics, one man from each of the twelve Elean tribes was chosen as a Hellanodicus.

6] When pressed in war by the Arcadians they lost a part of their territory including the townships that had been in the forfeited districts. Accordingly the one hundred and fourth Olympics were managed by eight tribes, the numbers of the Hellanodicae equalling the number of tribes. But with the one hundred and eighth Olympics they reverted to the use of ten officials, and this has continued to my day.

*　　*　　*

xxi

2] Following the road from the Metroüm[22] towards the stadium, on the left side towards the bottom of Mount Cronus you will see a stone foundation close by the mountain and with steps leading up through it. Beside this foundation bronze statues of Zeus have been dedicated. These were set up with the money paid in fines by athletes for cheating, and the statues are called "Zanes"[23] by the natives.

3] The first six were set up in the ninety-eighth Olympiad, when Eupolus of Thessaly bribed the boxing contestants Agetor the Arcadian, Prytanis of Cyzicus and in addition to them Phormio the Halicarnassian, who had won the victory in the preceding Olympics. They say this was the first instance of fraud by an athlete in the games, and that Eupolus and those he bribed were the first to be fined money by the Eleans. Two of the statues were made by Cleon of Sicyon but we do not know who made the other four.

4] All but the third and fourth images have inscriptions in verse. The first purports to demonstrate that victory in the Olympics is not to be obtained by money but by swiftness of foot and strength of body. The second proclaims that the image is set up in honor of the god by the piety of the Eleans, to inspire terror in athletes who cheat. Of the fifth and sixth inscriptions the former praises the Eleans on various counts and particularly for fining the boxers, while the other says these figures will serve to warn the Greeks never to offer money for an Olympic victory.

5] After Eupolus, they say the the Athenian Callippus, a contestant in the pentathlon, bribed his adversaries, and that this occurred in the one hundred and twelfth Olympics. When the Eleans demanded fines from Callippus and his fellow contestants the Athenians sent Hypereides to persuade the Eleans to remit the fine. When they refused this favor the Athenians were so contemptuous that they did not send the money and stayed out of the Olympics until the Delphic god announced that he would refuse an oracle to the Athenians on any subject until they paid the fine to the Eleans.

6] So the money was paid, and again six statues were erected to Zeus. They were inscribed in verses that were in no way superior to those concerning Eupolus' fine. These are their content: on the first, the statues are said to have been set up to honor the god for his oracle supporting the Elean decision about the pentathlon contestants; on the second and likewise on the third, the Eleans are praised for fining the pentathlon contestants.

7] The fourth aims to show that the Olympics are contests of valor rather than money; of the fifth and sixth inscriptions the former explains why the statues were erected and the latter commemorates the oracle given the Athenians in Delphi.

8] Next to the ones I have mentioned there are two statues that were set up from fines for wrestling. But what their names were has escaped me and also the Elean guides.

*　　*　　*

12] Later, others were fined by the Eleans, including a boxer from Alexandria in the 218th Olympics.[24] His name was Apollonius and his cognomen was Rhantes, for it is customary for the Alexandrians to have a cognomen.

13] He was the first Egyptian to be convicted of wrongdoing by the Eleans. He was not fined for giving or taking a bribe, but for another offense connected with the games. He failed to arrive at the appointed time and therefore, in accordance with the law, the Eleans barred him from the competition. His excuse that he had been held back in the Cyclades by winds was refuted by Heracleides, himself an Alexandrian by birth, who said he was delayed by making money in the Ionian games.

14] Therefore the Eleans barred Apollonius from the contest along with any other boxers who had not arrived at the appointed time, and they then awarded the crown to Heracleides without a contest. Thereupon Apollonius donned his boxing gloves as if for a fight, and ran after Heracleides. The latter had already put on his olive crown and had taken refuge among the judges when Apollonius struck him. For this bit of folly he was to be severely punished.

Notes

1. From a lost fifth-century comedy. The speaker is probably from Rhodes.
2. An unknown comic poet.
3. A third-century poet.
4. In a lost play.
5. Little is known of Laon, except that he was a comic poet.
6. N.B. The main road would be the way to Chalcis.
7. Perhaps the sea god of Plato's *Republic*, 611D.
8. I.e., natural formations regarded as of divine origin.
9. A fifth-century comic poet.
10. Probably a poet of the Middle Comedy.
11. I.e., Demetrias.
12. The famous centaur medicine man.
13. *Iliad*, II, 684.
14. Probably from the prologue of his lost *Aeolus*.

15. The text is corrupt here.
16. I.e., Sicily.
17. Or, as we would say, every four years.
18. *Iliad*, XXIII, 295.
19. A combination of wrestling and boxing.
20. I.e., in 776 B.C. To convert Olympic dates into B.C. dates, multiply the number of the Olympiad by 4, then subtract from 780; thus the 15th Olympics were held in 720 B.C.
21. I.e., for two stades, or 400 yards.
22. Temple of the Mother.
23. I.e., statues of Zeus.
24. 93 A.D.